Developing Change Leaders

"Dr Paul Aitken and Prof. Malcolm Higgs' book "Developing Change Leaders" is refreshingly unusual as it provides a fruitful combination of well-researched academic authority and rich description of how to develop the individual and create a change leader environment.

The book expertly fills the gap between leadership, change management and personal and organisational development. The text draws on a wealth of evidence from key authors in the field and combined this with checklists and case studies which illustrate the main learning with enormous relevance. There is a logical flow through the major issues of leadership, change management, the change leader, value-led change, creating an appropriate environment for change, developing capabilities, identifying the impact of change and leading talent. Throughout, the authors draw on many theoretical fields which include the behavioural, coaching and personal development literature.

This book delivers a comprehensive, multi-dimensional work which will inform both the individual and organization on the necessary environment for and best practice in developing change leaders."

Claire Collins, Director, Henley Partnership, Subject Area Leader, Leadership & Change, Henley Business School, UK

"This book is based on high quality research. It uses practical real-life case studies around which to implement the learning generated from research. Case studies from the UK and New Zealand complement research undertaken around the world. As a result, this book is applicable across organizational cultures and national boundaries. Paul and Malcolm were at the forefront of change leadership interventions in the New Zealand public sector, and have worked widely with public and private sectors for many years. This is required reading for students of business and more-than-useful general reading for managers in all industries and sectors across the world. This is executive education in a book."

Professor Ken Parry, Director of the Centre for Leadership Studies, Bond University, Australia
Founding Director, Centre for the Study of Leadership, New Zealand

"When you work with Paul you appreciate and value not only his academic skills but also his practical side. Everything in this very interesting book helps busy leaders understand how and what to do in a way that is both relevant and helpful. This is because Paul understands the 'real' world and the demands all stakeholders put on those of us who lead and are involved in business transformation."

Mark Saxton C Dir., BA (Western Australia), MSc (Bath), MD of The Ballintrae Partnership (South West England) and former VP HR Cadbury Beverages and Group HR Director Arriva PLC

"As a leader and now consultant I have experienced operating in turbulent, volatile environments characterised by continuous change and changing demands on leadership and management capability. Setbacks are inevitable and it is important to have a set of personal values and anchors against which to recalibrate thinking and behaviour. Paul Aitken and Malcolm Higgs have delivered a text of refreshing clarity enabling understanding of the change journey and provide a wealth of reference points for leaders to develop personal capability and effectiveness"

Steve McLauchlan, MBA , Principal Consultant at The Ballintrae Partnership and former change leader in LloydsTSB Commercial Banking

"This book represents an achievement in drawing together three core concepts; leadership, culture and change. It asks and answers some critical questions to bring wonderful clarity to a complex area, concerning how to develop change leadership capability across organistions. A timely publication!"

Dr Gareth Edwards, Head of Research and Academic Exchange, Centre for Applied Leadership Research, The Leadership Trust Foundation

Developing Change Leaders
The Principles and Practices of Change Leadership Development

Paul Aitken and Malcolm Higgs

Routledge
Taylor & Francis Group

LONDON AND NEW YORK

First published by Butterworth-Heinemann

First Edition 2010

This edition published 2011 by Routledge
2 Park Square, Milton Park, Abingdon, Oxon OX14 4RN
711 Third Avenue, New York, NY 10017, USA

Routledge is an imprint of the Taylor & Francis Group, an informa business

Notice
No responsibility is assumed by the publisher for any injury and/or damage
to persons or property as a matter of products liability, negligence or otherwise, or from
any use or operation of any methods, products, instructions or ideas contained in the
material herein

British Library Cataloguing in Publication Data
A catalogue record for this book is available from the British Library

Library of Congress Cataloging-in-Publication Data
A catalog record for this book is available from the Library of Congress

ISBN: 978-0-7506-8377-7

Dedications

For my parents Robert and Florence who from afar continue to release my spirit to change and my wife Sue, together with FJ, for their close support, love and perspective which sustains me day to day.

–Paul

To my wife Sue who has been so supportive throughout the many hours of working on this and provided so much encouragement when the task seemed impossible.

–Malcolm

Contents

Introduction

Why this book was written?

There is no doubt billions of words have been written on the topic of leadership. Notably, Goffee and Jones (2000) estimated that in an eighteen-month period some 2000 books had been published on this topic. In a similar vein we have witnessed an outpouring of books and papers on the topic of change and its management. Yet, in spite of this we face the reality that a huge proportion of change initiatives fail to realize their goals. Indeed it has been claimed (Carnall, 1999; Higgs & Rowland, 2005) that as many as 70% of change initiatives fail to achieve their intended goals. Surprisingly less has been written about change leadership, although this is a growing area of interest (Aitken, 2007; Rowland & Higgs, 2008). Against this background we would argue that in today's environment the overarching agenda for leadership development is the implementation of change.

However, in the midst of the outpouring of theories, cases and models in these vast literatures we encounter relatively little which begins to address the question:

'How do we develop effective change leaders?'

Exploring this question is central to this book. In writing this book we have reflected on our experience of consulting with organizations, researching and designing leadership development programmes and educating/coaching individual change leaders and change leadership teams.

Who this book is for?

We have sought to provide a range of practical guidelines derived from practice and research insights which can be of value to:

(i) leaders in organizations faced with implementing change,

(ii) those with roles advising organizations on leadership development,

(iii) executive educators and

(iv) the broader HR community, including those involved with supporting change initiatives or organizational development.

In addition we hope this book will provide an up-to-date resource for students studying for DBA, MBA or specialist Masters degrees in related subject areas. In fact one business school has already used elements of our work in designing a core curriculum for the topic of leadership and change.

How this book works?

Given the range of readerships identified earlier we have structured this book in a way in which it can be used as a flexible resource. Whilst some may wish to read this book sequentially, others may wish to focus on specific aspects. Thus Part 1 provides a review of the contemporary context within which change leadership needs to be considered. Part 2 focuses specifically on values and leadership culture research insights which play an important, often overlooked, part in shaping, defining and evaluating the organizational impact of the necessary change leadership capabilities we detail here. Finally, Part 3 explores broader organizational considerations which affect the nature, development and impact measurement of change leadership capability. We finish with an overarching framework which makes sense of our core material and acts as a starting point for those responsible for developing change leaders. A concluding commentary pitches forward to describe potential new demands and roles for contemporary change leaders.

A summary of the content for each part is outlined in the following paragraphs.

Part 1: The Contemporary Context for Developing Change Leadership

Chapter 1 begins by exploring the broader context which gives rise to a need to examine the nature of change leadership and the importance of developing associated capabilities. In doing so, this part begins with an overview of developments in our thinking about the nature of leadership and the significance of exploring leadership within specific organizational contexts, including the highly significant impact of organizational culture. Chapter 2 reviews the challenges involved in implementing change effectively. This entails a discussion of barriers to change and differing approaches to change implementation. We also examine recent research into change management and frameworks which provide insights into potentially effective approaches to managing change. Chapter 3 concludes Part 1 with a review of our understanding of what it takes for leaders to contribute to the effective implementation of change. This review begins by considering the range of roles which individuals and leaders play in the change process. Building on recent research the chapter ends with an overview of generic change leadership competencies, behaviors and practices.

Part 2: How to Develop Change Leadership Capability

Whilst Part 1 sets the scene for developing effective change leaders, Part 2 covers the necessary development interventions. Chapter 4 explores what lies beneath the surface of leadership behaviors and looks at values which may drive or restrict change. Chapter 5 then takes us beyond individual leader development to consider the importance of collective and distributed leadership as expressed through leadership culture. In the course of this discussion the importance of authenticity and role-modeling of behavior is emphasized and the impact of an integrated transformational leadership culture is highlighted. Chapter 6 uses the prevailing practice and research to chart the journey of a developing change leader and specifies what we consider to be the top 10 'must have' dynamic capabilities required by leaders tasked with leading and implementing change. Chapter 7 explores a broad range of development tools and techniques which are anchored in our 10 dynamic capabilities, also including some illustrative cases that demonstrate how capability development programmes can be designed in a way which models our core learning principles.

Part 3: Organizational Considerations

Part 3 of this book provides linkages between the first two parts. As with any development activity, sustained effort to build change leadership capability has to demonstrate a clear return on investment. Chapter 8 includes some different and more relevant metrics to monitor and evaluate interventions designed to build change leadership capability. Chapter 9 explores the accountabilities for managing change talent and the debate around differing roles in the change talent management processes. In this discussion the respective roles of line leaders and HRD specialists are explored. The chapter concludes with a clear view that line leadership accountability for change talent management is more significant than technical processes in ensuring success. However, this accountability has to be underpinned by effective processes. Chapter 10 rounds off this book by providing an organization-wide framework for developing change leaders that integrates the generic and context-specific strands covered throughout this book, giving change leader developers somewhere to begin if they are coming to this topic for the first time, or a powerful way of positioning the purpose of development activities for experienced practitioners advising senior managers.

Given this structure those already familiar with the context for change leadership summarized in Part 1 may wish to go straight to Part 2. Similarly, those who feel they have effective development programmes and mechanisms, but are not achieving sustainable impact, may wish to focus on Part 3. Exploring a main focus of interest may raise questions or issues which warrant dipping into other Chapters of this book. In any event we would not want you to miss our top 10 research and practice derived 'must have' capabilities for exceptional change leaders, together with allied development activities, described in Part 2.

As mentioned earlier, this book is designed to meet a diverse range of reader interests and needs. Along the way we have tried to combine theory and practice; rigor and relevance. We also recognize that any form of learning is a journey. We do not claim to have all the answers, neither to have covered every aspect of the subject. In line with this we have provided signposts to further resources throughout this book. If we have one overall aim for this book it is to contribute to the development of more effective change leadership in organizations. This will not only help organizations to flourish, but also hopefully reduce the pain and suffering of the 'targets of change' and their leaders alike. We hope to achieve this through encouraging our readers to become more reflective practitioners of change leadership development.

References

Aitken, P. (2007) "Walking the Talk – the nature and role of leadership culture within organisation culture/s", *Journal of General Management, Vol. 32, No. 4,* Summer.

Carnall, C. (1999). *Managing change in organizations.* London: Prentice-Hall.

Goffee, R., & Jones, G. (2000). Why should anyone be led by you? *Harvard Business Review,* (Sept–Oct), 63–70.

Higgs, M. J., & Rowland, D. (2005). All changes great and small. *Journal of Change Management, 5*(2), 121–135.

Rowland, D., & Higgs, M. J. (2008). *Sustaining change: leadership that works.* London: Jossey-Bass.

Part 1

The Contemporary Context for Developing Change Leadership

Introduction

In this part of the book we provide a broad context within which the development of change leaders needs to occur. In exploring this development it is important to consider both what we know about leadership and the context of change within organizations.

We begin by exploring the way in which our understanding of leadership has evolved. It has been argued that our attempts to understand leadership have represented a search for the 'Holy Grail' (Higgs, 2003). In the course of this search we have consistently critiqued the journeys and conclusions of our predecessors and attempted to supplant them with 'new truths'. However, as Weick (1995) pointed out:

> *Social and organisational sciences, as opposed to physics or biology, do not discover anything new, but let us comprehend what we have known all along in a much better way, opening up new, unforeseen, possibilities of reshaping, re-engineering and restructuring our original social environment.*

Thus, we should perhaps attempt to understand this journey as a process of 'sense-making' rather than one of discovery. Importantly in this context Chapter 1 points to the importance of understanding the impact which corporate culture has on the nature of developing effective change leadership.

Within this sense-making frame Chapter 2 explores the challenges of change faced by organizations today. In doing this we not only explore the drivers of change, but also the reasons why it is so difficult to implement change successfully. This entails not only enumerating the barriers to change, but also attempting to understand the causes of the difficulties we face and the need to challenge many of our assumptions about the reasons for behavior which makes change so difficult to implement.

Finally, Chapter 3 brings together these different contextual themes and explores a number of ways in which we attempt to define the requirements of an effective change leader. In doing so, we explore lessons from research and practice and examine differing frameworks which range from role-based to competence-based models. In doing this we explore an emerging framework which links leader behaviors and the contextual approach required for the leadership of organizational change implementation.

References

Higgs, M. J. (2003). Developments in leadership thinking. *Journal of Organizational Development and Leadership*, 24(5), 273–284.
Weick, K. E. (1995). *Sense-making in organisations*. Thousand Oaks, CA: Sage.

Chapter 1

The Change Leadership Context

I wanna be the leader!
I wanna be the leader!
Can I be the leader?
Can I? I can?
Promise! Promise!
Yippee! I'm the leader!
I'm the leader!
OK, what shall we do?

Roger McGough

Introduction

It is increasingly evident that change is not a process which can be simply managed. Change needs to be led and research has shown the way in which change if led can make a significant difference to the chances of success in achieving change goals.

Before exploring the specific challenges and requirements of leading change successfully (which we will do in Chapters 2 and 3), it is worth reflecting on what we have learned about leadership in general. In doing so, we will explore the following:

■ Developments in thinking about the nature of leadership and understanding what it takes to deliver successful performance as a leader.

■ The changing context within which leadership is both required and being exercised, plus developing an understanding of the dynamic between context and leadership behaviors.

■ The significant role of organizational culture in the selection and development of leaders and the interaction between leader behaviors and organizational culture. In doing this, we will also explore the relationship between culture and change within an organization.

Developments in our understanding of leadership

It is worth beginning our exploration of developments in thinking about leadership by reflecting on Roger McGough's poem at the beginning of this chapter. What meaning do you take from this poem? In using this poem in introducing leadership development workshops over many years, some of the common responses to this reflection we have encountered include:

■ 'No one understands what leadership is'.

■ 'People pursue leadership for its status and recognition of their ambition'.

■ 'You need to be driven by a desire to be a leader in order to become a leader'.

■ 'You can only become a leader, if you have permission from others to lead'.

■ 'We do not have a clear understanding of what it is that leaders do'.

■ 'Leadership involves engaging others in determining our priorities and plans'.

■ 'Leadership is a team game'.

This experience is by no means restricted to our own interactions with leaders and potential leaders. Burns (1978) pointed out that we do not have a clear view of the nature of leadership. In his research, he identified some 284 different definitions of leadership. The progression of time and further research has clearly failed to clarify this ambiguity. Kets de Vries (1993) commented that:

The more leaders I encounter the more difficult I find it to identify a common pattern of effective leadership behaviours.

Ultimately this leads to a view expressed in this adaptation of a comment by the Canadian educationalist, Lawrence Peters:

Leadership, like truth, beauty and contact lenses, lays in the eye of the beholder.

Indeed the above quotation provides the basis for an important insight; this being that follower's needs and requirements play a significant contextual role for understanding the nature of effective leadership. We will return to this point later.

Faced with this apparently impossible compendium for thinking about leadership, how can we make sense of what we know and what we have learned? If we consider leadership as a long line of study, it could be argued that societies have had an interest in leadership which stretches back over millennia. Core to this tends to be views concerning the purpose of leadership, the nature of power, the sources of leadership and the nature or source of leadership excellence. Considering these issues could be the subject of a book (or even a treatise) in its own right. However, it may be useful to attempt to chart the developments in this debate over the course of the period during which we have more systematically studied leadership as a significant aspect of organizational behavior (arguably beginning in the 1930s).

The key developments would seem to be:

- ■ The purpose of leadership
  Thinking about leadership has been dominated for a significant period of time by the view that the purpose of leadership is to deliver results. In much of the literature, this perspective has been focused on the specific delivery of financial results. During the 1970s, a somewhat different view of the purpose began to emerge. This saw, in some cases, a shift from seeing the purpose as delivery of results to that of effecting a transformation in the organization. In essence this view saw the purpose of leadership as being to bring about significant change within an organization in order to deal with significant changes in the business environment.

  Many examples of effective leadership, from the business world, began to lose credibility when 'successful' CEOs left an organization only to see a significant dip in performance. This, in part, led to a view about the purpose of leadership being concerned with the delivery of sustainable performance. This view, which began to emerge in the late 1980s, positioned the purpose of leadership as being the development of capability. Building individual and organizational capability is seen as central to the delivery of sustainable organizational performance. Today, the thinking about the purpose of leadership is more concerned with an integration of the above three views. This viewpoint sees leadership as enabling results to be delivered through the development of capability; importantly, the capability to effect change, transformation and sustainability.

■ The focus of leadership studies
The focus of leadership studies has shifted notably over the period we are considering. This shift has occurred in two ways. First, our approach to leadership studies has begun to move away from a focus on top leaders, which has traditionally dominated research in this area, to a more distributed view of leadership within an organization. This leadership has moved from being purely associated with position within an organization to being seen to be concerned with the process by which anyone who needs to engage followers in the organization achieves such engagement. In part, this shift responds to the critique that leadership studies have been in essence little more than studies of the traits and behaviors of white, male American CEOs (Alimo-Metcalfe, 1995). In seeing leadership as more widely distributed within the organization, we are now able to move from a constant focus on 'distant' leaders to exploring the behaviors and practices of 'near' leaders.

The second shift we have seen under this heading is a move from seeing leadership as an individually centered phenomenon to being more of a collective activity. Hence, leadership is now being seen by many as a team game.

■ Sources of power
In broad terms, the relationships between leadership and power have been underexplored in research into leadership. However, in framing leadership studies it is evident that there have been underlying assumptions made about the source of leadership power. From the early studies of leadership until the 1970s, the dominant assumption about power tended to be that a leader's power was derived from their position within the organization. In the course of the 1970s, the power base tended to be seen as being less concerned with positional power and more concerned with personal power. This tended to be illustrated by a growing focus on the charismatic aspects of leadership. More recently, as organizational life has become more complex, the power of the leader is being seen to be more concerned with the ability to create connections within the organization. This is clearly linked to the development of the view that the purpose of leadership is to build capability in the organization.

■ Existence of leadership
Underpinning much of the research into leadership has been the 'nature/nurture' debate. For a considerable time, views on leadership tended to be dominated by a belief that leaders are born. Clearly, such a belief influences the focus of research and indeed led to a significant focus on attempting to identify traits which were associated with effective and successful leaders. In the 1960s, an opposing belief emerged. The focus in this period was based on a view that effective leaders can

be made. Operating on this belief led to a focus on identifying specific behaviors which could be incorporated into the development of leaders. More recently, the view has emerged that leadership is both nature and nurture – leaders are both born and made. This is not an attempt to avoid taking a position. It is a view which suggests that certain traits or characteristics may be necessary to provide a base upon which leadership capabilities might be developed.

In practice, these developments in underpinning assumptions and beliefs relating to the framing of leadership studies have not moved tidily from one stage to another. In reality, many of these exist today in different forms and combinations. What is important, however, is to understand leadership in the context of these assumptions. Against this background, it is worth reflecting on the approaches we have adopted in attempting to describe and understand the nature of effective leadership.

It has been suggested that the study of leadership has a history stretching back over many centuries. Indeed, an historical review of the development of attempts to understand leadership may be illuminating. Below is a brief review of trends and developments in thinking on leadership from such a perspective. However, in presenting developments in this way, it is important to be aware that the process is not linear and early frameworks remain potential lenses for viewing leadership today.

THE LONG LINE IN RETROSPECT

Clemens and Mayer (1999) draw on literature to illustrate periods of leadership. The use of literature provides a means of identifying stories, which help us to understand the dominant discourse, which in turn enables us to understand and make sense of a construct within a context. An illustration of this development is provided in Table 1.1. The importance of understanding perceptions of leadership contextually is illustrated by Plato's observation.

Society values whatever is honoured there.

However, the key value of reviewing the historical discourse lies not in finding selective evidence for today's views, but in understanding the dynamic between society and the dominant perspectives on leadership. From the above overview of leadership, it is evident that, until the late twentieth century, the paradigm was determined by the rational/analytical perspective of Weber. This led to the emergence of 'Taylorism' and 'Fordism' which has dominated, and to an extent continues to dominate, thinking on business organization and leadership. The impact of the 'modern' school, influenced by Freud, Jung, Skinner, etc., provides the second major leadership behavioural/relational discourse in the latter part of the twentieth century. In some respects the current financial/economic/environmental crisis in western capitalism is encouraging leadership observers to re-visit the more philosophical 'classical' period, albeit now in global terms, with an emphasis on who and what leadership serves.

Table 1.1 Leadership discourses: A historic perspective

Era	Dominant discourse	Examples of authors
Classical	▪ Dialogue ▪ Society ▪ Democracy	▪ Plato ▪ Aristotle ▪ Homer ▪ Pericles ▪ Sophocles
Renaissance	▪ Ambition ▪ Individual ▪ Great man not great event	▪ Petrarch ▪ Chaucer ▪ Castiglione ▪ Machiavelli ▪ Shakespeare
Industrial	▪ Survival of the fittest ▪ Control ▪ Rationality	▪ Weber ▪ Darwin ▪ Durkheim ▪ Marx
Modern	▪ Psychological ▪ Behavioral	▪ Freud ▪ Skinner ▪ Jung

Source: Adapted from Clemens and Mayer (1999).

TRAIT THEORIES OF LEADERSHIP

The 'modern' study of leadership is viewed as having begun with trait theory in the late 1920s. This was a personality-based approach, and one which led to generally inconclusive findings. However, three key traits associated with effective leadership were identified (and indeed are still evident in recent research). These were:

1. Cognitive abilities
2. Drive
3. Conscientiousness

BEHAVIORAL AND SITUATIONAL THEORIES OF LEADERSHIP

The limitations of trait theory were responded to by examining the behaviors and style of leaders. A classic example of this approach is provided by the Blake and Mouton 'managerial grid' model. This approach was underpinned by a point of view, or belief, that there was a 'best' style. Reality, however, provided numerous examples of success employing 'less desirable' styles. The limitations of the 'style theories' were the catalyst for the application of contingency theory to leadership. A classic example of the contingency leadership model is that developed by Hersey and Blanchard (1993) who maintained that it was not the leader's style per se which led to effectiveness, but rather the ability of the leader to adapt the style to the needs of the followers. This approach drew on the relatively underexplored work on understanding leadership from the follower perspective, originally developed from research carried out by Fiedler (1964).

Whilst the trait theory tended to imply that effective leadership is a matter of selection, the behavioral and situational theories focused more on the development of leadership capabilities. Once again, research using both style and contingency theories failed to provide consistent and compelling evidence for their validity across a wide range of contexts.

CHARISMATIC THEORIES

In focusing on top-level leadership performance, Shamir (1992) returned to the qualities of the leaders and identified, through studying cases of successful leaders, the common thread of 'charisma'. He described charisma as being the ability to inspire others to act in a way, which is required to realize the leader's vision. This approach led to a period in which the focus of much of the leadership research was on the qualities of the 'heroic CEO'. This approach not only failed to produce compelling results, but it also tended to be very US focused.

TRANSFORMATIONAL AND TRANSACTIONAL THEORIES

In the late 1970s, the state of leadership research was such that methodological and terminological debates were causing more confusion than enlightenment. The rational paradigm derived from a Weberian perspective was in conflict with the psychological paradigm. Zalesnik (1977) summarized the issue, and indeed failures of leadership research as follows:

Theoreticians of scientific management, with their organisational diagrams and time and motion studies were missing half the picture – the half filled with inspiration, vision and the full spectrum of human drives and desires.

In many ways, this statement captured the key debate around the difference between leadership and management. In parallel with and possibly influenced by this stream of thought, Bass (1985) developed a leadership model, which identified different sets of behaviors and characteristics required in situations of organizational transformation and situations of stability. Bass labeled these as transformational and transactional leadership. Further work using this model identified the main characteristics and behaviors associated with each context as being:

a. Transformational leadership
   - *Charismatic/inspirational*: inspiring and aligning others by providing a common purpose allied with optimism about the 'mission' and its attainability.
   - *Intellectual stimulation*: encouraging individuals to challenge the status quo, to consider problems from new and unique perspectives and to be innovative and creative.
   - *Individualized consideration*: a genuine concern for individuals' feelings, aspirations and development. They pay special attention to each individual's needs for achievement and growth, they coach and mentor. Followers are treated differently and equitably.
b. Transactional leadership
   - *Contingent reward*: encouraging specific performance and behaviors by making rewards (in the broadest sense) contingent on delivery.
   - *Management by exception*: only intervening actively when a delegated task or function is failing to perform to expectations.

Bass and Avolio (1996) operationalized this model in the form of a questionnaire (the Multifactor Leadership Questionnaire, MLQ) which has been used as the basis for much empirical work in the field. Whilst the instrument has not been without its critics, there is little doubt that it has been influential in building understanding of leadership in a changing environment.

An emerging perspective on leadership

The diverse, and often contradictory, findings on the nature of effective leadership share two common factors. They are: (1) a focus on top-level leaders and (2) the measure of success employed is the financial performance of the business. This criticism implies an alternative means of assessing the effectiveness of leadership behaviors, a route initiated by Fiedler (1964) and further developed by Alimo-Metcalfe (1995), in terms of the impact of leader behaviors on the followers.

In addition, it has been suggested that the extensive literature on leadership, and changing schools of thought and models, contain much re-working of earlier concepts. Perhaps, the frustration with the inability of leadership research is rooted in a paradigm which suggests that there is a fundamental truth which is yet to be discovered. Shifting the lens through which leadership is observed may bring new and useful insights. Viewing leadership through a different lens suggests a potential change in the measure of leadership effectiveness from hard business results to the impact of leaders on their followers. This view resonates with the view that leadership in a change context requires focus on building the capability of people within the organization to deal with continuing change, a dynamic, rather than static, view of enhancing organizational performance over time.

Although not explicitly acknowledging this shift in paradigm, there is a body of literature which is beginning to look at leadership through a 'new lens' in order to attempt to make sense of this complex concept in today's business environment. Within this 'emerging theory' school of thought, there are two common strands which are: (1) the focus of study is on what leaders actually do and (2) the determinant of effectiveness includes the leader's impact on followers and their subsequent ability to perform over time.

It may have been Kotter's (1990) study which prompted a move from studying personality or testing theoretical models in the search for understanding the nature of leadership. His study of the work of leaders certainly appears to influence many of the studies, which may be placed in this 'emerging school'. Typical of these studies is the work reported by Kouzes and Posner (1998), which identified the following elements of effective leadership (with effectiveness judged from the follower's perspective).

(i) *Challenging the process* – a constant questioning of why things are being done in a certain way combined with openness to having their own actions challenged.

(ii) *Inspiring shared vision* – engaging others with a vision of how things can be and how progress may be made.

(iii) *Enabling others to act* – working on a belief in the potential of people and creating the conditions to enable people to realize their potential.

(iv) *Modeling the way* – acting as a role model and demonstrating integrity in terms of congruence of words and actions.

(v) *Encouraging the heart* – providing recognition tailored to an understanding of the needs and personalities of each person.

In reviewing these findings, clear overlaps with elements of transformational leadership become apparent. However, this does not diminish the potential contribution of Kouzes and Posner when seen in a 'sense-making' context. Examining leadership through this new lens produces insights not normally associated with the 'financial performance' lens. Indeed, some writers are quite explicit in their acknowledgement that a number of 'effective' leaders they studied would not necessarily have been considered so in the absence of the followers' perspective. In reviewing studies such as those outlined above, it becomes evident that this 'emerging school' sees leadership as being a combination of personal characteristics and areas of competence. The re-emergence of personality implied in this school of thought, seen as a component of effective leadership, is evident in some of the more recent studies of leadership where the focus in on building capability.

A POTENTIAL FRAMEWORK FOR UNDERSTANDING LEADERSHIP

Having reviewed the development in thinking about the nature of effective leadership and, in particular, having looked at the literature from a 'sense-making' rather than discovery perspective, a pattern is beginning to emerge. One part of this pattern is that the personality of the leader is a determinant of their effectiveness. The second element is that effective leaders are differentiated from other leaders through the exercise of a relatively small range of skill or competence areas. The way in which these skills and competencies are exercised is not prescribed, but is the function of the underlying personality of the leader. Building on this view, it is possible to suggest a framework which reflects the research and thinking on leadership emerging from a 'sense-making' paradigm. This is shown in Figure 1.1.

The elements in this framework are summarized below:

a. Skill/competence areas
    - *Envision*: the ability to identify a clear future picture, which will inform the way in which people direct their efforts and utilize their skills.
    - *Engage*: finding the appropriate way for each individual to understand the vision and, hence, the way in which they can contribute.
    - *Enable*: acting on a belief in the talent and potential of individuals, and creating the environment in which these can be released.

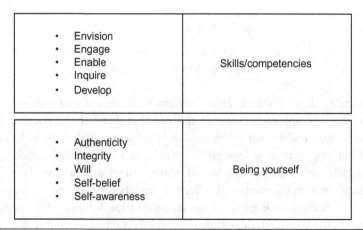

Figure 1.1   An emerging model of effective leadership.

- *Inquire*: being open to real dialogue with those involved in the organization and encouraging free and frank debate of all issues.
- *Develop*: working with people to build their capability and help them to make the envisioned contribution.

b. Personal characteristics
  - *Authenticity*: being genuine and not attempting to 'play a role', not acting in manipulative way.
  - *Integrity*: being consistent in what you say and do.
  - *Will*: a drive and persistence in working toward a goal.
  - *Self-belief*: a realistic evaluation of your capabilities and belief that you can achieve required goals.
  - *Self-awareness*: a realistic understanding of 'who you are', how you feel and how others see you.

IMPLICATIONS OF THE FRAMEWORK

If personality is a significant determinant of effective leadership, then a purely developmental focus will not contribute sufficiently to building an organization's leadership capability. This implies that any approach to building leadership capability needs to be underpinned by rigorous and effective selection procedures.

The skills encompassed within the framework outlined in Figure 1.1 do not lend themselves to 'traditional' training interventions. They require a longer term development approach combining workshops, coaching and monitored implementation and re-inforcement through work-based projects. Higgs and Rowland (2000) reported a study, which demonstrated the effectiveness of such an approach in the context of developing change leadership capability. In the same study, they highlighted the importance of appropriate performance measures which go beyond the 'traditional' financial or short-term goal/output-related measures. Thus, in addition to selection and development, the 'emerging' framework for understanding leadership has implications for organizations in terms of metrics to track the performance and development of leaders. Such metrics may well include climate studies/employee feedback and measures of follower capability development. We list some indicative measures in Chapter 8. Without appropriate metrics, the required leadership behaviors are unlikely to be identified, developed or open to reinforcement through 'reward'.

SUMMARY OF THIS EMERGING PERSPECTIVE

From the above, we can see that there have been significant developments in our thinking about the purpose and nature of leadership. These have impacted on the focus of research and the development of our understanding of the nature of effective leadership. In broad terms, our framing of effective leadership has shifted notably

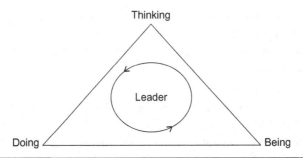

Figure 1.2 The leadership learning and enacting balance frame.

from the 'Heroic', leader-centric viewpoint to a more 'Engaging' one which focuses on working with followers to address the leadership of organizational challenges.

Although the 'emerging' frame encompasses both behaviors and personality, it is important not to neglect some of the consistent findings from trait-based studies. Importantly, we should remember that effective leadership requires high cognitive ability. Overall, it is feasible to view effective leadership in terms of a balance between skills/behaviors, personality and cognitive abilities. Figure 1.2 presents this schematically.

Within this model the 'Thinking' relates to the cognitive abilities and their application in an organizational context. For example, this could include areas such as critical analysis and evaluation of plans, proposals and ideas; decision-making and judgment and strategic thinking. The 'Being' relates to core aspects of the leader's personality and, importantly, awareness of how they impact on the leader's behaviors and actions as well as understanding how these need to be deployed and managed. 'Doing' covers the leader's actions and behaviors in terms of how the leader works with and engages followers. The model is not intended to be static. Rather, it provides a frame for the leaders to reflect on their effectiveness and consider the need to balance the three components when enacting their leadership. Through this process of active reflection, the leaders should be in a position to learn and develop in a way which improves their effectiveness. We return to this development frame in Chapter 10, superimposed on which, we locate the top 10 dynamic capabilities we consider are required for effective change leadership.

The significance of organizational context and culture

There are several contextual factors underpinning the increasing pressures on organizations to respond to growing complexity and environmental volatility. In brief, these are (see Chapter 2 for more detail):

- increasing levels of competition;
- investor and stakeholder demands;

■ globalization;

■ changing nature of the workforce;

■ technology;

■ legal and regulatory changes;

■ societal changes.

To a large extent, these same factors underpin the ever increasing focus on leadership in organizations and the drive to identify what it takes to exercise effective leadership. Indeed, it is these factors which provide the macro-context within which leaders today need to operate. Whilst all of these factors are of significant importance for leadership, it is worth highlighting the particular impact of the changing nature of the workforce. For some while now, we have known that there is a strong positive relationship between the levels of employee commitment to an organization and the performance of the organization.

However, changing employees' values and expectations are creating conditions which can weaken levels of loyalty and commitment (see Chapter 4). For example, recent surveys have shown declining levels of employee trust in their organizations; without trust it is difficult to build high levels of commitment (see Chapter 8). This represents a significant leadership challenge and illustrates well the interplay between leadership and the context in which it is being exercised. The commitment challenge is illustrated by the rapid growth in employee engagement (a version of commitment) benchmarking by organizations and the burgeoning business of providing advice on actions to increase engagement. However, what we do know is that without leadership attention and action such initiatives have limited (if any) sustainable impact (see Chapter 5).

Whilst it is important that leadership is understood within a macro-context, it is also necessary to consider leadership within the more specific micro-organizational context. In reality, there is a dynamic between leadership and the organizational context (both macro and micro). There is certainly evidence that the nature of an organization, its purpose, strategies and plans play a part in determining the type of leadership which is considered necessary, the type of people who are placed in leadership roles and the types of actions and behaviors which are recognized and rewarded. There is also good evidence to show that leaders can impact significantly on the nature of an organization and its strategic direction. This dynamic is shown schematically in Figure 1.3. In reflecting on the dynamic, it is evident that there is an organizational equivalent of the leadership balance shown in Figure 1.2.

The organizational equivalent of the leader's cognitive abilities (Thinking) may be represented by the organization's strategy. This represents the organization's thought through response to its environment and the intent in terms of achieving its core purpose in the face of an evaluation of the environmental challenges and opportunities. The organizational equivalent of the leader's personality (Being) may

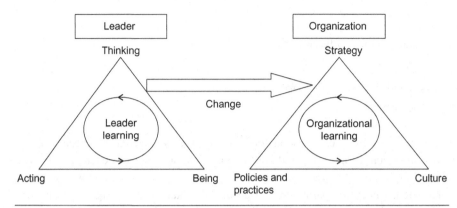

Figure 1.3 Leadership in context.

be seen as being the overall culture of the organization. Indeed in the vast literature associated with the concept of organizational culture, culture is referred to as the 'personality of the organisation'. We will explore the nature and significance of culture in a little more detail in the next section. Finally, the organizational equivalent of the leader's behaviors (Doing) may be seen as being the framework of policies and practices deployed throughout the organization. Combining the leader, and organizational processes creates the opportunity for organizational learning and development, in effect becoming the organizational development agenda, driven by appropriate leadership development. As can be seen from Figure 1.3, there is also a clear interaction between the leader and the organizational context. For example, changes to strategy will create a need for a change in the focus for the leader and often the need to deploy leadership skills in a different way to address changing contexts and priorities.

Much of the thinking and writing on leadership focuses on the leader and leader behaviors. What is often neglected in this area is consideration of the nature of the leadership agenda and the priorities for action. The model described provides a useful framework for helping leaders to identify their action agenda and priorities. If leaders review the key elements of the organizational strategy alongside the current culture and the key organizational policies and practices, they can begin to identify an agenda for actions with a clear sense of priorities and sequencing. This may be best illustrated by considering a brief case study example.

An organization in the United Kingdom financial sector has a major strategic goal of increasing market share by 10% over the next five years. In order to do this, they have identified a number of critical strategic priorities which are:

(i) Improving the speed of getting new products to market. This will entail increasing the ability to work across organizational functions and boundaries.

(ii) Encouraging higher levels of innovation across most areas of the organization.

(iii) Identifying new distribution channels and rapidly establishing means of utilizing them for both new and existing products.

The current culture of the organization is characterized by:

(i) *Risk aversion*: This tends to be reflected in slow decision-making and a need for the development of lengthy business cases to underpin any decisions.

(ii) *Hierarchical*: There are a significant number of organizational levels. Decision-making tends to be fairly centralized with relatively limited delegation of authority. In addition, the organization tends to be largely silo-based with limited cross-functional communication or cooperation.

(iii) *Bureaucratic*: The organization tends to make extensive use of committees for decision-making purposes and for reviewing practices and performances. There are extensive and complex processes for reporting, analysis and communication of information.

Flowing from this culture, some of the relevant policies and practices include:

(i) Communication flows tend to be downward and upward through the chain of command within each functional area. Communication between functions tends to be formal and largely occurs between functional heads.

(ii) Objective-setting tends to be carried out on a top–down basis. In practice, individual objectives only tend to emerge some five–six months into the planning cycle.

(iii) Detailed and tight job descriptions exist for the majority of jobs within the organization. Formal performance reviews focus on individual objectives which are tightly linked to individual job descriptions.

(iv) Reward is largely related to a combination of organizational level and length of service. Incentive bonuses tend to be restricted to sales force and a few senior executive positions.

From this synopsis, it becomes apparent that in order to achieve the strategic goal, the leadership agenda will need to address the cultural, policy and practice dimensions as an early priority. In reality, cultural change tends to take quite some time (see below) and therefore, the priority areas for leadership to address will be associated with policies and practices. This dimension also tends to encompass structures. Therefore, in this example, a potential priority leadership focus may entail an initial intervention which would establish cross-functional teams to work on improving the effectiveness of product development processes. This example highlights the importance of considering the interaction between leadership and the organizational context in framing and prioritizing the change and development agenda for leaders.

In the above discussion, the importance of culture as a significant aspect of the organizational context for leadership was highlighted. In the example, we considered how an understanding of the organizational context could help to frame the leadership agenda. However, the model in Figure 1.3 indicates a two-way dynamic relationship between the leader and their context. This invites consideration of how a leader can impact on the context and, in particular, on the culture of the organization.

In order to explore the relationship between organizational culture, leadership and change, it is necessary to be clear as to what is meant by organizational culture. This is an area of considerable debate and a voluminous literature. Whilst it is beyond the scope of this paper to explore this vast literature, it is necessary to establish a frame for considering organizational culture. There are numerous definitions of culture that have been produced over the years. In searching for an appropriate definition, it would appear that there are many facets, with emphasis shifting according to the individual author. In addition, culture is impalpable, making definitions hard to relate to. For many, simply describing what culture means let alone managing it can be difficult. Hofstede (1991) describes culture as '...software of the mind – a collective programming of the mind that distinguishes the members of one group of people from another'. Schein (1985) defines culture as '...the deeper level of basic assumptions and beliefs that are shared by members of an organization, that operate unconsciously, and that define in a basic taken-for-granted fashion an organization's view of itself and its environment'. A more long-standing definition by Hall (1959) suggests that 'culture is the pattern of taken-for-granted assumptions about how a given collection of people should think, act and feel as they go about their daily affairs'. Even though this definition is over fifty years old, it does not appear out-of-date today.

There are many other definitions of culture, but most commonly, it is colloquially described as 'the ways in which things are done around here' and, as a form of social glue that holds a group of people together. However, there is an increasing recognition that culture may be viewed at two levels which are: (1) what is thought and the way of thinking – implicit beliefs, values and basic assumptions and (2) explicit or observable phenomena – procedures, structures, rituals, logos, etc.

The difficulty in pinning down the nature of culture has led to challenges in finding ways of assessing or measuring an organization's culture. Although many different approaches are adopted, a relatively recent framework proposed by Goffee and Jones (1996) has proved to be helpful in practice. This framework explores an organization's culture through examining both of the levels described above. They use two dimensions to describe the way human beings form groups and how they relate to each other: sociability and solidarity. They define sociability as: 'a measure of friendliness among members of a community'. This measure considers how people relate to each other. High levels of sociability are likely amongst people who share similar ideas, values, personal histories, attitudes and interests. Solidarity is defined as being: 'based on common tasks, mutual interests and clearly understood shared goals that benefit all the involved parties'.

This measure considers a community's ability to pursue shared objectives quickly and effectively, regardless of personal ties. It is more about how people think and act than how they feel. Comparing these two dimensions within organizations resulted in a matrix of four culture types, each of which can be present in a positive (functional) or negative (dysfunctional) form within an organization. These are: networked, communal, fragmented and mercenary, shown below (Figure 1.4) in their double S cube model. This model was underpinned by four major points relating to business culture that emerged from their research. These were: (1) most organizations are characterized by several cultures at once, (2) some companies experience an archetypal life cycle of their culture/s, (3) there is not one 'right' or 'best' culture for an organization – only the appropriate culture for the business environment and (4) any form of culture can be functional or dysfunctional. It is the third of these that begins to establish a link between leadership, change and culture.

In considering organizational culture, there is a widely held view that culture is difficult to change and any change takes a long time. An understanding of the two levels described is helpful in identifying ways in which the culture may be moved. The first level is concerned with core values and beliefs. This is certainly difficult to change rapidly, as outlined in Chapter 4. However, there is some evidence that, over time, leaders' actions and behaviors can bring about a change at this level (see Chapter 5 which focuses on the creation and use of leadership culture to effect change). The second level is more concerned with the manifestations of culture and how people

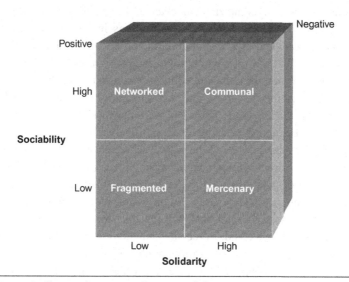

Figure 1.4   Goffee and Jones' culture model.

experience the culture of the organization (often referred to as the organizational climate). This is more amenable to change in a shorter timescale and is an area in which leaders' actions and behaviors can have a significant short-term impact.

There is a considerable amount of research which highlights the importance of leaders paying attention to achieving cultural change in a way which creates a culture capable of supporting an organization's strategic direction. The research evidence of direct linkages between leadership behaviors and organizational performance is, surprisingly, relatively sparse and, to an extent, somewhat inconclusive. However, there are consistent research findings which cover a period of more than thirty years, showing clear links between organizational culture and organizational performance. This stream indicates that around 50% of variance in organizational performance can be explained by differences in organizational culture. Furthermore, this pattern of relationships is encountered within organizations as well as across organizations. Individual business unit, or work group, performance differences can also be explained by different 'sub-cultures'.

A separate stream of research has shown clear linkages between leader behaviors and the level two aspects of both organizational and business unit cultures. Indeed, some studies have indicated that up to 80% of the variance in this level of culture can be explained by differences in leadership behaviors. Considering these various streams together provides a strong indication that leader's impact on organizational performance through their impact on aspects of the organizational culture.

The dynamic between leadership and culture does, however, also impact on leader behaviors. This is well illustrated by a recent study carried out by Higgs and Rowland (2005). In this study, they used the Goffee and Jones' model of culture and explored the relationship between organizational change, leadership behaviors and organizational culture. They found that in organizations in which the dimension of sociability was a dominant aspect of culture, the predominant leadership behaviors were leader-centric and followed the 'heroic leadership' model. On the other hand, in organizations in which the dominant cultural dimension was solidarity, the dominant leadership behaviors fell more into the 'Engaging' framework. Furthermore, they found that the leader-centric behaviors were negatively related to change success, whereas the 'Engaging' behaviors were positively related to change success.

In this chapter, we have explored the way in which changes in the broad organizational environment are resulting in an increasing focus on leadership and a search for a clear picture of what effective leadership looks like. However, there are no easy solutions – there is no 'Holy Grail'. In the course of this journey, we have seen that the long-established and traditional 'heroic leadership' framework is of increasingly questionable relevance and, as recent events have shown, these can have detrimental, even disastrous implications for national and global economies. In today's complex environment, an approach to leadership which is more 'Engaging' appears to offer some useful pointers to more sustainable success.

It has also become evident that leadership not only takes place within a macro-context, but also in a dynamic relationship with the immediate organizational context. Understanding and exploring this dynamic enables change leaders to develop a clear focus and agenda both for action and their related development priorities. One of the most significant areas of focus is that of the culture of the organization. It is through the leader's impact on the culture that effective and long-lasting performance may be delivered.

In our exploration of the interaction between leadership and internal culture and, indeed, between leadership and the external context, it is apparent that much of the leadership agenda is core to the effective implementation of change. In Chapters 2 and 3, we explore in more detail the specific requirements involved in facing up to and leading change.

References

Alimo-Metcalfe, B. (1995). An investigation of female and male constructs of leadership. *Women in Management Review*, MCB, Bradford.

Bass, B. M. (1985). *Leadership and performance beyond expectations*. New York: Free Press.

Bass, B. M., & Avolio, B. J. (1996). *Postscripts: recent developments for improving organisational effectiveness*. London: Sage.

Burns, J. M. (1978). *Leaders' work*. New York: Harper & Row.

Clemens, J. K., & Mayer, D. F. (1999). *The classic touch: Lessons in leadership from Homer to Hemingway*. Chicago, IL: Contemporary Books.

Fiedler, F. (1964). A contingency model of leadership effectiveness. In L. Berkowicz (Ed.), *Advances in experimental and social psychology*. New York: Academic Press.

Goffee, R., & Jones, G. (1996). What holds the modern company together? *Harvard Business Review*, November–December, 137–148.

Hall, E. (1959). *The silent language*. New York: Anchor Press.

Hersey, P., & Blanchard, K. H. (1993). *Management of organizational behaviour; utilising human resources*. Englewood Cliffs, NJ: Prentice Hall.

Higgs, M. J., & Rowland, D. (2000). Building change leadership capability: 'The quest for change competence'. *Journal of Change Management*, 1(2), 116–131.

Higgs, M. J., & Rowland, D. (2005). All changes great and small. *Journal of Change Management*, 5(2), 121–135.

Hofstede, G. (1991). *Cultures and organizations*. Maidenhead: McGraw-Hill International (UK).

Kets De Vries, M. R. (1993). *Leaders, fools, imposters*. San Francisco, CA: Jossey-Bass.

Kotter, J. P. (1990). What leaders really do. *Harvard Business Review*, May–June, 37–60.

Kouzes, J. M., & Posner, B. Z. (1998). *Encouraging the heart*. San Francisco, CA: Jossey-Bass.

Schein, E. H. (1985). *Organizational culture and leadership*. New York: Wiley.

Shamir, B. (1992). Attribution of influence and charisma to the leader. *Journal of Applied Social Psychology*, 22(5), 386–407.

Chapter 2

The Challenge
of Change

Introduction

This chapter focuses on the critical challenges faced by organizations in implementing change. In considering how change leadership can be developed, it is important to consider the emerging changes impacting organizational life in more detail. In particular, it is relevant to reflect on:

- the drivers of and difficulties associated with change;
- the differing types of change;

■ experience of organizations in implementing change and lessons which may be learned;

■ developing an understanding of what works and what does not work in implementing change.

In exploring these issues here, a significant range of research into change implementation will be examined, together with experiences from practice.

Why is change so important and difficult?

We consistently hear that the external environment is increasing in its complexity and volatility and by extension this becomes a significant driver within organizations. This is not to say that all organizational change is reactive. The environment establishes a broad context; much organizational change represents either a response to this changing context or an anticipation of future contextual changes. In broad terms, there is much agreement that the main contextual change drivers are:

■ *Increasing levels of competition*: The competitive landscape is impacted by changes in entrants to the market as well as changes in consumer demands and expectations.

■ *Investor and stakeholder demands*: In the private sector, investors' demands for improved performance and returns are a frequent driver of organizational change. The relatively recent emergence of the impact of private equity funds has, to a significant extent, increased this drive for change. At the same time, in the public sector (particularly in the UK), demands from both service users and government create pressures for organizational change.

■ *Globalization*: The emergence of a global economy gives rise not only to changing competition but also to challenges relating to working across cultural boundaries and managing culturally diverse workforces often in diverse locations. In broad terms, this places pressures on organizations to change ways of working, leading and developing their business.

■ *Changing nature of the workforce*: Whilst the process of globalization leads to greater workforce diversity, organizations are also faced with a workforce with different values, expectations and communication media useage. 'Traditional' ways of leading and managing are no longer acceptable to many employees. Increasingly, organizations are wrestling with ways of securing employee commitment and attracting and retaining key talent. This creates significant pressures to change and develop appropriate leadership behaviors, human resource systems and ways to share knowledge.

■ *Technology*: Few of us have not been touched by the ever-advancing pace of technological developments. Such developments create conditions which demand organizational changes in terms of finance, production, marketing, work processes communication and even location (both of business units and employees).

■ *Legal and regulation*: It is a paradox that as business acts globally and requires flexibility in order to respond to the challenges of a local and global marketplace, they are faced with an increasing level of legal interventions and regulation. Whilst the details vary from country to country, there are also changes which have global effects. For example, the Sarbanes–Oxley legislation has had a significant impact in terms of governance structures and processes for any business with some degree of connection to the USA. Recent machinations at the G20 summit are likely to lead to global and local financing scrutiny.

■ *Societal changes*: Broader societal developments can lead to significant pressures on organizations to change their business practices and ways of working. The current concerns relating to 'global warming' are leading to pressures for change to both public and private sector organizations, through corporate social responsibility agendas, clean and energy efficient technologies, social entrepreneurship and not-for-profit agencies.

These change drivers create an organizational context in a way which leads to ever-increasing levels of complexity. In addition, there is a growing recognition that in order to achieve longer term viability, organizations need to become more flexible, adaptive, innovative and reputation savvy.

TYPES OF CHANGE

Many interventions in organizations are described as changes. However, in reality it is important to understand that there are different types of change, each of which presents differing challenges and may require differing approaches. One way of characterizing types of changes is essentially based on the extent or degree of change being considered. Three broad categories may be identified. These are:

1. Developmental
   Developmental change can be either planned or emergent; it tends to be incremental. It is change that enhances or corrects existing aspects of an organization, often focusing on the improvement of a skill or process.

2. Transitional
   Transitional change is intended to achieve a known desired state that is different from the existing one. It is episodic, planned and often radical. Much of the organizational change research and literature is based on this type.

3. Transformational
   Transformational change is sustainable in nature and requires a shift in assumptions made by the organization and its stakeholders. Transformation can result

in an organization that differs significantly in terms of structure, processes, culture and strategy. It may, therefore, result in the creation of an organization that subsequently operates in a way in which it continuously learns, adapts and improves.

Carnall (1999) proposed a somewhat different typology which he described as follows:

■ Organization-specific change
  This category relates to single change initiatives applying to a bounded part of the organization. For example, the development of a new product or goods/services distribution channel.

■ Generic organization-wide change
  This covers changes which tend to have an impact across the whole of the organization. For example, the introduction of Business Process Re-engineering, Total Quality Management programs, or their offshoots like 'lean', tend to touch all parts of the organization.

■ Generic multiorganizational change
  These are changes which involve more than one organization. Examples here would include mergers and acquisitions.

Within this framework, a further categorization emerges which is concerned with the distinction between episodic and continuous change. Episodic change tends to be infrequent, discontinuous and intentional. In essence episodic change tends to be radical and frequently entails the replacement of one strategy or program with another. On the other hand, continuous change is ongoing, evolving and cumulative. It is seen as 'improvement' change and is characterized by people constantly adapting ideas they acquire from different sources. At an organizational level, these continuous adjustments made across all parts of the organization can create significant leadership challenges. The principles of continuous change engender the flexibility to accommodate and experiment with everyday contingencies, breakdowns, exceptions, opportunities and unintended consequences that punctuate organizational life.

In considering types of change, it is also important to think about the part (or parts) of the organization which is the focus of the change. Those changes which impact on the core activities, structures or processes of the organization are likely to be more difficult to manage than those which impact on peripheral activities. Combining the dimension of radical:incremental change with the dimension of core:peripheral provides a framework for assessing the degree of challenge involved in any change. This framework is shown in Figure 2.1.

From this it is clear that the changes which present the greatest leadership challenge are those which impact core activities and where a radical approach is

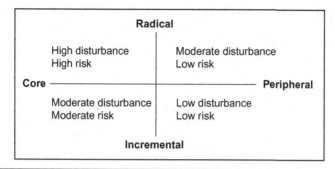

Figure 2.1   Framework for assessing change initiatives.

adopted. These introduce a high level of complexity into the change process. Yet it is to this quadrant that many organizations are increasingly drawn and attempt to deal with the complexity through the development of comprehensive and detailed process and project planning mechanisms.

More recent research has indicated that the 70% failure rate mentioned previously may overstate the degree of challenge faced in implementing change. However, these studies still indicate significant levels of change failure. So what are the reasons for consistent failure and what leads to success?

Research has shown that one of the causes of the failure to manage change is that managers have neither the expertise nor the capacity to implement change successfully and that managing change according to 'textbook theory' is difficult (Buchanan & Boddy, 1992). Others argue that the prevailing theoretical paradigms are based on assumptions that: (1) managers can choose successful changes in advance of environmental changes, (2) change is a linear process and (3) organizations are systems tending to states of stable equilibrium. This paradigm has a long history, perhaps beginning with Lewin (1947) who proposed the classic three-stage model of the change process that is shown in Figure 2.2. This model has been central to much of our thinking about how change works for many decades.

These views on the difficulty of change tend to be relatively 'high level' and often somewhat theoretical. Furthermore, much of the research and writing which examines change difficulty tends to look at the radical/core section of the change framework shown in Figure 2.1.

RESISTANCE TO CHANGE

In working with practicing managers in organizations, a major common difficulty associated with implementing change is the challenge of dealing with the resistance to change which is inevitably encountered. As witnessed in discussing the problems of successfully implementing the changes associated with Business Process

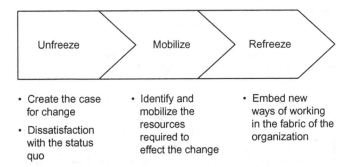

Figure 2.2   The three-phase model.
Source: Adapted from Lewin (1947).

Re-engineering, 'people are the problem!', even though change initiatives tend to forget, or over or underestimate, the likely responses of the people.

In exploring the nature and causes of resistance to change, the following have been identified as significant factors:

■ When the reason for the change is unclear. Ambiguity (whether it is about costs, equipment or jobs) can trigger negative reactions among employees.

■ When those impacted by the change have not been consulted about the change and it is offered to them as a fait accompli.

■ When change threatens to modify established patterns of working relationships between people.

■ When communication about the change (purpose, scope, timetables, personnel, etc.) has been inadequate. Employees need to know what is going on especially if their jobs may be affected. Informed employees tend to have higher levels of job satisfaction than uniformed ones.

■ When the benefits and rewards for making the change are not seen as adequate for the trouble involved.

■ When the change threatens jobs, power and status in an organization.

Associated with resistance is the challenge of securing the performance of all of the people impacted by the change. There is no doubt that performance dips during the early part of the change. If the 'natural' change cycle is achieved and managed, then, over time, performance can be rebuilt. The concept of a change cycle (or change curve) is illustrated in Figure 2.3.

What is clear from Figure 2.3 is that achieving individual and personal performance in relation to a change takes time (and effort). However, all too often the change imperative and related plans fail to allow for the personal transition of people. Resisters tend to be labeled as 'bad people' and frequently coerced into accepting

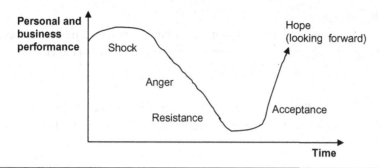

Figure 2.3   The change curve.

Source of change

		Me	Other
Target of change	Me	In control	In response
	Other	In direction mode	In support

Figure 2.4   How change is experienced.

the change. As a result, resumption of performance is rarely achieved and the levels of personal commitment of the 'resisters' decline. In order to develop strategies for managing resistance to change, it is helpful to consider how people in the organization experience the change. One useful way of thinking about this is illustrated in Figure 2.4.

This considers where the change is coming from and who is impacted by it. In a sense, it identifies the locus of control and an individual's position in the frame tends to lead to different experiences of change and, consequently, the nature and degree of resistance. For example:

■ In control
    This is the change we tend to feel best about. 'I am initiating it and it only impacts me' (e.g. losing weight, initiating a job transfer).

■ In response
    This is the change where we usually feel most resistant or 'victimised'. The change is being 'done' to us (e.g. top–down restructuring, being asked to develop a new skill).

- In direction mode

  We tend to feel pretty OK about this kind of change, although we usually encounter resistance from others, e.g. trying to change your partner's habits, setting staff performance objectives.

- In support

  We are not usually in this mode of change; however when we are (e.g. as a consultant or facilitator), it can feel strangely out of control and invisible which makes us anxious.

Within this framework, effective strategies for managing resistance tend to entail:

- Helping individuals and teams understand how they are responding to the change and why.

- Identifying opportunities to help individuals and teams to develop stronger feelings of control. In general terms, this tends to entail ensuring increased involvement in the creation of change activities. Achieving this entails a combination of facilitation (e.g. working with them to help them in achieving the change goals), and education (e.g. spending time on helping them to understand why the change is required).

In practice organizations have found that working with resistance, rather than trying to overcome it, is a more effective strategy. This way of viewing resistance places greater emphasis on understanding the impact of how we approach change on the ultimate effectiveness of its implementation. Furthermore, it emphasizes the need to do change with others rather than doing change to them.

Any approach to managing resistance is, in part, dependant upon being able to identify signs of resistance. There are potentially four distinct types of resistance. These are:

1. Covert resistance

   Covert resistance is deliberate resistance to change, but done in a manner that allows the perpetrators to appear as if they are not resisting.

2. Overt resistance

   Overt resistance does not try to hide and is a result either of someone comfortable with their power, someone for whom covert acts are against their values or someone who is desperate. This may take forms such as open argument, refusal or attack.

3. Passive resistance

   Passive resistance occurs where people do not take specific actions. At meetings, they will sit quietly and may appear to agree with the change. Their main tool is to refuse to collaborate with the change. In passive aggression, for example, they may agree and then do nothing to fulfil their commitments.

4. Active resistance
Active resistance occurs where people are taking specific and deliberate action to resist the change. It may be overt, such as public statements and acts of resistance, and it may be covert, such as mobilizing others to create an underground resistance movement.

Clearly both passive and covert resistance are the most difficult to identify quickly. If a change leader relies on purely responding to resistance, when encountered, these two categories may take too long to uncover and thus the resistance will have an opportunity to impact adversely on change implementation. It is a more productive strategy to try to anticipate reactions to the change and deploy the overall strategies outlined above.

Whilst resistance is generally perceived as being a negative within a change process, it is important to consider that resistance can be an indicator that change is having an impact. Furthermore, it surfaces the key issues and concerns which need to be addressed in order to ensure effective implementation in the long run. Finally, resistance can play a positive role in surfacing challenge and insights which can prove beneficial in achieving the change goals or indeed discovering more appropriate ones.

WHAT HAS BEEN LEARNED FROM WORKING WITH ORGANIZATIONS?

Much has been written about change based on experiences of organizations attempting to implement significant changes. One of the seminal works, based on the experience of working with organizations, is presented by John Kotter (1996). In his *Harvard Business Review* article, Kotter identified eight core reasons for change failure. These were:

1. *Allowing too much complacency*: Failing to make a sufficiently compelling case for change and allowing people within the organization to believe that the status quo is a viable option for the organization.

2. *Failing to find champions*: This leads to a focus on dealing with resisters rather than identifying, and utilizing, those who identify with the change and are able to influence others within the organization.

3. *Underestimating the power of vision*: In broad terms, the belief that the metrics relating to the change provide the impetus leads to minimal engagement. In reality, engagement with change is a combination of rational and emotional engagement, with the latter being the more powerful driver of action.

4. *Under-communicating the vision*: Relying on formal and rational communication of the change vision. Successful organizations communicate the vision on a face-to-face basis and leaders have conversations around this on an ongoing basis.

5. *Allowing obstacles to block the new vision*: Simply, in many organizations resistance and difficulty in implementation is allowed to halt the change implementation.

6. *Failing to create short-term wins*: In many organizations, the achievement of successful change implementation requires significant effort which needs to be sustained over a long period. However, unless there are visible signs of progress, it is difficult to sustain the required effort.

7. *Declaring victory too soon*: Too often change implementation success is monitored in terms of achievement of process and system change. However, true change only occurs when changes in individual behavior are realized.

8. *Neglecting to anchor changes firmly in the corporate culture*: In many cases, change is a 'silo' activity. The linkages with all aspects of the organizational system are ignored. For example, a change designed to develop higher levels of innovation based on effective teamworking is unlikely to be sustained unless the reward structures recognize both individual and team contributions.

Kotter proposed that if organizations addressed all of the above issues, they would be more successful in implementing significant change initiatives. However, in the decade following Kotter's insights, the level of change failure has not reduced. This indicates that addressing the important (if not critical) but challenging issue of implementing change warrants consideration of how implementation can be approached.

Approaches to change and how change happens

In practice, relatively few organizations consciously consider the options available to them in terms of how they might approach the implementation of a significant change. Approaches to change may be summarized under five headings, viz:

1. Directive
2. Expert
3. Negotiating
4. Educative
5. Participative

Brief descriptions of these approaches are as follows:

■ Directive

This strategy focuses on the leaders' right to manage change and the use of authority to impose change with little or no involvement of other people. The advantage of the directive approach is stated to be that change can be undertaken quickly. However, the disadvantage of this approach is that it does not take into consideration the views, or feelings, of those involved in, or affected by, the imposed change. This approach may lead to valuable information and ideas being missed and there is usually strong resentment from employees when changes are imposed rather than discussed and agreed.

■ Expert

Within this approach, the management of change is seen as a problem-solving process that needs to be resolved by an 'expert'. In general, the approach is applied to more technical problems and is normally led by a specialist project team or senior manager. There is likely to be little involvement with those affected by the change. The advantages to using this strategy are that experts play a major role in the solution and the solution can be implemented quickly as a small number of 'experts' are involved. Again, there are some issues in relation to this strategy as those affected may have different views from those of the 'expert' and may not appreciate the solution being imposed or the outcomes of the changes made.

■ Negotiating

This strategy emphasizes the willingness on the part of leaders to negotiate and bargain in order to effect the desired change. In employing such an approach, leaders need to accept that adjustments and concessions may need to be made in order to implement the change. The approach acknowledges that those affected by change have the right to have a say in what changes are made, how they are implemented and the expected outcomes. A major perceived disadvantage is that the approach takes more time to effect change, the outcomes cannot be predicted and the changes may not fulfil the total expectations of the leadership team. However, a significant advantage is that individuals will feel involved in the change and be more supportive of the changes made.

■ Educative

Within this approach, the emphasis is on changing people's values and beliefs, 'winning hearts and minds', in order for them to fully support the changes being made and move toward the development of a shared set of organizational values that individuals are willing and able to support. As with a negotiating approach, the disadvantage is that the approach is asserted to take longer to implement. However, the advantage is that individuals within the organization will have positive commitment to the changes being made.

■ Participative

This strategy emphasizes extensive involvement of all of those involved and affected by the anticipated changes. Although driven by leaders, change processes are less management dominated and driven more by groups or individuals within the organization. The views of all are taken into account before changes are made. The main disadvantages of this approach are the length of time taken before any changes are made and it can be more costly due to the number of meetings that take place. However, the benefits are that changes made are more likely to be supported due to the involvement of all those affected. The commitment of individuals and groups within the organization will increase because they will feel ownership of the changes.

Since the early 1950s, the dominant thinking about change (and consequent approaches) may be described as largely programmatic. This results in change approaches which are characterized by:

■ *Linear and sequential thinking*: A mindset which sees change implementation as employing clearly defined steps with an ability to predict the outcomes of each intervention.

■ *Change is initiated and implemented on a 'Top down' basis*: The need for change is identified and the plans for implementation are developed by the senior leadership group and then cascaded through the organization (or impacted part of the organization).

■ Without the intervention of the senior leadership group, no change in response to a changing context would occur. In other words, there is a significant level of inertia amongst those who work within the organization.

■ *The role of change leaders is interventionist*: Through interventions the leaders drive the change forward.

Underpinning this frame is a 'mind-set' which sees change as essentially episodic with a goal of creating or enhancing economic value. Since the mid-1990s, lessons from research into 'Complex Adaptive Systems' from fields such as physics, biology and the natural world have greatly influenced thinking about organizational change. This world view assumes that change is happening all the time, it is 'emerging' all around us, it is a feature of living systems where equilibrium would equal death. Can we therefore treat human communities in organizations as living systems? The leadership challenge turns the programmatic sequence on its head – it is to discover existing pockets of innovation ('freeze'), work with that energy and shape it ('adjust') and then set the organization free again ('unfreeze'). It assumes a more organic, yet also unpredictable change sequence.

Employing this way of thinking leads to what have been described as 'Emergent' change approaches which are characterized by:

- *Systems thinking*: Viewing the organization as a complex system and understanding the connections and interactions in order to stimulate change.
- *Change can start anywhere in the system*: In complex organisms, the largest changes often start at the periphery of the system. This is the point where the organism interacts with its environment. In an organizational context, the parallel is that the need for change, and related adaptations, is often found at the interface between the organization and its customers (the front line).
- *People in the organization are naturally self-organizing*: They are capable of identifying and responding to changes in the external environment.
- *The role of change leaders is to help the people in the organization make sense of the challenges and issues they face*: This is achieved through dialogue and the leader becomes a facilitator of change rather than a driver of change.

This framework operates on the belief that change is a continuous, adaptive, process. The goal of such change is seen as not only creating economic value, but also developing the capability of the organization. For some while, these differing frames for thinking about change tended to be seen as competing views. However, in practice, change approaches can vary depending on the context and needs for change. The advantages and disadvantages of each approach are summarized in Table 2.1.

Higgs and Rowland (2005) in reviewing the research on change built on the programmatic versus emergent debate identified that approaches to change could be categorized using two axes which reflected core mindsets adopted by leaders in the change process. These were:

- *Simple to complex*: At the simple end of this axis change is seen as a linear process in which actions can be planned and consequences predicted. At the complex end of the axis change is seen as a complex phenomenon in which outcomes cannot be readily predicted and the process of change cannot be assumed to be linear.
- *Uniform to distributed*: This axis relates to the extent to which change has to be standardized throughout the organization. At the uniform end, standardization dominates. However, at the distributed end of the axis, whilst the intent and direction of change is shared throughout the organization, the implementation of the change can vary in different parts of the organization.

Much of the writing on change is either descriptive of a specific case or somewhat theoretical. Higgs and Rowland (2005) conducted an extensive research project to explore how change really happens. In doing this, they collected data from over 50

Table 2.1 Reviewing alternative change approaches

	Advantages	Disadvantages
Emergent	■ Adaptability/ breakthrough ■ Local sensitivity ■ Works with natural energy ■ Exploits tacit knowledge ■ Develops self-capacity ■ Quick feedback and learning	■ Too slow/not good facing threats ■ Not bold or visionary enough ■ Paradigm shifts not visible ■ Against the grain – control of outcomes/hierarchy ■ Limited by pre-existing skills
Programmatic	■ Captures attention and focus ■ Aligned to power distribution ■ Conveys rationality to shareholders ■ Easier to diffuse	■ High probability of relapse ■ Less suitable for opportunity driven change ■ Patchy implementation ■ Has unanticipated consequences ■ Temptation toward hypocrisy

Source: Adapted from Weick (1995).

change leaders drawn from 12 organizations. Each change leader was asked to recount stories relating to changes in which they had been involved. In all, they collected nearly 100 change stories. Analyses of this data identified four distinct approaches to change. These are placed within the axes described above and are shown in Figure 2.5.

Further analyses of this data explored the relative success of the changes described together with a range of contextual factors (e.g. speed of change, scale, complexity, etc.). From these analyses they found:

(i) In high magnitude change (i.e. change which impacts a large number of people and entails changes to multiple parts of the system), the most effective change approach is an Emergent one. This approach accounted for nearly a third of the variance in change success.

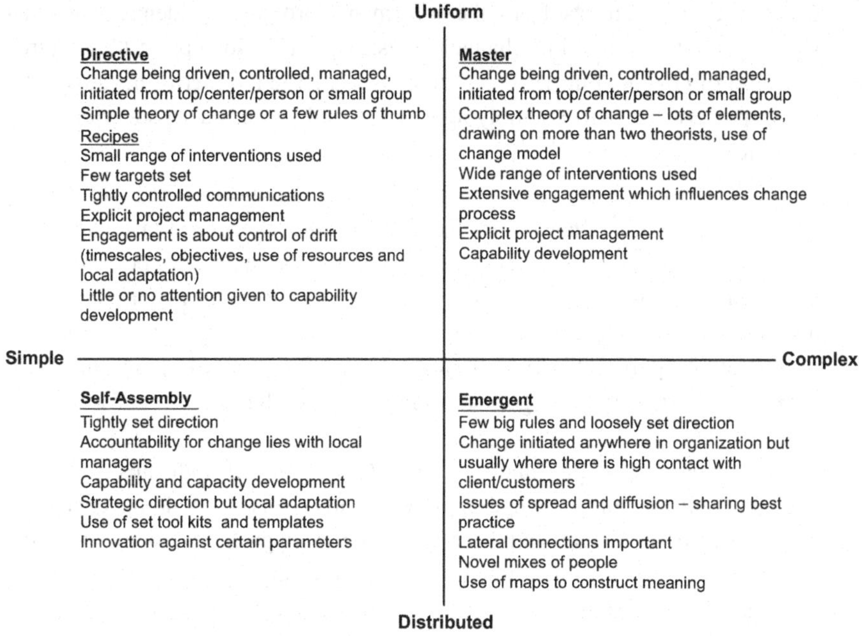

Uniform

Directive	Master
Change being driven, controlled, managed, initiated from top/center/person or small group	Change being driven, controlled, managed, initiated from top/center/person or small group
Simple theory of change or a few rules of thumb	Complex theory of change – lots of elements,
Recipes	drawing on more than two theorists, use of
Small range of interventions used	change model
Few targets set	Wide range of interventions used
Tightly controlled communications	Extensive engagement which influences change
Explicit project management	process
Engagement is about control of drift	Explicit project management
(timescales, objectives, use of resources and	Capability development
local adaptation)	
Little or no attention given to capability	
development	

Simple ─────────────────────────────┼───────────────────────── Complex

Self-Assembly	Emergent
Tightly set direction	Few big rules and loosely set direction
Accountability for change lies with local	Change initiated anywhere in organization but
managers	usually where there is high contact with
Capability and capacity development	client/customers
Strategic direction but local adaptation	Issues of spread and diffusion – sharing best
Use of set tool kits and templates	practice
Innovation against certain parameters	Lateral connections important
	Novel mixes of people
	Use of maps to construct meaning

Distributed

Figure 2.5 Four change approaches explained.
Source: Copyright RFLC 2007.

(ii) Change is a complex activity. Those approaches identified as being underpinned by assumptions at the simple end of the simple:complex axis shown in Figure 2.5 above (i.e. Directive change and Self-assembly change) are less effective in most scenarios than those which recognize the underlying complexity of the phenomenon (i.e. Master and Emergent approaches). Indeed both Directive and Self-assembly approaches were negatively related to success in most contexts.

(iii) An Emergent approach to change appeared to be more successful than any of the other three change approaches in most contexts. Analyses indicated that an Emergent approach explains greater proportions of variance in success. However, informants were often describing an Emergent approach from an intuitive rather than theoretically informed perspective. From the interviews, it was apparent that the Emergent approach occurred in the context of a change framework that was more planned and structured. It is feasible, from this data, to propose that the Emergent approach describes how change actually happens as opposed to how change is articulated.

(iv) An approach to change that is both simplistic and widely differentiated (see Figure 2.5, i.e. a Self-assembly approach) appears to be unsuccessful in any context. Change stories from the informants provided evidence that what was referred to as 'tool kit' change consistently failed to support the required direction of change. Furthermore, there were a large number of negative relationships between Self-assembly approaches and success across a wide range of contexts.

(v) In long-term change initiatives (i.e. those with a time horizon of more than 18 months), and within organizations facing continuing change, a Master approach appears to be an effective strategy. Evidence for the interviews pointed to the importance, in such contexts, of creating an overall framework for change and developing both individual and organizational capacity for change. Analyses of the data supported this view showing that a Master approach accounted for 21% of the variance in change success in long-term change.

In broad terms, the Higgs and Rowland (2005) model indicates that both Directive and Self-assembly change approaches are focused on doing change to people; whereas both Master and Emergent change approaches focus on doing change with people. The results indicate that doing change with people is a more effective change strategy in most contexts including short-term change. Thus the more participative practice of change is more effective and less disadvantageous than has been suggested by many writers on change.

The high failure rates of change implementation present organizations with a major challenge. This is particularly so as there are increasing pressures on organizations to change in response to a volatile and rapidly changing environment. What is clear is that the problem of implementing change is not something which lends itself to simplistic solutions. Indeed, the process of change implementation is described by many leaders as being a 'very messy business'.

The exploration of alternatives to the dominant 'programmatic' view of change has provided valuable insights into some of the approaches which have a greater chance of success. What is clear is that many of the more promising approaches require a shift in our view of the change leader's role and the associates capabilities required.

In broad terms, this chapter has shown that although it is clearly difficult to implement change effectively, there is a growing volume of evidence which indicates that success is more likely if:

■ change is understood as a complex leadership, management and follower phenomenon;

■ change approaches and processes genuinely involve all of those impacted by the change;

■ change leaders have the capabilities necessary to lead the implementation of change in complex and volatile settings, in a more involving manner.

To a large extent, this book is designed to explore in more detail the last of these points. Further chapters will examine the nature of the capabilities required by change leaders and how these may be developed, leading to the specification of our top 10 capabilities emanating from practice and research.

References

Buchanan, D., & Boddy, D. (1992). *The expertise of the change agent.* London: Prentice Hall.

Carnall, C. (1999). *Managing change in organizations.* London: Prentice-Hall.

Higgs, M. J., & Rowland, D. (2005). All changes great and small. *Journal of Change Management,* 5(2), 121–135.

Kotter, J. P. (1996). *Leading change.* Boston, MA: Harvard Business School Press.

Lewin, K. (1947). *Field theory in social science.* New York: Harper & Row.

Weick, K. E. (1995). *Sense-making in organisations.* Thousand Oaks, CA: Sage Publications.

What Does It Take to Lead Change?

Introduction

The overall aim of this book is to identify strategies and tactics for developing change leaders. In order to develop such leadership capability, it is important to have a clear picture of what is required to lead change effectively. This chapter is designed to provide a view of the areas of focus required in any change leadership development process.

Having explored the context and challenges of change, the significance of the role of leadership is notable. In this chapter, we build on the general developments in our thinking about leadership and explore the specific aspects which are important to enable effective leadership of the implementation of change.

In doing this, the chapter begins by exploring the range of roles encountered in a change process. Understanding the nature of the role being played is an important prerequisite for understanding the nature and style of leadership behavior which is required for each specific role. The chapter then explores a range of views and models encountered in developing an understanding of what it takes to lead effective change interventions. This exploration covers views on skills, competencies and leadership practices.

Critical roles in a change process

In any change process, there are four critical roles, which are:

1. *Change Advocates*: The individual (or group of individuals) who are primarily concerned with the initiation of the change.
2. *Change Sponsors*: The senior-level individuals within the organization who place their support behind the change and give legitimacy to the interventions required to implement the change.
3. *Change Agents*: The individuals charged with the implementation of the change process.
4. *Change Targets*: The individuals impacted by the change and whose practices and behaviors need to be modified in order to achieve the goals of the change.

In the light of this categorization of roles, it is evident that three of them immediately relate to leadership, either based on position, power or practice (i.e. advocate, sponsor or agent). However, leaders can also be change targets and, therefore, the roles are not necessarily arranged in a hierarchical manner. Indeed there is a dynamic relationship between the roles. This is shown diagrammatically in Figure 3.1.

For example, an individual senior manager may have identified a need for a change which has an impact beyond their immediate remit. In this case the senior manager may be the change Advocate. However, in order to achieve the support and resource necessary to make this change happen, they need access to senior levels within the organization and need to secure the support of a senior member of the executive who will act as the change Sponsor. Given a clear case and relevant sponsorship, the change Agent is the individual who has the role of leading the implementation of the change. The change Target is the individual impacted by the change. The target could indeed be an individual in the organization who is at a higher level in the organization than the change Agent. This is an example of where the dynamic relationship between the roles becomes notable. The Agent may need

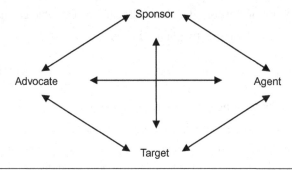

Figure 3.1 Dynamic change role relationships.

the support of the Sponsor in securing behavioral change in a Target who is at a higher organizational level than the Agent. Of these four roles, three require proactive leadership skills and behaviors (i.e. Advocate, Sponsor and Agent), whilst the fourth (i.e. Target) requires somewhat different skills and behaviors. In broad terms, the key leadership skills required within each role may be seen as being:

■ *Change Advocate*: Ability to exercise environmental scanning, identify the need for change, ability to formulate and articulate the case for change, influencing and persuasion skills.

■ *Change Sponsor*: Networking skills, political awareness and role modelling skills.

■ *Change Target*: A leader in the role of change Target – it is important that skills relating to challenging constructively, assumption surfacing and clarifying through inquiry are important. These skills ensure that the Target is not a passive participant in the change process, but can contribute to effective implementation through skilled engagement with the change.

■ *Change Agent*: Much of the literature and research associated with change leadership focuses on the role of the change Agent.

In reviewing the role of the change Agent, Buchanan and Boddy (1992) identify the importance of effective Agents by understanding that the reality of change implementation requires a combination of ability to manage the explicit change plans and processes, and the ability to operate separately within the organization's political and power structures. They refer to this as being the 'performing' and 'backstaging' skills and abilities.

The public 'performing' skills relate to:

■ following the ritual, and legitimizing the script, relating to the rational/linear model of change project management;

- implementing rationally considered and logically phased change plans;
- visibly encouraging participation in the change process.

However, they propose that the 'backstage' activity requires skills relating to:

- engaging and maintaining support for the change;
- identifying and overcoming resistance to the change;
- influencing others, deploying power, negotiating, selling the case for change, and managing the interpretation of the purpose and meaning of the change.

Weick (1995) sees the focus for change leadership as being to help those involved in the change to make sense of what is happening and what needs to happen. 'Given the ambiguity created by change, the effectiveness of any intervention is determined not so much by the content of the change initiative as by the quality of the interaction available to deal with the ambiguity created by that project' (Weick, 1995, p. 48). Core to this sense-making process is the leader's skilled use of inquiry as an aid to uncovering the systemic issues underpinning the need for change and which either support or impair change implementation. Building on this view, Isaacs (2000) sees two major skill areas for change Agents. He identifies these as being Advocacy and Inquiry, both of which need to be exercised in a skilled and balanced manner. He sees the focus of advocacy as being a process of influencing which requires the leader to:

- state his/her opinion and providing a description of the data which informs this opinion;
- provide an overview of their reasoning, in particular explaining their assumptions;
- test his/her conclusions; having provided their opinion and the leader invites input from others, having encouraged this input.

Isaacs (2000) describes the focus of inquiry being that of learning. This, he proposes, requires the leader to:

- ask questions as a means of drawing out the reasoning of others;
- stating why he/she is asking this question; this provides a means of connecting individuals' responses to the leader's intent in relation to the change;
- explore the responses to the questions, in particular this requires the ability to elicit specific examples to illuminate the responses;
- check his/her understanding of the responses; the purpose here is to build a new or deeper understanding rather than to close down dialogue or promote their own ideas.

Overall, leaders need to deploy a balanced mix of advocacy in acting as a change Agent. In this way, Isaac suggests they achieve effective dialogue which, in itself, progresses the change. In a similar vein, Shaw (1997) suggests that conversations are central to change. She proposes that the most effective thing a leader can do in order to bring about change in an organization is to change the nature of the conversations which take place in the organization.

Whilst much of the work around implementing change has focused on understanding the roles and responsibilities, research into causes of change failure has demonstrated that little emphasis has been placed on the importance of a broader understanding of the role and behavior of change leaders. Indeed Buchanan and Boddy (1992) have suggested that a major cause of the endemic failure of change can be attributed to the failure to understand that change leadership capability needs to be developed and to invest in this development. It has been suggested that typical leadership development activities build the capability to leaders to solve problems rather than deal with ambiguity, paradoxes and dilemmas. Yet it is the latter which are central to the process of change within an organization. Within this context, many have argued that the skills and competencies required by leaders in general need to be reappraised in the context of their significant role and impact on the effectiveness of change implementation (Conner, 1999). Further, it has been suggested that the development of change leadership capability can, in itself, provide organizations in today's context with significant competitive advantage. However, much of this debate takes a relatively traditional/hierarchical view of leadership. This raises a question concerning who we see as being involved in the leadership of change. Senge et al. (2002) suggested that the traditional leadership view may constrain an organization's ability to build change leadership capability. His following observation appears particularly apposite to the debate.

Might not the continual search for the hero-leader be a critical factor in itself, diverting attention away from building institutions that by their very nature, continually adapt and reinvent themselves, with leadership coming from many people and many places and not just from the top.

Senge et al. (2002, p. 64)

In pursuing this line, a broader view of change leadership emerges, which is largely focused on the view that certain change leadership competencies are prerequisites for successful implementation, irrespective of the hierarchical level of the 'change leader'. This developing 'competency' school is explored further in the next section.

Change leadership competencies

There have been a number of attempts to categorize and explain the major competencies associated with effective change leadership. At a very high level, the core change leadership competencies required to develop change capability within an organization can be seen to be:

(i) change mastery (i.e. a deep understanding of change and challenges and approaches);

(ii) managing resistance;

(iii) an appetite to learn;

(iv) an ability to influence without authority.

Working at a more detailed level, Buchanan and Boddy (1992) conducted a survey within a broad range of organizations. From an analysis of the responses, they identified the following areas of competence:

(i) sensitivity to key personnel changes and their impact on goals;

(ii) clarity in specifying goals and defining the achievable;

(iii) flexibility in responding to change and risk taking;

(iv) team building;

(v) networking;

(vi) ambiguity tolerance;

(vii) communication skills;

(viii) interpersonal skills;

(ix) personal enthusiasm;

(x) stimulating motivation and commitment in others;

(xi) selling plans and ideas to others;

(xii) negotiating with key players for resources and change;

(xiii) political awareness;

(xiv) influency skills;

(xv) helicopter perspective.

Although there are a diverse range of such frameworks, some emerging patterns can be identified. Higgs and Rowland (2001) conducted a review of both academic and practitioner literature and produced the overall review summarized in Table 3.1.

Based on this review, Higgs and Rowland (2001) undertook an action research project, working with a global energy company, to develop a change leadership competency framework. This research led to the development of a reliable framework which proved to be valuable in building this organization's change leadership capability and has subsequently been validated in further research projects.

Table 3.1   Change management competency profiles in the literature

Source	Key elements
Ulrich & Brockbank (2005)	Business Acumen, HR Practices and Managing Change (latter accounts for 42.7% of the variance in HR professionals' competency levels)
General Electric; Definition of HR Competencies	Knowledge of Business, Delivery of HR, Personal Credibility, Ability to Manage Change (Change Advocacy, Process Orientation, Facilitation)
Cornell University: Change Skills for HR Managers	Facilitation of Organizational Change (defining change goals, identifying obstacles and resistance, establishing change strategy, implementing interventions, techniques for managing transitions, empowering line managers)
PepsiCo's Change Leadership Profile	Roger Enrico Leading Change Seminar Skills Profile for HR Professionals (acting as a catalyst for change, being a facilitator, providing support to team members)
Conner (1999); Organization Development Research	ODR Candidate Selection Form (sponsor trust, challenge, group dynamics, change agent knowledge) ODR Change Resilience Profile (Positive, Focused, Flexibility, Organized, Proactive)
How to Be an Internal Consultant	Challenger, Interventionist, Provider of Insight, Process Analyst, Listener/Observer, Developer of Ownership
Oliver Wyman & Company; Criteria for Choosing Effective Change Agents	High levels of political support, works well across organizational boundaries, personally resilient, produces accurate perception of reality, direct and open)

This framework is summarized in Table 3.2.

In a detailed study which followed up a change leadership competency development program, Higgs and Rowland (2002) demonstrated clear and significant relationships between the development of each of the competency areas and the change leaders' impact on the implementation of specific change initiatives which they were working with.

Table 3.2 Change management competency framework

Competency cluster	Competency indicators
Change Initiation (CIN); ability to create the case of change and secure credible sponsorship	Surface issues Demonstrates impact of issues on performance Influences key sponsors Secures sponsor commitment
Change Impact (CIM); ability to scope the breadth, depth, sustainability and returns of a change strategy	Scope of thinking Depth of impact (systemic thinking) Reframing Identifies 'returns on change'
Change Facilitation (CF); ability to help others, through effective facilitation, to gain insight into the human dynamics of change and to develop the confidence to achieve the change goals.	Manages human dynamics Encourages and supports self-management Conflict management Process management
Change Leadership (CL); ability to influence and enthuse others, though personal advocacy, vision and drive, and to access resources to build a solid platform for change.	Networking Relationship building Personal impact Sells ideas
Change Learning (CLE); ability to scan, reflect and identify learning and ensure insights are used to develop individual, group and organizational capabilities.	Coaching Listening and inquiry Knowledge management
Change Execution (CEX); ability to formulate and guide the implementation of a credible change plan with appropriate goals, resources, metrics and review mechanisms.	Organizational savvy Manages resistance Journey design Journey management
Change Presence (CP); demonstrates high personal commitment to achievement of change goals through integrity and courage, while maintaining objectively and individual resilience ('a non-anxious presence in a sea of anxiety')	Courage Resilience Authenticity Objectivity
Change Technology (CT); knowledge, generation and skilful application of change theories, tools and processes.	Theories Tools Processes

Reproduced under licence to TRANSCEND.

The results of this study provided significant support for the view that building change leadership capabilities provide a solid platform for successful change. An interesting finding which emerged from this study was that the participants did not follow a set or common approach to the overall change implementation process. Indeed as both Moss Kanter (1996) and Senge et al. (2002) have commented 'there is no one right way to implement change'. What is important is that the leadership of the change is developed to diagnose, understand, confront and reshape the reality as people see it. It is only by learning new things about ourselves, our relationships with others and discovering new ways of seeing reality that we can start to implement new business practices that ultimately will lead to different (and improved) business results. To a large extent this links to the significance of self-awareness in leadership which we refer to in Chapter 6. In the next section we will explore this linkage in a little more detail.

DOES IT TAKE EMOTIONAL INTELLIGENCE TO LEAD CHANGE EFFECTIVELY?

For some considerable time, research has shown significant links between self-awareness and broader managerial competence. However, in the course of the last decade, the significance of self-awareness has received increasing attention with the emergence of the concept of Emotional Intelligence. This concept became widely discussed in both academic and practitioner communities following the publication of Goleman's (1996) book. In essence, Goleman provided a thought-provoking summary of the development in the academic world of the concept of Emotional Intelligence and translated this thinking into a business context. At its core the concept of Emotional Intelligence relates to the ability to recognize emotions in both oneself and others, to understand the impact of these emotions on behaviors and interactions, and to be able to regulate these emotionally driven behaviors.

Research based on this context has broadly demonstrated, in an organizational context, that Emotional Intelligence is positively related to career progression, managerial performance, leadership potential and psychological well-being. More recent research in this area has paid increasing attention to the relationship between Emotional Intelligence and leadership effectiveness. Whilst there are numerous models of Emotional Intelligence, one developed by Higgs and Dulewicz (2002) has been used extensively in leadership research. This model proposes that Emotional Intelligence results from a combination of the following seven components:

1. *Self-awareness*: The awareness of your own feelings and the ability to recognize and manage these.
2. *Emotional resilience*: The ability to perform well and consistently in a range of situations and when under pressure.

3. *Motivation*: The drive and energy which you have to achieve results, balance short- and long-terms goals and pursue your goals in the face of challenge and rejection.

4. *Interpersonal sensitivity*: The ability to be aware of the needs and feelings of others and to use this awareness effectively in interacting with them and arriving at decisions impacting on them.

5. *Influence*: The ability to persuade others to change their viewpoint on a problem, issue or decision.

6. *Intuitiveness*: The ability to use insight and interaction to arrive at and implement decisions when faced with ambiguous or incomplete information.

7. *Conscientiousness and integrity*: The ability to display commitment to a course of action in the face of challenge, to act consistently, and in line with understood ethical requirements.

In reviewing their work in change leadership competencies, Higgs and Rowland (2001) hypothesized that a relationship existed between the competencies they had identified which were associated with successful change implementation and the seven elements of Emotional Intelligence. To test this hypothesis they developed a reliable questionnaire to assess change leadership competencies and used this together with the Higgs and Dulewicz Emotional Intelligence questionnaire with a sample of 84 change leaders drawn from a range of private sector organizations. The data from this study demonstrated clear and significant correlations between Emotional Intelligence and change leadership competencies. This research provides support for the view that effective change leadership requires the leaders to have a high level of Emotional Intelligence. In Chapter 6 we explain how Emotional Intelligence can be developed.

Change leadership practices

Whilst there is a vast literature on leadership, there is comparatively little written about change leadership as a specific area of study. Furthermore, a general critique of the body of work suggests it is relatively generic and derivative. Studies which explore specific leadership behaviors and practices in a change context are rare. Higgs and Rowland (2005) have responded to this critique. In a major and long-term study, they examined specific change leadership practices and behaviors. Their studies involved extensive interviews with leaders who had been involved in change. Leaders were asked to relate stories of changes they had been involved with and provide detailed examples of their practices and behaviors. The first study focused on the behaviors of leaders. In this study they collected over 100 change leadership stories. Analysis of these identified three broad groupings of behaviors. These were:

(i) *Shaping Behavior*: The communication and actions of leaders related directly to the change, 'making others accountable', 'thinking about change' and 'using an individual focus'.

(ii) *Framing Change*: Establishing starting points for change, 'designing and managing the journey' and 'communicating guiding principles in the organization'.

(iii) *Creating Capacity*: Creating individual and organizational capabilities, communication and making connections.

The specific behaviors they identified within these categories were:
Shaping Behavior

■ Leaders play a significant role and tend to act as the 'movers and shapers'.

■ The leader sets the pace for others to follow.

■ Leaders expect others to do what they do; they look to others to work as hard and enthusiastically in the implementation of the change.

■ The leader is personally expressive and tends to be very persuasive.

■ Leaders hold others accountable for performing allocated tasks and delivering results.

■ Leaders personally control what gets done in implementing the change.

Framing Change

■ Leaders work with others to create a vision and direction for the change.

■ The leader helps others to understand why things need changing and, importantly, that the change is not temporary (i.e. there is no going back).

■ Leaders share with others the overall plans of what has to be done in order to implement this change.

■ Having established the framework, leaders give others the space and freedom to do what needs to be done to realize the change goals.

■ Leaders work with others to find ways of changing how things get done, not just what gets done.

Creating Capacity

■ Leaders develop the skills of others in implementing change.

■ Leaders provide feedback to let others know how they are doing and coaches them in order that they can improve their abilities and performance in implementing the change.

■ The leader works with people across the organization in order to get individuals working across organizational boundaries. In addition, the leader gets people to focus on processes across the organization rather than within their own areas of responsibility.

■ Leaders notice what is happening within the wider system and ensure that the organization's processes and systems support the change.

From their research, Higgs and Rowland (2005) found a relationship between these leadership behaviors and the approach to change which was being adopted. In broad terms they found that:

■ In Directive change Shaping Behaviors tended to dominate.

■ In Master change Framing Behaviors were dominant.

■ In Emergent change Creating Capacity tended to be the dominant set of leadership behaviors.

It was interesting to see that in Self-Assembly change, there was no clear dominance of any of the three types of leadership behavior.

The relative impact of the different sets of leadership behaviors on the success of the change was explored. The context of the change was considered in assessing the impact of the leadership behaviors on the success of the change. Overall, they found that:

■ In all contexts Shaping Behavior was negatively related to the success of the change. In other words, Shaping Behavior reduces the likelihood that the change will be successful.

■ Framing leadership behaviors were particularly successful in large-scale and short-terms change.

■ Creating Capacity was a particularly successful leaderships approach in long-term change and in a context in which organizations had a long history of change.

Based on these findings, Rowland and Higgs (2008) conducted a study to explore in more detail the leadership practices which tend to lead to successful change implementation. To do this, they interviewed leaders involved in change in some 30 organizations. Again, they asked the leaders to tell stories about specific changes and obtained data covering over 60 change stories. Analysis of this data identified four core leadership practices which were associated with successful change implementation. These are illustrated in Figure 3.2.

(i) Attractor
  • Connects with others at an emotional level, embodies the future intent of the organization.

Attractor

Creates an
energy for the
change

Edge and tension

Amplifies
disturbance
around the change

**Transforming
space**

Creates
movement

**Creates a
container**

Holds the tension
around the change

Figure 3.2 Behaviors which make a difference. Leaders UK Consortium ©RFLC 2006.

- Tunes in to day-to-day reality, sees themes and patterns that connect to a wider movement and from this creates a compelling story for the organization.
- Uses this to set the context of how things fit together, working the story into the life of the organization so that every conversation and decision 'makes sense'.
- Visibly works beyond personal ambition to serve higher purpose, the organization and its wider community.
- Is consciously aware of one's own leadership and adapts this for a specific purpose.

(ii) Edge and tension
- Tells it as it is – describes reality with respect yet without compromise
- In times of turbulence, has constancy; does not withdraw from tough stuff; keeps people's hands in the fire.
- Can spot and challenge assumptions – creates discomfort by challenging existing paradigms and disrupting habitual ways of doing things.
- Sets the bar high and keeps it there – stretches the goals and limits of what is possible.
- Does not compromise on talent – pays attention to getting and keeping top talent.

(iii) Container
- Sets and contracts boundaries, clear expectations and hard rules so that people know what to operate on (performance expectations) and how they need to operate (values and behaviors).

- Is self-assured, confident and takes a stand for one's beliefs – is non-anxious in challenging conditions.
- Provides affirming and encouraging signals; creates ownership, trust and confidence.
- Makes it 'safe' to say risky things and have the 'hard to have conversations' via empathy and high-quality dialogue skills.
- Creates alignment at the top to ensure consistency and constancy of approach.

(iv) Creates movement
  - Demonstrates a commitment that engenders trust, enabling the system to go to new places, learn about itself and act differently.
  - Frees people to new possibilities through making oneself vulnerable and open.
  - Understands what is happening in the moment and breaks established patterns and structures in ways that create movement in the 'here and now'.
  - Powerfully inquires into ripe systemic issues to enable deep change to happen.
  - Creates time and space (including attending to its physical quality) for transforming encounters.

In this study they found that the combination of all four of these practices explained around 50% of the variance in change success. Building on this they examined in more detail the practices of those leaders who deployed a balance of all four of these practices. In doing this they found that the differentiating practices were:

(i) They understand and incorporate the wider change context: they lead upwards and outwards to create space for the organization and catalyze energy for change.

(ii) They build their leadership teams to think and act for the whole: requiring them to step up and back to hold a bigger space and be strategic, interdependent and systemic – thereby creating an aligned transforming energy at the top.

(iii) They work on the underlying system that produces the performance outcomes: they show an intense ability to 'tune in' to their organization, see patterns, notice how things are said not just what's being said, identify the few key assumptions and patterns that if shifted would transform everything, and then take creative moves to make those shifts.

(iv) They are then patient with people to make the transition: while still keeping the change on course (others by contrast were passive, and just stood back and waited).

(v) They display extremely high levels of self-awareness: are able to sense the impact they have on others, seek feedback and exchange on this, and consciously use their presence in the organization to create shifts ('evidencing leadership').

(vi) They set tangible measures for the change: they open up the system to share information and performance data to both 'hold up the mirror' and catalyze people to take personal ownership for improving things.

In order to develop change leaders, it is important to begin with a clear picture of what it takes to lead change effectively. Whilst there are some broad views on the roles and competencies of change leaders, there have been relatively few studies which have examined specific leadership practices and behaviors which can make a real difference. However, recent research has provided useful insights into what successful change leaders do in practice and how they behave. From this research it is evident that leader-centric behaviors and practices are more likely to reduce the potential success of a change. However, more facilitative and engaging practices are shown to have a significant and positive impact on leadership of change implementation.

In Part 2, utilizing our coverage in Part 1, we develop and define what we consider to be our top 10 capabilities and associated development activities for priority investment of the development resource allocated to change leaders. However, before we arrive at this point, we consider what the research on leader's values, the leadership culture they create and the nature of their own leadership learning journey tells us in terms of a deeper understanding of the less tangible conditions and interplays associated with effective change leadership development.

References

Buchanan, D., & Boddy, D. (1992). *The expertise of the change agent.* London: Prentice Hall.

Buchanan, D., Claydon, T., & Doyle, M. (1999). Organisation development and change: the Legacy of the nineties. *Human Resource Management Journal, 9*(2), 20–37.

Conner, D. (1999). *Leading at the edge of chaos.* New York: John Wiley.

Goleman, D. (1996). *Emotional intelligence.* London: Bloomsbury.

Higgs, M. J., & Dulewicz, S. V. (2002). *Making sense of emotional intelligence.* London: ASE.

Higgs and Rowland (2002)

Higgs, M. J., & Rowland, D. (2001). Developing change leaders: assessing the impact of a development programme. *Change Management Journal, 2*(1), 47–64.

Higgs, M. J., & Rowland, D. (2005). All changes great and small. *Journal of Change Management, 5*(2), 121–135.

Isaacs, W. N. (2000). Taking flight: dialogue, collective thinking and organizational learning. In R. L. Cross & S. M. Isralit (Eds.), *Strategic learning in a knowledge economy.* London: Butterworth-Heinemann.

Kanter, R. M. (1996). *World class.* London: Simon & Schuster.

Rowland, D., & Higgs, M. J. (2008). *Sustaining Change: Leadership that Works.* Chichester: Jossey-Bass.

Shaw, P. (1997). Intervening in the shadow systems of organisations: consulting from a complexity perspective. *Journal of Organisational Change Management, 10*(3), 235–250.

Senge, P., Kleiner, A., Roberts, C., Ross, R., Roth, G., & Smith, B. (2002). *The dance of change.* San Francisco: Nicholas Brealey Publishing.

Ulrich, D., & Brockbank, W. (2005). *The HR value proposition.* San Francisco, Boston, MA: Harvard Business School Publishing.

Weick, K. E. (1995). *Sense-making in organisations.* Thousand Oaks, CA: Sage.

Part 2

How to Develop Change Leadership Capability

Introduction

The ability for leaders to change their own and others behavior and working practices depends to a large degree on understanding and connecting with the deeper motivational drivers which engage hearts as well as minds. People are more likely to accept and connect with change if the leadership actions they see in the workplace are authentic (where deeds match words) and where the messages surrounding change sent to their workplace resonate with their own sense of vision, purpose and values. Much of the dysfunctional behavior seen in working environments during periods of significant change are caused by change leaders not practicing what they preach and/or personal values clashes between managers, employees, suppliers, customers and stakeholders.

So, change leaders need to be cognizant of these dynamics, if when embarking on initiatives which appear plausible and logical to them, they find themselves not listened to or understood; or resisted, either actively or passively. It also helps if the leadership (represented by collective and distributed leaders throughout the organization) is able to send amplified and consistent signals about the new values and associated behavior priorities alongside the most pressing business goal demands. Development of such a strong 'leadership culture' is more likely to gain the change traction required.

This is the rationale for spending more time in Chapters 4 and 5 unpacking the detail of personal values and leadership culture respectively, with new research insights and case illustrations inserted along the way. Our contention is that leadership cultures which value values diversity and learn to work with these grains of difference, rather than reject what they find, or worse, ignore them altogether, are more likely to take people along with them, which is the whole purpose of change leadership. Change leaders are required to lead whole cultures, having moved beyond their managerial, functional and professional values reference points.

Following this exposition, in Chapter 6 we undertake an exploration of how leaders develop through time and experience to highlight the point that when we see them in 'here and now' development situations or events, we must recognize the different learning pathways or stages of journeys they are on. Failure to acknowledge this will lead to low take up of development offerings, inappropriate development solutions and/or frustration with poor translation of learning into leadership practice. To overcome this hurdle of 'development fit in real time', we use our analysis of the coverage in this book to identify what we consider to be the top 10 dynamic capabilities change leaders should be working toward acquiring, regardless of their current operational contexts, although they might choose to speed up their learning by selecting some from the list which are more suited to immediate leadership challenges.

We also include a range of development tools, techniques and activities, and some examples of development cases we were/are closely involved with, which reflect some of the ideas in this book, albeit viewed in retrospect. Our reflections on change leadership development practice and research, released by writing this book, means we can now present a capabilities-and-applications menu to draw upon for future programme design and implementation.

A Values Dialogue for Change Leaders

Chapter 4

Two Wolves:

One evening an old Cherokee told his grandson about a battle that goes on inside people. He said, 'My son, the battle is between two wolves inside us all. One is evil. It is anger, envy, jealousy, sorrow, regret, greed, arrogance, self-pity, guilt, resentment, inferiority, lies, false pride, superiority and ego. The other is good. It is joy, peace, love, hope, serenity, humility, kindness, benevolence, empathy, generosity, truth, compassion and faith'. The grandson thought about it for a minute and then asked his grandfather, 'Which wolf wins?' The old Cherokee simply replied, 'The one you feed'.

Introduction

Personal values, forming our own unique identity or 'brand', affect how we construct meaning in our world, and impact the way we perceive and understand our personal, business and social life. They act as a powerful filter for receiving communication and color our lens for making choices about with whom we are prepared to connect, trust, do business with, work for and invest our time and energy in. Values are a central feature of the intangibles impacting current and predicted business value, such as market confidence, brand loyalty, staff morale, customer retention and reputation. In periods of significant change, it is crucial for leaders to diagnose, discuss and clarify the nature of the entire 'values chain', beginning with the potentially different personal values held by the board, senior executive team members, managers and staff. Sometimes, an entirely new values system emerges through a shift in leadership culture, as witnessed with Barack Obama and his new administration (informed by Abraham Lincoln and the leadership culture he developed, described in Goodwin, 2009). Messages from leaders related to change, whilst resonating with the challenges of the time and forging a new zeitgeist (or spirit of our time), have to appeal emotionally to the different values audiences present if the changes laid out are to be acted upon.

Unfortunately, much confusion exists within business about whose values are referred to when considering the values which drive business behavior and strategic approaches to creating shareholder value. Problems of definition center on differences between corporate governance values, organizational values and the personal values of leaders. This is compounded by the diversity of personal values found within and across employee, customer and stakeholder groups, particularly if the business has international operations.

Business universally adopts value creation as the primary leadership role. Strategy literature rightly includes requisite leadership approaches, whilst largely ignoring the individual executive and his or her motivational drivers based on values (Finkelstein & Hambrick, 1996). For example, Schmidt and Posner (1982, p. 12) assert, 'The direction and vitality of corporate America and its managers cannot be fully understood without knowing more about the values and visions of the men and women who manage it'. With images of the impact of Enron, Lehman Brothers and RBS fresh in our minds, Aitken (2006) and Lichtenstein (2005) have respectively argued that if executives make strategic decisions either alone or together, and implement these through collective leadership to shape business culture, how can their personal values differences and mix be ignored?

Whilst many nonexecutive directors, chief executives and senior managers will be at ease pushing the organization beyond its natural limits, whatever the consequences, this may create conflict and de-motivate other managers and employees who are motivated by different values. Such discord may well destroy value if it is ignored and with the interconnected nature of global business, the effects on commerce and nations can be profound, as we have recently seen. As an example of possible disagreement in the next decade, the UN Global Compact and the European Foundation for Management Development (EFMD) have called for 'Globally Responsible Leadership' as a 'global exercise of ethical, values-based leadership in the pursuit of economic and societal progress and sustainable development' (EFMD, 2005, p. 2). This counters predominant market capitalism with its underpinning neo-liberal values and is the half-turn that Obama and others less wedded to 'year on year growth at any cost' economics are now espousing.

Gibson (1995) listed the significant changes in organizational life that remain relevant today: increasing diversity of the workforce, a shift in working environments from local to international markets, increasing numbers of mergers and acquisitions among organizations from different countries, re-structuring across national boundaries and emergence of information and telecommunication technologies, increasing and speeding up global communication traffic that affects types, ways and means of conducting business. She suggests that each of these changes will have a profound impact on the psychology of individuals in organizations given that studies have tended to focus on intra-personal events, rather than on happenings between people, including for example, the influence of culture and societal roles on social behavior within organizations. Values affect leaders in several ways.

They:

1. affect leaders' perceptions of situations;

2. affect the selection of solutions to problems;

3. play a role in interpersonal relationships;

4. influence perceptions of individual and business success;

5. provide a basis for differentiating between ethical and unethical behavior;

6. affect the extent to which leaders accept or reject business goals and pressures;

7. affect motivation and therefore leadership performance.

Indeed, Dolan and Garcia (2002) note a shift over time from an emphasis on 'Management by instruction' (based on hierarchies, procedures and controls), through 'Management by objectives' (MBO – using quality outputs and outcomes as motivational devices) to 'Management by values' (MBV). For them, true strategic leadership is at its most fundamental a dialogue about values, made more important because of the current need for: quality and customer orientation; greater professionalism, autonomy and responsibility in production and delivery; bosses who can evolve into transformational leaders (facilitators of organisational learning) and flatter and more agile organizational structures. Additionally, Ellis and Hall (2002), in considering the application of systems thinking as a key management tool to assist business in lifting the fog of change, regard values as the missing link. They call for a new, unified science of values, formed by integrating systems thinking, human values and 'transformative leadership' to enable organizations to sustain and thrive.

Since values differences are found everywhere in a globally connected and inter-dependent business and world environment, leaders (particularly Board and senior executive team members) need to create a shared 'values radar' to successfully navigate the business implications of this diversity together. The management focus for the first part of the twenty-first century will be the management of meaning through the demonstration of values in management behavior. How leaders respond to the dilemmas created by the interaction of diverse values through their everyday behavior will send strong signals to the internal culture and external business and community environment about what is truly and demonstrably valued around here (Schein, 1992; Trompenaars & Hampden-Turner, 2002).

MacMillan, Money, Downing and Hillenbrand (2004) argue that a focus on relationships allows directors to manage issues of governance, reputation and responsibility in a practical way such that they can address the dilemma of pursuing year on year improvements in financial performance, whilst protecting intangible assets such as their reputation with stakeholders. Clarification of predominant executive's values structures may encourage the Board and the senior executive team to acknowledge, discuss and understand different personal windows on ways to embark on and conduct business, commencing with self-insight into their own values drives.

The world of executive's personal values

Our intention here is not to provide an exhaustive review of the values literature. Rather, we concentrate on major contributions to the study of executive's values as expressed in their impact on leaders and their environments. Indeed, a recent survey found that 82% of UK professionals would not work for an organization whose values they did not believe in, (Levene, 2001); whilst another suggests one-third of graduates claim that working for a caring and responsible employer was more important than salary, while 44% would n't work for an employer with a bad reputation (Katbamna, 2007).

When considering manager's values, England (1967, p. 54) defined a 'Personal Value System' as 'a relatively permanent perceptual framework that shapes and influences the general nature of an individual's behavior. Values are similar to attitudes, but are more ingrained, permanent and stable in nature. (They are) closer to ideology or philosophy...'. Kenny (1994) defines values as principles or standards of an individual, group, organization or society as a whole. They reflect an individual or collective judgment as to what is valuable or important in life and provide a yardstick against which personal, organizational and societal behavior can be evaluated. He maintains that business visions can only be realized through the development and operation of a values base. For Posner and Schmidt (1994), 'Values are a silent power for understanding interpersonal and organisational life. Because they are at the core of people's personality, values influence the choices they make, people they trust, the appeals they respond to, and the way they invest their time and energy. In turbulent times values give a sense of direction amid conflicting views and demands'.

Dolan and Garcia (2002) position their MBV framework as one that is useful for a continual re-design of corporate culture, by which collective purpose and commitment is generated for new projects that address future based business positioning. The biggest limitation of MBO, they maintain, is it makes the assumption that objectives make 'sense' to everyone, whereas this can only be realized if they are founded on shared values. Thus, values serve to endow action with sense and guiding principles, whilst objectives serve to translate action into results and rewards. Or, in other words, leadership remains geared to the transactional level unless it is endowed with shared values that forge transformational approaches. Moreover, they maintain that this differentiation between 'final' values and 'operating' values is vital for the definition of strategy. The former are essential for giving meaning and cohesion to the collective effort required to move the business toward its long-term position by determining the kind of business it wants to become, the reason for its existence, its fundamental dimensions, competitor differentiators and community interests; whilst the latter is concerned with the daily tactics, conduct and ways of working in order to get the job done.

For them shared values are the 'glue' that allows these two elements of organizational life to work in concert, because they provide common guidelines to people making choices and decisions that affect operations against the background of strategy. Cross-cultural studies also indicate the importance of personal values. Tapsell (1998) reports preliminary (1997) findings from 35 countries (represented by 9,500 managers in 606 organizations) taking part in the GLOBE (Global Leadership and Organisational Behaviour Effectiveness) study of cross-cultural leadership theory validity, by House et al. (1999); indicating that 'values based' leadership was nearly universally endorsed. Schwartz (2005) suggests there are three fundamental values dilemmas that confront all societies, impacting on the expectations people hold and the predominant cultural atmosphere (Table 4.1).

A study by Sarros and Santora (2001) of the top 500 Australian companies found that values orientations of Australian executives, when compared with their Russian, Japanese and Chinese counterparts, revealed as many similarities as there were differences. Those executives whose values were grounded in values constructs such as benevolence and honesty (self-fulfilment), but who also retained a need for personal gratification and success (self-approval), were closely related to transformational leadership behaviors, particularly the encouragement of personal and professional development (see Figure 4.1).

One can see, therefore, that a leader's personal values will influence the primary drivers for their behavior during change. Clearly owner-manager's and executives' personal values influence the strategies adopted in running their businesses and consequent business performance (Kotey & Meredith, 1997; Lichtenstein, 2005). Strategic leadership includes, amongst other things, monitoring how well organizational culture,

Table 4.1 Fundamental values dilemmas

Autonomy versus embeddedness	*Autonomy* (emotional and intellectual) – promoting and protecting uniqueness *Embeddedness* – sharing a collective ambition and goals
Egalitarianism versus hierarchy	*Egalitarianism* – equals in opportunity and co-operation *Hierarchy* – allocation of fixed roles and resources based on authority
Harmony versus mastery	*Harmony* – at one with the world around us *Mastery* – control and exploitation of the world's resources

Source: Schwartz (2005).

including values, is supporting the business vision and mission (Gill, 2002). In strategic terms, Fiedler (1978) points out that organizational effectiveness is a function of the interaction between characteristics of the organization and the external environment, and characteristics of the members of the organization. And, executive's perceptions are a function of a number of factors, such as their experiences, capabilities, tenure, personality, functional backgrounds, values and national cultures (Finkelstein & Hambrick, 1996). In Sturdivant, Ginter and Sawyer's (1985) study of executive values and their impact on financial performance they state, 'In most organizations, it will be the collective personal values of senior management which will have the greatest influence on corporate goals' (p. 18); and older managers are associated with risk-aversion and being conservative (Thomas & Ramaswamy, 1996).

Beyer (1981), in her exhaustive review of the personal and corporate values literature, asserts that organizations use ideologies and values to legitimate their activities and to justify their decisions to members and the environment. People behave in accordance with their ideologies and values, and also in accordance with the ideologies and values of powerful superiors. However, the mechanics and effects of the values interaction between leaders and their immediate team members remain unexplored. Kabanoff, Waldersee and Cohen (1995) conclude their paper by suggesting that research into organizational values has a number of shortcomings, including an absence of theory, resulting in: an inability to deal with higher level values concepts, such as values structures, that may be key to understanding differences in social groups and values systems (Schwartz, 1992); uncertainty about how and why different organizational values' patterns develop in different contexts (Trice & Beyer, 1993) and although there is a perennial interest in whether values influence performance this is met by a shortage of longitudinal data on values from a sufficiently large sample (Siehl & Martin, 1990).

Aitken (2002) summarized the importance of personal values exploration as:

Personal values interaction is an influential leadership culture dynamic for leading and effecting change, e.g. Dolan and Garcia (2002), Hammer and Champy (1993), Schein (1992), Nadler and Tushman (1990), Burke and Litwin (1989).

Personal values are key factors influencing the 'transformational' leadership behavior required for continuous business 'sense making' by leadership teams, e.g. Higgs (2002), Bass and Avolio (2001), Alimo-Metcalfe and Alban-Metcalfe (2001), Parry (1998), Katzenbach (1998), Kouzes and Posner (1990).

Personal values variation has implications for leadership team behavior, functioning and effectiveness, e.g. Brodbeck et al. (2000), Kupperschmidt (2000), Joynt and Morton (1999), Gibson (1995), Alimo-Metcalfe (1995), Schwartz (1992), Etzioni (1988), Hofstede (1980a, b).

Personal values are potential leadership team identity and alignment characteristics within the leadership team member relationship and interaction process, e.g. Hogg and Terry (2000), Hogan and Holland (2000), Lau and Murnighan (1998), Ashkanasy and O'Connor (1997), Erez and Earley (1993), Louis (1983), Dansereau, Graen and Haga (1975).

The Hay Group (1999) conducted a survey of the most admired companies (who do a better job of attracting and retaining talent) and some of their peers. When asked about their approach to leadership, a significant number confirmed the importance of aligning the behavior of leaders with the values and culture of the organization. However, in this sense 'aligned' values may be dysfunctional if an organization's environment goalposts suddenly change (Denison, 1990), or they could produce 'strategic myopia' (Lorsch, 1986), by placing an emotional shield around the cognitive and intuitive processes of strategic thinking and business positioning, thereby limiting business responsiveness (Hambrick and Mason, 1984).

To break through this dilemma and to support ongoing adaptability, Bass and Avolio (1993) recommend a transformational culture based on 'transformational leadership'. In this vein, Kotter and Heskett's (1992, p. 56) 'adaptive culture' perspective contains a view that, 'holding on to an adaptive culture requires being both inflexible with regard to "core adaptive" values and yet flexible with regard to most practices and "other" values', although the identification and differential impact of 'core adaptive' and 'other' values does not seem to have been tested empirically. Any potential business response is made more complex by the diversity in people's personal values and the match/mismatch with the prevailing leader's values and working culture values credo, as illustrated by Table 4.2.

As Kabanoff et al. (1995) note all organizations need to solve a fundamental problem during change – how to maintain internal cohesion while continuing to produce

Table 4.2 Generational differences in values

Generational category	Entered workforce	Approximate age now	Individual work values	Organizational work values
Protestant work ethic	1945–1959	60+	Hard work, conservative, loyalty to organization	Command, control, efficiency, compliance, dehumanization
Existentialism	1960–1979	45+	Quality of life, nonconforming, seeks autonomy, loyalty to self	Teamwork, quality, respect for individual, involvement
Pragmatism	1980–1989	25+	Success, achievement, ambition, hard work, loyalty to career	Efficiency, cost reduction, effectiveness
Generation X	1990s	Under 20	Lifestyle, self-development, loyalty to peers	Empowerment, organizational learning, employability

Source: Joynt and Morton (1999).

economic outputs. They cite Polley (1987) who described this 'task versus person' conflict as an enduring common thread in organizational behavior research and as a fundamental source of tension within the 'deep structure of organizations (Gersick, 1991). The authors argue that a key source of tension lies in the competing distributive justice system principles embedded within the two sets of concerns. This results from the pressure to adopt organizational values reflecting equitable distribution of resources, for economic efficiency needs, whilst at the same time attempting (particularly in organizational change initiatives) to promote equal allocation of resources, based on values of cohesion and solidarity, to remain fair to everyone.

The researchers claim that the different ways that organizations try to find a sustainable balance between these competing values shapes the overall values structures of managers, as discussed by Quinn (1988). Quinn and Rohrbaugh (1983) produced the 'competing values' model for assessing organizational culture according to four categories, each containing their own values set. These are, 'Human Relations' and 'Open Systems' based on 'flexibility' and 'Rational Goal' and 'Internal Process' based on 'control'. Quinn (1988) argued that in practice all four approaches coexist and should be balanced in their application by leaders of modern organizations, with some values more dominant and functional than others depending on the organization's sector, stage of development and mandate. We return to this framework later in this chapter

Waddock and Post (1991), with an example from the public sector, have stressed the importance of values in those executives they term 'social entrepreneurs'. The social entrepreneur, they argue, generates followers' commitment to public-good projects by framing it in terms of important social values, rather than in economic terms, which results in a sense of collective purpose amongst those involved. The vision created by these values is so powerful that it overcomes some of the project complexity and problems associated with collective action through commitment gained by tapping into deep rooted personal and social values, (Etzioni, 1988). The authors note that such catalytic social entrepreneurs epitomize the 'transforming' leadership described by Burns (1978, p. 20), which 'occurs when one or more persons engage with others in such a way that leaders and followers raise one another to higher levels of motivation and morality'. Another characteristic of this collective purpose is that the goals or purposes were 'end values' and not 'modal values'. According to Burns (1978), the chief monitors of transactional leadership are modal values or values of means such as honesty, responsibility, fairness, the honoring of commitments, without which this form of leadership would not work. Transformational leadership, he argues, is more concerned with end-values such as justice, liberty and equality.

In concluding this background to prior research on executive's personal values, Maio (2002, p. 299) notes, 'What makes values so special? Perhaps they carry import precisely because they are truistic. In other words, the significance of values is attributable to the strong social consensus supporting them. As a result of this consensus, values become empowered by a strong sense of emotional conviction. This emotional conviction may be primarily responsible for the impact of values on a variety of psychological phenomena, making it vital that research continues to explore this issue'.

The Business Sector Advisory Group on Corporate Governance states in its agenda for modernization under 'Recognising societal interests', 'Companies do not act independently from the societies in which they operate, (Corporate Governance, 1998, p. 18). Accordingly, corporate actions must be compatible with societal objectives concerning social cohesion, individual welfare and equal opportunities for all', and 'For dynamic enterprises operating in a rapidly changing world, corporate governance adaptability and flexibility – supported by an enabling regulatory framework – is a prerequisite for better corporate performance' (p. 17). In summary, organizational and stakeholder values may well be aligned but could also, given the latter's diverse nature, be diametrically opposed. Values are not brought to life by stating them in corporate publications. Their kaleidoscopic quality represents uniquely personal views about the way business, personal and community life should look and feel.

Six leadership values challenges emerge from the above, each generating their own dilemma for change leaders. These are represented in Table 4.3.

It appears that the most critical dilemma for Board members and senior executives to grapple with is to ensure they and their fellow leaders direct and uphold the

Table 4.3 Leadership and values (challenges and dilemmas)

Challenges	Dilemma
We all differ in the personal values we hold, whatever we claim the organizations to be.	Choice between my, your and our values?
We underestimate the power of personal values.	Choice between recognizing and ignoring their impact?
We rarely know or talk about what we personally value.	Choice between knowing and guessing?
We invariably try to agree on which values everyone should hold.	Choice between individuality and group belonging?
We have little idea about which values are good for business, generally or specifically.	Choice between generalization and specialization AND between common practice and research?
We rarely seek feedback about whether or not we role model our values through our everyday behavior.	Choice between identity (what we think we represent) and reputation (what others think of us, based on the way they see us behave)?

values that sustain business identity and reputation, whilst simultaneously leveraging off the stakeholders' values chain diversity and the window this opens on different ways of generating and conducting business. For this to happen, everyone in the Board and their wider leadership culture may have to personally value 'diversity in values'. Significantly more research is required to determine if this statement, or any other position on values, will impact on the behavior of leaders and the life of their business. The rest of this chapter aims to highlight executive's values systems (Ellis & Hall, 2002) which can be used for additional exploration.

Discovery of diverse executive's personal values

Before suggesting a new direction for research and practice assessing the likely impact of executive's personal values on their working environment, including how they form their personal, business and world views, the research background for suggesting our recently created personal values framework is set out below.

STUDY 1 – AITKEN (2004)

A study of 211 middle and senior in-work managers, measured their personal values using the 57-item Schwartz (1994) Values Survey (SVS), with a reliability of 0.94 for the study. To test whether personal values were structured as predicted by Schwartz, both of his motivational domains were tested for construct validity:

(i) The four domains (1994) of conservation, self-enhancement, openness to change and self-transcendence.

(ii) The seven domains (1999) of conservatism, hierarchy, mastery, affective autonomy, intellectual autonomy, egalitarianism and harmony.

To test the former, an a priori based four factor extraction was carried out. The four factor solution explained a total of 42% of the variance. All four factors of the rotated solution showed a number of strong loadings using Hair et al.'s (1998) guidelines for statistically significant factor loadings of 0.45 for the sample size of the current research ($n = 161$). To test the latter, an a priori based seven factor extraction was carried out. The seven factor solution explained a total of 53% of the variance.

STUDY 2 – LICHTENSTEIN (2005)

In a study of 167 work owner, senior and middle managers, Kotey and Meredith's (1997) List of Values (LoV) 28 item personal values scale (high reliability score of 0.87 for the current research) was used to categorize variables into values structures by subjecting it to principal components analysis. Utilizing Maslow's (1970) theory of inner directed (ID), outer directed (OD) and sustenance driven (SD) values structures, the a priori criterion (Sharma, 1996) was used to derive a three factor extraction. The three factor solution below explained a total of 41% of the variance.

(i) The core SD traditional values of loyalty, trust, compassion and affection of factor 1 has a reliability score of 0.79.

(ii) The core esteem-seeking OD values of power, prestige, ambition and aggression of factor 3 has a reliability score of 0.64.

(iii) The core of the ID entrepreneurial values of innovation, risk and creativity of factor 2 has a reliability score of 0.72.

This appears to be the first attempt to compare results of two managerial values surveys, each using a different values dimensions heritage from the two 'founding fathers' (Maslow and Schwartz) of needs and values research, respectively. The main finding is there are more similarities than differences in the approaches and results. Firstly, regarding constructs, it is clear that Maslow's (1970) and Schwartz's (1994, 1999) approach approximate each other (see Table 4.4).

Secondly, when items within the constructs are scrutinized, there remains the possibility that executives within the Board and senior executive team may hold peculiar personal values structures, which drive very different leadership behavior. Most notably from this study, a significant tension may exist between those who feel most comfortable with tried and trusted ways of doing things (Sustenance Driven, bottom row above), those focusing on getting their self-esteem needs fulfilled (Outer Directed, middle row) and those who focus on novelty, self-development and reflection (Inner Directed, top row). Responsible business change agents will be required to balance these three values structures when reconciling competing interests.

Thirdly, for executives embarking on organizational change, a more accessible values framework is required which uses everyday language to facilitate dialogue between stakeholders. As yet unpublished research suggests executives' and employees' personal values fall into the six personal brand values (PBV) clusters shown in Figure 4.1 (mirroring some of the values constructs outlined by authors such as Trompenaars & Hampden-Turner, 2002 and Schneider & Barsoux, 2003), and as you can see from the descriptions, this recent discovery has profound implications for how leadership is actually practiced and who it ultimately benefits. Although these personal values can be considered as universal (Schwartz, 1994), the mix and strength with which they are held by individuals and within organizations, communities and nation states will vary and are open to change over time, as well as being dependent on shifting circumstances and the prevailing zeitgeist (spirit of the time) – for example, the rapidly strengthening environmental and

Table 4.4 Comparing Maslow (1970) and Schwartz (1994, 1999)

Lichtenstein (2005) and Maslow (1970)		Schwartz (1994)	Schwartz (1996)	Aitken and Lichtenstein interpretation
Inner directed	Self-actualization Transcendence of all needs Aesthetic Cognitive To know, understand, beauty	Self-transcendence; Openness to change	Harmony	Self-development
			Intellectual Autonomy	Exploring a new beginning
Outer directed	Self-esteem from self-achievement	Self-enhancement	Mastery	Striving
	Self-esteem from others Approval Recognition		Hierarchy Affective Autonomy	All about my needs
Sustenance Driven	BelongingLove, Acceptance	Conservation	Egalitarianism	Self-preservation
	Safety Security, comfort Physiological Air, food, water, sex		Conservatism	Staying stable

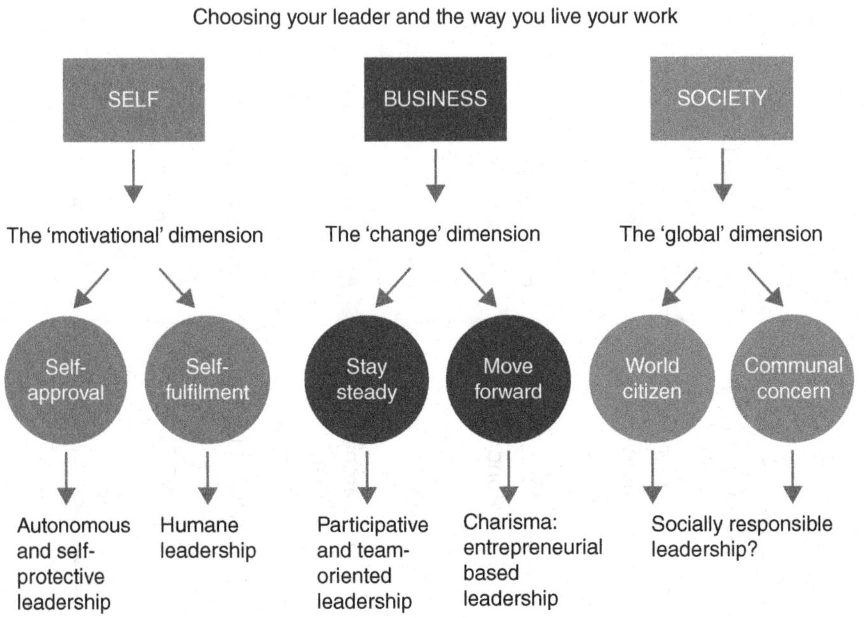

Choosing your leader and the way you live your work

Figure 4.1 Personal Brand Values and the six globe leadership dimensions (set out on the diagram's bottom line).
Source: Copyright Concordia International Ltd.

sustainability agenda in the developed and emerging-economy worlds. Indeed, you can see from Figure 4.1 that four of the six values systems can be mapped onto universal dimensions of leadership, as per the results of the 'Globe' leadership study (House, Hanges, Agar and Quintanilla, 1995). It appears that the new zeitgeist, although often acknowledged in organizations' corporate social responsibility statements of intent and reporting, has yet to be adopted globally by leaders, or indeed sufficiently represented in Schwartz's original framework.

Table 4.5 presents lists of personal values, each related to a PBV values cluster, showing the connection to forms of employee engagement and the type of change we might encounter at work, together with an indication of their fitness for change purpose.

How change leaders can utilize values for change leadership?

Change leaders are required to understand their own and others personal values drivers in sufficient detail to take stock of the prevailing personal and business sub-cultures. Doing so will enable them to identify and secure the potential levels

Table 4.5 Personal brand values and their relationship with forms of work engagement and change leadership

PBV values cluster	Type of motivation and engagement	Personal values (examples)	Indicative 'fitness for change' purpose
Self-approval	Motivated by external and self-centered measures of success Engaged by appealing to self-interest	Wealth (material possessions, money) Social power (control over others, dominance) Ego-driven (seeking self-esteem)	'Leader centric' driven change producing short-term performance focus
Self-fulfilment	Motivated by internal and pro-social measures of success Engaged by appealing to personal growth and the development of others	Meaning in life (a purpose for living) A spiritual life (emphasis on spiritual, not material matters) Selfless (putting others' needs before my own, compassionate)	Altruistic change primarily driven by the accrual of benefit for others with a focus on capability building
Stay steady	Prefers a stable environment with reciprocal respect Engaged by appealing to sense of belonging	Sense of belonging (feeling colleagues are closely connected to me) Loyal (faithful to my colleagues or group at work) Respect for tradition (preservation of customs, honoring those who have come before me)	Slow burn change where incremental improvements are sought, although not at the expense of long-held relationships

(Continued)

Table 4.5 Continued

PBV values cluster	Type of motivation and engagement	Personal values (examples)	Indicative 'fitness for change' purpose
Move forward	Prefers a fast-moving environment with opportunity for personal impact Engaged by appealing to entrepreneurial spirit	Successful (achieving, stretching) Innovation (engaging with novel and creative ideas) Resourceful (finding ways to make things happen)	Self-starter change which challenges the status-quo
World citizen	Connects with the world at large Engaged by appealing to worldly responsibility	Unity with nature (fitting myself into nature) Diversity (tolerant of different cultures) One worldliness (sensitive to interconnectivity of people)	Whole system change on a global platform
Communal concern	Connects with the local community Engaged by appealing to community spirit	Social justice (correcting injustice, care for the weak) Social order (stability of society) Civic pride (taking responsibility for maintaining local reputation)	Public system change on a local platform

Source: Copyright Concordia International Ltd.

of engagement and evaluate potential resistance to the change signals sent out to internal and external stakeholders and customers. Communication of organizational intent are also more likely to be listened to and acted upon if the message appeals to particular values sets. For example, although the same behavior may be demonstrated, there will often be different values-based reasons for committing to change action, as can be seen below.

I reach high performance objectives (stretch targets) because...

...I want to stand out and get recognised

(appeal to 'Self-approval' values system)

...I want to secure my job

(appeal to 'Stay steady' values system)

...how else am I going to learn?

(appeal to 'Self-fulfilment' values system)

Clearly change leaders can use the PBV in different ways. Starting by developing their own self-insight into the values that drive them they could ask the following. Based on your predominant values systems:

- Do your own values fit well with those espoused by your organization?
- Which combination of values (and the leadership behavior they drive) is 'best fit' for the organization's current and future direction – producing an organisational gap analysis?
- Are your espoused values supported by your appropriate demonstrable behaviour – producing an individual gap analysis?
- What type of leadership would you be most suited to?
- What type of leader would you work best for/with?
- Have your values systems changed over time or are they currently undergoing some change?
- How might your values systems impact on the type of organization/sector you feel most comfortable working in?
- If you are currently in an executive team, how similar or different are your values to those of your colleagues?
- How might this similarity/difference affect the impact of your combined leadership (the prevailing leadership culture) on your workplace culture?

Change leaders might also ask which particular values are most likely to release the opportunity for continuous improvement. Aitken (2004) found the 'Move Forward' values cluster (see Table 4.6) was most desired by executives for change leaders, as long as it was accompanied by the demonstrable transformational leadership behavior covered in Chapter 5. Continuous improvement, defined as a company-wide process of focused innovation sustained over a long period of time, was shown by Jabnoun (2001) to be best served by 'driving' values like respect, responsibility and empathy and 'enabling' values like trust, humility, openness and cooperation. Indeed, a study by Abbott et al. (2005) found that companies adopting 'prosocial' values such as vision, self-direction and humanity may enhance organizational commitment and therefore the likelihood that someone will stick around in order to make a performance difference.

As suggested above, the PBV can also be used to determine the most appropriate values–culture mix for the business, depending on its stage of development and strategic intent. Grist (2009) suggests the following four links between the Schwartz (2005) model, adapted here for the PBV values clusters (listed in brackets), and the previously mentioned cultural measurement device called the competing values framework (CVF) (Cameron & Quinn, 2006) used, for example, in turnarounds at Philips and Reuters: (1) self-transcendence (or self-fulfilment) – Clan; (2) openness-to-change (or move forward) – Adhocracy; (3) self-enhancement (or self-approval) – Market; (4) conservation (stay steady) – Hierarchy.

The CVF is outlined in Figure 4.2.

Table 4.6 'Move forward' personal values system defined

Freedom	Freedom of action and thought
Creativity	Uniqueness, imagination
Wisdom	A mature understanding of life
Independent	Self-reliant, self-sufficient
Moderate	Avoiding extremes of feeling and action
Broad-minded	Tolerant of different ideas and beliefs
Choosing own goals	Selecting own purposes
Capable	Competent, effective, efficient
Intelligent	Logical, thinking
Successful	Achieving goals

Source: Aitken (2004).

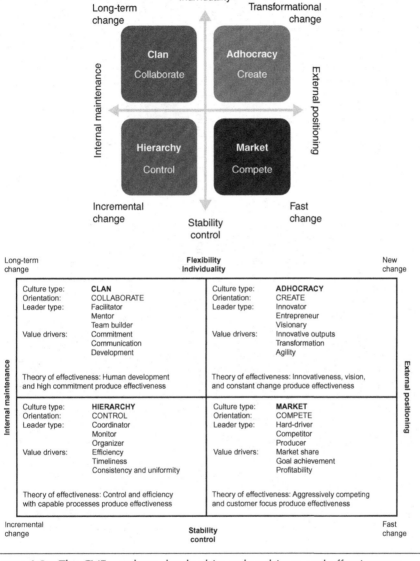

Figure 4.2 The CVF – culture, leadership, value drivers and effectiveness. *Source: Cameron et al. (2006).*

And through other research links with the CVF, the PBV can be used as guide for assessing predominant leadership culture archetypes currently at play in business life and their future fitness for purpose, given changing market conditions, internal focus and external socio-economic-political environment (see Table 4.7).

Table 4.7 The competing values framework and links to the PBV

Deal and Kennedy (1983)	Graves (1985)	Dobson and Williams (1989)	Hampden-Turner and Trompenaars (2006)	Cameron and Quinn, (2006)	Personal Brand Values (PBV)
Tough guy culture Risk taking individualistic	Barbarian Ego-driven Workaholic	Power-orientated Competitive Responsibility to personality rather than expertise	Guided Missile Project-oriented culture	Market Compete	Self-approval
Work/play hard Persistent Sociable	Presidential Democratic Hierarchical	People-orientated Consensua lRejects management control	Family Person-orientated culture	Clan Collaborate	Self-fulfilment
Bet your company Ponderous Unpressurized	Monarchical Loyalty Doggedness	Task-orientated Competency Dynamic	Incubator Fulfilment-orientated	Adhocracy Create	Move forward
Process culture Bureaucratic Protective	Pharaonic Ritualized Changeless	Role-orientated Legality Legitimacy Pure bureaucracy	Eiffel Tower Role-orientated culture	Hierarchy Control	Stay steady

Source: Adapted from Gunter and Furnham (1996) cited by Furnham (2008), Garrison (2006), Cameron and Quinn (2006).

A useful summary of the four CVF archetypes, which includes links to related change leadership styles, and a sample culture change plan, is provided by Grist (2009) below:

THE CLAN CULTURE

Clan organizations have parallels with family run organizations, characterized as a friendly place to work, with shared values and goals, a strong cohesiveness and sense of 'we-ness' permeates throughout the organization. The work environment is designed to be a human place to work, where employee empowerment and participation is encouraged to foster commitment and loyalty. The clan culture is typically found in Japanese companies.

Assumptions that operate include: the external environment is handled by teamwork, employee training and development and treating customers as partners. The clan organization is effective in coordinating organizational activity, in fast changing, turbulent external environments, where the outcome of decision-making is uncertain. Leaders are seen as mentors. Loyalty and tradition bind the organization together and organizational commitment is high. A concern for people is at its heart, where employee long-term development and high morale is the deemed the pathway to success.

THE ADHOCRACY CULTURE

The adhocracy culture emerged, as the economies in the developed world, shifted from the industrial to information age. This was in response to rapidly accelerating changes at the beginning of the twenty-first century driven by powerful forces of globalization, improvements in technology and communications. Organizations also faced increasingly shorter product and service life cycles. This led to innovation and new product development becoming key strategies for success, requiring organizations to foster an environment of entrepreneurship and creativity. Examples include companies in aerospace, software development and film-making industries.

In an adhocracy culture typically, power is decentralized, effective leaders are visionary, innovative and risk taking. Preparedness for change and dealing with challenges as they arise are fundamental. Teams may form on a temporary basis to work on projects or particular tasks. Individuality and experimentation is encouraged, where each employee has a stake in the future direction of the organization. The long-term strategy is centered on rapid growth and acquiring new resources. Success is achieved by creating unique product or service propositions.

THE MARKET CULTURE

The third typology, the market culture became popular in the 1960s as organizations experienced greater competition. This new set of assumptions that Wilkins and Ouchi

(1983) proposed were based on efficient transaction costs between stakeholders, for example suppliers, customers, contractors, unions and regulators.

The fundamental assumptions of the market are the external environment is hostile and customers are demanding and seeking value. Management's primary goal is to drive the organization to improve its financial performance with higher sales, productivity and profits. This is achieved through an unequivocal and aggressive strategy that strongly emphasizes external positioning and internal control. Leaders are typically hard-driving, who are tough and demanding to work. The organization is bound together by its emphasis on winning. Success is all about beating the competition, achieving higher market share, market penetration and ultimately market leadership.

THE HIERARCHY CULTURE

The fourth organizational form, the hierarchy emerged at the beginning of the twentieth century. Goods and services needed to be produced efficiently and reliably with smooth-flowing and predictable output. This was in response to the growth in large-scale organizations and the development of mass production.

The hierarchy organization is characterized as formal and structured where procedures govern how people work. Effective leadership includes good coordination and organization, where the maintenance of a smooth-flowing operation is the key. The long-term focus is on providing stability, predictability and efficiency. Examples include a mass production company like Toyota, a mass service company like McDonalds or a mass public service governmental organization like the Inland Revenue.

A sample Culture Change plan and related behaviours (*Source*: Adapted from Cameron & Quinn, 2006) is provided below.

Clan culture increase means: More employee empowerment More participation and involvement More cross-functional teamwork More horizontal communication A more caring climate More recognition	*Adhocracy culture increase means*: More employee suggestions More process innovativeness More thoughtful risk taking Tolerance of first-time mistakes More listening to customers
Clan culture decrease does not mean: A culture of 'niceness' Lack of standards and rigor An absence of tough decisions Slacking off Tolerance of mediocrity	*Adhocracy culture decrease does not mean*: Everyone for himself or herself Covering up errors Thoughtless risk taking Taking our eye off the ball Spending money on the latest fad No coordination and sharing ideas

Hierarchy culture decrease means:	*Market culture decrease means*:
Fewer sign-offs for decisions	Ongoing commitment to excellence
More decentralized decisions	A world-class organization
Fewer roadblocks and less red tape	Goal accomplishment
Less micromanagement	Energized employees Less myopic
Trying out more crazy ideas	thinking about targets
Eliminating paperwork	A less punishing environment
Hierarchy culture decrease does not mean:	*Market culture decrease does not mean*:
Lack of measurement	Less pressure for performance
Not holding people accountable	Ceasing to listen to customers
Not following the rules	Less satisfied customers
Not monitoring performance	Missing deadlines
A nonorientation toward change	Lower quality standards
	Less competitiveness

By using the above, change leaders can consider how well their own and others values fit with the type of culture or culture change the business requires going forward, thereby producing a values and culture gap analysis for workplace dialogue. We return to the idea of a culture development plan, instigated and driven by change leaders, in Chapter 5.

Implications for the change leadership development community

Preliminary findings from our ongoing research indicate significant differences found in the personal values of senior executives. As a result, an emerging proposition suggests the most critical personal value for Board members and their senior managers to share is 'acknowledging, recognising and valuing diversity in values'. Moreover, results on the structure of values show clear signs of different executive values dimensions and clusters, with implications for practitioners and researchers in corporate governance and change leadership; looking at how executive's values impact personal and organizational approaches to business value creation.

There are several implications for research. A worthwhile literature meta-analysis could usefully identify the theoretical and empirical strands between values, motives and personality traits, possibly representing universal dimensions of human expression within the workplace. In addition, a longer term investigation of the links between leadership behavior and personal values held by those leaders would enable us to identify the leadership culture conditions necessary for creating sustained and sustainable (in the sense of corporate social and environmental aims) business innovation, excellence and achievement; as opposed to cross-sectional studies using short-term business outcome measures. In particular, which executive's personal values might, for example, facilitate or restrict organization movement from 'good to great' (Collins, 2001), whilst also accommodating the new ecological zeitgeist?

And, as Drucker (2001) reminds us, 'To survive and succeed every organisation will have to turn itself into a change agent…. .an important task for top management in the next society's corporation will be to balance its three dimensions: as an economic, human and as an increasingly important social organisation…the biggest challenge will become its social legitimacy: its values, mission & vision, increasingly top management will represent the unique personality of the company'. Post Enron and alongside the business carbon footprint debate, the collegial and reflective deep dialogue skills of executives will continue to be severely tested where value creation cuts across divergent personal approaches and responses to the business of business, with the inherent dilemmas created by diverse self, business and societal values drivers. Follow-up studies could usefully delineate which personal values structures fit within these overarching 'windows on life' drivers in specific organisational contexts (Louis, 1983).

There are also implications for practitioners. The preoccupation of using past experience, competencies and demographic variables such as age, education and functional experience to determine the 'right' person for the job, whilst neglecting executive's values, is clearly a mistake. To avoid the multimillion dollar disasters of hiring the wrong CEO and leadership team, Boards must put values-based selection on the Board agenda. For leaders, this research indicates there is a diversity of values operating throughout business life. Effective leaders lead a whole culture of diverse values, not just people who happen to share their values. As 'value is in the eye of the beholder' (Andriessen, 2003), those responsible for delivering shareholder value must understand these different value structures and be able to communicate with people in a language that resonates with their unique values drivers; and, if change and strategy initiatives are to be successfully implemented, must be able to audit the current values held by people across the business, using personal values identifiers which are contemporary, comprehensive and accurately defined.

Change leaders, in building their own and others change leadership capability, need to recognize that managers tend to operate from their own narrow, personal interest values (functional/professional allegiance) and mainly concentrate on the formal business arrangements, whereas leaders have to learn to communicate purpose and direction with a whole culture made up of different personal values, concentrating on shaping informal organizational life. We might call this 'strategy by the coffee machine', consisting of dialogue about what we are told we should be doing, what our leaders are actually doing and how we feel about joining them to make change happen. For coherence and credibility, business leaders – acting as a culture influence team – should remain true to themselves, live by what they espouse and do what it says on their corporate jackets. Effective change leaders must continually check what their heart, head and hands communicate.

Unfortunately, the exercise of change leadership appears to be at the mercy of organizational culture, with the potential benefits of transformational leadership thwarted if the culture is so transactional (geared to defining and monitoring the outputs from processes and systems) that it stifles and suppresses its exercise (Parry & Proctor, 2003). Sending out signals through deliberate role modeling, physical work conditions that support nonhierarchical workplace connections and more flexible cross-organisation means of co-operating will also induce a culture more amenable to beneficial change (Aitken, 2007). For business to compete and differentiate, this cannot be left to chance or to consultants. A niche business requires its own unique leader-led values-culture formula for success, as Figure 4.3 indicates.

How change leaders create and utilize such a leadership culture is the subject of the next chapter.

To summarize, business spends time and money on producing missions, values statements and corporate branding, often without paying sufficient attention to the personal brands held by leaders and other members of the workforce. The result can be a culture of misaligned purpose and motivation, together with different interpretations of what matters. This creates variability in internal and external customer service and, if not addressed, an undercurrent of resentment because uniqueness is neither valued nor leveraged for everyone's benefit. Understanding the diversity of personal values present in a business has the following benefits for change leaders:

■ Attempts to change business direction and culture are more likely to succeed if you know what people's drivers are before you start.

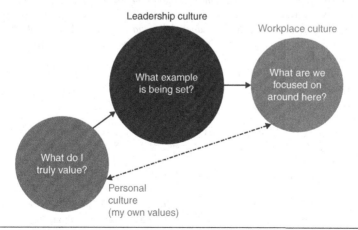

Figure 4.3   Leaders role-model business uniqueness.
Source: Concordia International Ltd, 2006.

■ Boards and their senior executive teams can identify mismatches amongst their own values before they develop vision, purpose, mission and strategy together.

■ Leaders can identify how similar/different their motivations and beliefs are from the people they lead.

■ Selection, using PBV assessment, will save you considerable cost and angst down the line, when people fail to 'fit' the organization, business unit, workgroup, role.

■ People, whatever their role, are often not aware of the internal drivers of their behavior – a deeper understanding will allow more productive dialogue when finding new ways forward or addressing conflict, as so often occurs in leadership attempts to implement organizational change.

Obviously, organisations will also need to understand the specific blend of personal brand values they require of their people, both in connecting to the sector, market and customer values and internally to drive different values based business functions and components. For example, embedding and maintaining work systems requires a 'stay steady' motivational driver. The change leader's challenge is to become more sophisticated in attempts to release discretionary performance by discovering, connecting and engaging with the personal values mosaic colouring their world.

References

Aitken, P. (2002). An investigation of the relationships between leader and team member personal values, their alignment and team transformational leadership – an emergent research model. *Henley Working Paper Series*. HWP0222.

Aitken, P. (2004). The relationships between Personal Values, Leadership Behaviour and Team Functioning. *Doctor of Business Administration Thesis*, Henley Management College/Brunel University.

Aitken, P (2006). *Board Leadership Values Dilemmas*. Paper delivered at the Henley Management College, UK: *9th International Corporate Governance and Board Leadership Conference*.

Aitken, P. (2007). Walking the Talk – the nature and role of leadership culture within organisation culture/s. *Journal of General Management*, 32(4, Summer), p. 17–37.

Ali, M., Sharma, M., & Subhash, C. (Mar/Apr 1996). Robustness to nonnormality of regression F-tests, Amsterdam. *Journal of Econometrics*, 71(1–2), 175.

Alimo-Metcalfe, B. (1995). An investigation of female and male constructs of leadership and empowerment. *Women in Management Review*, 10(2), 3–8.

Alimo-Metcalfe, B., & Alban-Metcalfe, R. J. (2001, March). The development of a new transformational leadership questionnaire. *Journal of Occupational and Organisational Psychology*, 74(Part 1).

Andriessen, D. (2003). IC valuation and measurement – why and how? *Paper for the PMA IC Research Symposium October 2003*. Cranfield School of Management. Retrieved <www.weightlesswealth.com>

Ashkanasy, N. M., & O'Connor, C. (1997). Value congruence in leader–member exchange. *The Journal of Social Psychology, 137*, 647–662.

Bass, B. M., & Avolio B. J. (1993). Transformational Leadership and Organisational Culture (pp. 112–121). PAQ, Spring.

Bass, B. M., & Avolio, B. J. (2001). *Permission set for the multifactor leadership questionnaire*. California: Mind Garden.

Beyer, J. (1981). Ideologies, values and decision-making in organisations Chap. 8. In P. C. Nystrom, & W. H. Starbuck, (Eds.) *Handbook of organisational design: Vol. 2* (pp. 166–202). New York: Oxford University Press.

Brodbeck, F. C., et al. (2000). Cultural variation of leadership prototypes across 22 European countries. *Journal of Occupational and Organisational Psychology, 73*, 1–29.

Burke, W.W., & Litwin, G. H. (1989). A causal model of organisational performance. In J. W. Pfeiffer (Ed.), *The 1989 Annual: Developing Human Resources*.

Burke, W.W., & Litwin, G. H. (1989). *A causal model of organisational performance.* In J. W. Pfeiffer (Ed.), The 1989 Annual: Developing Human Resources.

Burns, J. M. (1978). *Leadership*. New York: Harper & Row.

Cameron, K. S., & Quinn, R. E. (2006). *Diagnosing and changing organizational culture: Based on the competing values framework* (revised ed.). San Francisco, CA., USA: Jossey-Bass.

Cameron, K. S., Quinn, R. E., Degraff, J., & Thakor, A. V. (2006). *Competing values leadership: Creating value in organizations*. Cheltenham, Glos, UK: Edward Elgar Publishing.

Charles, H.-T., & Trompenaars, F. (Feb 2006). Cultural intelligence: Is such a capacity credible? Thousand Oaks. *Group and Organization Management, 31*(1), 56.

Collins, S. (2001). *Good to great*. New York: HarperCollins Publishers.

Corporate Governance: improving competitiveness and access to capital in global markets – a report to the OECD by the business sector advisory group on Corporate Governance', OECD, 1998.

Dansereau, F., Graen, G., & Haga, W. J. (1975). A vertical dyad linkage approach to leadership within formal organisations: A longitudinal investigation of the role making process. *Organisational Behaviour and Human Performance, 14*, 46–78.

Deal, T. E., & Kennedy, A. A. (Nov. 1983). Culture: A new look through old lenses Arlington. *The Journal of Applied Behavioral Science, 19*(4), 498.

Denison, D. R. (1990). *Corporate culture and organisational effectiveness*. John Wiley & Sons.

Dobson, P., & Williams, A. (Dec 1989). The validation of the selection of male British Army Officers. *Journal of Occupational Psychology, 62*(4), 313.

Dolan, S. L., & Garcia, S. (2002). Managing by values – cultural redesign for strategic organisational change at the dawn of the twenty-first century. *Journal of Management Development, 21*(2), 101–117.

Drucker, P. (2001). *The Economist*, November.

EFMD. (2005). Globally responsible leadership: A call for engagement. Online. Available<HTTP:http://www.efmd.org/html/responsibility/cont-detail.asp?id=041207trl v&aid=051012qnis&tid=1&ref=ind> Accessed 18.10.05.

Ellis, R. K., & Hall, M. L. W. (2002). *Systems and values: An approach for practical organisational intervention*. Centre for Systems Studies, University of Hull, School of Management.

Ellis, R. K., & Hall, M. L. W. (2002). *Systems and values: an approach for practical organisational intervention*. Centre for Systems Studies, University of Hull, School of Management.

England, G. W. (1967). Personal value systems of American managers. *Academy of Management Journal, 10*, 53–68.

Erez, M., & Earley, P. C. (1993). *Culture, self-identity, and work*. New York: Oxford University Press.

Etzioni, A. (1988). *The moral dimension: Toward a new economics*. New York: Free Press.

Fiedler, F. E. (1978). The contingency model and the dynamics of leadership process. In L. Berkowicz (Ed.), *Advances in experimental social psychology*. New York: Academic Press.

Finkelstein, S., & Hambrick, D. (1996). *Strategic leadership: top executives and their effects on organisations*. St. Paul, MN: West Publishing Company.

Furnham (2008).

Furnham, A. F. (2008). *The psychology of behaviour at work – The individual in the organisation* (2nd ed.). Hove, East Sussex, UK: Psychology Press.

Garrison, T. G. (2006). *International business culture* (3rd ed.). Huntington, Cambs: Elm Publications.

Geoffrey, N. A., Fiona, A. W., & Margaret, A. C. (Dec 2005). Linking values and organizational commitment: A correlational and experimental investigation in two organizations Leicester. *Journal of Occupational and Organizational Psychology, 78*, 531.

George, W., & Lee, R. (Aug. 1974). The relationship between managerial values and managerial success in The United States, Japan, India, and Australia, England, Washington. *Journal of Applied Psychology, 59*(4), 411..

Gersick, C. J. G. (1991). Revolutionary change theories: a multilevel exploration of the punctuated equilibrium paradigm. *Academy of Management Review, 16*, 10–36.

Gibson, C. B. (1995). An investigation of gender differences in leadership across four countries. *Journal of International Business Studies, 26*(2), 255–279.

Gill, R., (2002). Towards an integrated theory of leadership, *Paper, European Institute for Advanced Studies in Management Workshop on Leadership Research*, Oxford, December 16–17.

Goodwin, D. K. (2009). *Team of rivals*. Penguin.

Graves, L. M. (Mar 1985). Effects of leader persistence and environmental complexity on leadership perceptions: Do implicit beliefs discourage adaptation to complex environments? *Group and Organization Studies, 10*(1), 19.

Grist, J. (2009). Does greater fit between an employee's ascendant personal values and perception of an organisation's culture lead to higher organisational commitment? *Unpublished MBA Dissertation*, Henley Business School.

Gunter, B., & Furnham, A. (Mar 1996). Biographical and climate predictors of job satisfaction and pride in organization, Provincetown. *The Journal of Psychology, 130*(2), 193.

Hair, J. F., Anderson, R. E., Tatham, R. T., & Black, W. C. (1998). Multivariate data analysis (5th ed.). Englewood Cliffs, NJ: Prentice Hall.

Hambrick, D. C., & Mason, P. A. (1984). Upper echelons, the organisation as a reflection of its top managers. *Academy of Management Review*, 195.

Hammer, M., & Champy, J. (1993). *Re-engineering the corporation*. New York: Harper Business.

Hay Group. (1999). *Moulding global leaders*. New York: Fortune.

Higgs, M. J. (2002). Leadership – the long line: a view on how we make sense of leadership in the 21st century. *Inaugural Paper*, Henley Management College.

Hofstede, G. (1980). Motivation, leadership, and organization: Do American theories apply abroad? New York: Summer. *Organizational Dynamics, 9*(1), 42.

Hofstede, G. (1980a). Motivation, leadership, and organisation: do American theories apply abroad? *Organisational Dynamics*, Summer.

Hofstede, G. (1980b). *Cultures consequences: international differences in work related values*. Beverly Hills, CA: Sage Publications.

Hogan, R., & Holland, B. (2000). *Leadership and values*. University of Tulsa Unpublished Manuscript.

Hogg, MA., & Terry, D. J. (2000). Social identity and self-categorisation processes in organisational contexts. *Academy of Management Review*, 25(1), 121–140.

House, R. J., Hanges, P. J., Ruiz-Quintanilla, S. A., Dorfman, P. W., Javidan, M., & Dickson, M. 170 co-authors. (1999). Cultural influences on leadership and organisations: Project GLOBE. In W. F. Mobley, M. J. Gessner, & V. Arnold, (Eds.) *Advances in global leadership: Vol. 1* (pp. 171–223). Stamford, CT: JAI Press.

House, R. J., Hanges, P., Agar, M., & Quintanilla, A. R. (1995). *GLOBE: The global leadership and organisational behaviour effectiveness research program*. Philadelphia: The Wharton School of Business, University of Pennsylvania.

James, C. S., & Joseph, C. S. (2001). Leaders and values: A cross-cultural study Bradford. *Leadership and Organization Development Journal. 22(5/6)*, 22(5/6), 243.

Joynt, P., & Morton, B. (Eds.), (1999). *The global HR manager – creating the seamless organization*. London: IPD.

Kabanoff, B., Waldersee, R., & Cohen, M. (1995). Espoused values and organisational change themes. *Academy of Management Journal*, 38(4), 1075–1104.

Katbamna, M. (2007, July). A change of heart. *The Guardian, 28*, 1.

Katzenbach, J. R. (1998). The irony of senior leadership teams Cincinnati. *The Journal for Quality and Participation, May/June*, 1.

Kelly, E. L. (1927). *Interpretation of educational measurements*. Yonkers, NY: World.

Kenny, T. (1994). From vision to reality through values. *Management Development Review*, 7(3), 17–20.

Kotey, B., & Meredith, G. G. (1997). Relationships among owner/manager personal values, business strategies and enterprise performance'. *Journal of Small Business Management*, 35(2), 37–64.

Kotter, J. P., & Heskett, J. L. (1992). *Corporate culture and performance*. New York: The Free Press.

Kouzes, J., & Posner, B. (1990). *The leadership challenge*. San Francisco: Jossey Bass.

Kupperschmidt, B. R. (2000). Multigeneration employees: strategies for effective management Gaithersburg, September 2000. *The Health Care Manager, 19*(1), 65–76.

Lau, D. C., & Murnighan, J. K. (1998). Demographic diversity and faultlines: the compositional dynamics of organisational groups. *Academy of Management Review*, 23(2), 325–340.

Levene, T. (2001). How to make your boss turn green?. *The Guardian, February 3*.

Lichtenstein, S. (2005). Strategy co-alignment: Strategic, executive values and organisational goal orientation and their impact on performance. *Doctor of Business Administration Thesis*, Henley Management College.

Lorsch, J. W. (1986). Managing culture; the invisible barrier to strategic change. *California Management Review*, 28(2), 95–109.

Louis, M. R. (1983). Organisations as cultural bearing milieux. In L. R. Pondy, G. Morgan, P. J. Frost, & T. C. Dandridge (Eds.), *Organisational symbolism*. JAI Press Inc.

MacMillan, K., Money, K., Downing, S., & Hillenbrand, C. (2004). Giving your organisation SPIRIT. *Journal of General Management, Winter*.

Maio, G. R. (2002). Values – truth and meaning British Psychological Society. *The Psychologist*, *15*(6), 296–299.

Maslow, A. H. (1954). *Motivation and personality*. New York: Harper.

Maslow, A. H. (1970). *Motivation and personality* (2nd ed.). New York: Harper and Row.

Naceur, J. (2001). Values underlying continuous improvement. *The TQM Magazine*, *13*(6), 381.

Nadler, D. A., & Tushman, D. L. (1990). Beyond the charismatic leader; leadership and organisational change. *California Management Review*, *32*(2), 77–97.

Parry, K. W. (1998). Grounded theory and social process: a new direction for leadership research. *Leadership Quarterly*, *9*(1), 85–105.

Parry, K. W., & Proctor, S. (2000). *New Zealand leadership survey*. Wellington, NZ: Centre for Leadership Studies, Victoria University.

Polley, R. B. (1987). Exploring polarisation in organisational groups. *Group and Organisation Studies*, *12*, 424–444.

Posner, B. Z., & Schmidt, W. H. (1994). An updated look at the values and expectations of federal government executives. *Public Administration Review*, *54*(1), 20–24.

Quinn, R. E. (1988). *Beyond rational management: Mastering the paradoxes and competing demands of high performance*. San Francisco: Jossey-Bass.

Quinn, R. E., & Rohrbaugh, J. (1983). A spatial model of effectiveness criteria: Towards a competing values approach to organisational analysis. *Management Science*, *29*, 363–377.

Sarros and Santora (2001)

Schein, E. H. (1992). *Organisational culture and leadership*. San Francisco: Jossey-Bass.

Schmidt, W. H., & Posner, B. Z. (1982). *Managerial values and expectations: The silent power in personal and organizational life*. New York: AMACOM.

Schneider, S. C., & Barsoux, J. L. (2003). *Managing across cultures*. HEC University of Geneva, INSEAD, Prentice Hall.

Schwartz, S. (1996). Value priorities and behavior: Applying a theory of integrated value systems. In C. Seligman, J. M. Olson, & M. P. Zanna, (Eds.)*The psychology of values: The Ontario symposium: Vol. 8* . Mahwah, NJ: Lawrence Erlbaum.

Schwartz, S. H. (1992). Universals in the content and structure of values: theoretical advances and empirical tests in 20 countries25, 1–65. In M. P. Zanna (Ed.), *Advances in experimental social psychology*. Orlando, FL: Academic Press.

Schwartz, S. H. (1994). Are there universal aspects in the structure and contents of human values? *Journal of Social Issues*, *50*(4), 19–45.

Siehl, C., & Martin, J. (1990). Organisational culture: A key to financial performance? In B. Schneider (Ed.), *Organisational climate and culture* (pp. 241–281) Newbury Park, CA: Sage.

Shalom, H. S., & Rubel, T. (Dec 2005). Sex differences in value priorities: Cross-cultural and multimethod studies Washington. *Journal of Personality and Social Psychology*, *89*(6), 1010.

Sturdivant, F., Ginter, J., & Sawyer, A. (1985). Managers: Conservatism and corporate performance. *Strategic Management Journal*, *6*, 17–36.

Tapsell, S. (1998). How leaders behave. Management, Auckland, February, reporting on the Global Leadership and Organisational Behaviour Effectiveness study, Bob House, Wharton School of Management, University of Pennsylvania.

Thomas, A. S., & Ramaswamy, K. (1996). Matching managers to strategy: further tests of the miles and snow typology. *British Journal of Management*, *7*, 247–261.

Trice, H. M., & Beyer, J. M. (1993). *The cultures of work organisations*. Englewood Cliffs, NJ: Prentice Hall.

Trompennars, F., & Hampden-Turner, C. (2002). *21 Leaders for the 21st Century – How innovative leaders manage in the digital age*. NY: McGraw-Hill.

Waddock, S. A., & Post, J. E. (1991, September/October). Social entrepreneurs and catalytic change. *Public Administration Review, 51*(5), 393–401.

Wilkins, A. L., & Ouchi, W. G. (Sep 1983). Efficient cultures: Exploring the relationship between culture and organizational performance, Ithaca. *Administrative Science Quarterly, 28*(3), 468.

Building a Change Leadership Culture

Chapter 5

We must become the change we want to see in the world.

Mahatma Gandhi

Introduction

'We' is the key word here. This chapter sets out to explain why individual change managers will never be able to create and sustain the critical leadership mass required to shift organizations along new paths. What is required is a whole 'leadership culture'. First of all in this chapter, leadership culture is broken down into its constituent components, showing the potential impact of the alignment between leaders' personal values and leadership team behavior on leadership team culture. These findings and future research implications have important ramifications for how change leaders develop and use leadership culture, with a particular focus on their potential role as organizational culture generators, carriers and shapers.

Evidence for the importance of leadership culture can be found in the work of Kotter and Heskett (1992) who studied 207 companies and drew the following conclusions: Companies that displayed leadership from managers at all levels in the organization achieved a net income growth of 756% versus 1% where this was not present; common shortcomings for leaderless performance-degrading companies were arrogance, inflexibility and an inability to see a need for adapting to change.

So, 'Walking the Talk' is a common phrase in the language of leadership (e.g. Miller, 2002; Taylor, 2005), but what does it entail and what effect might it have on organization culture(s)? Taylor (2005, p. 351) implores leaders 'to make the links specific between what you do and the values and beliefs that underpin this'. In this way, a leader's behavior and values are assumed to assist the development of organizational culture (Schein, 1992); but how might leaders, acting together to create leadership culture, utilize this in their role as organization culture shapers?

This chapter explores the notion and contribution of 'leadership culture', considered as a fusion of the collective conscious (leadership behavior) and unconscious (leaders' personal values) expression of leadership (Aitken, 2002). A previous study (Aitken, 2004) is summarized, providing evidence for the components of such a leadership culture. This chapter is a direct response to the call by Collinson and Grint (2005, p. 7) to 'challenge the conventions of leadership research (and practice) by exploring its existence beyond individual office holders or heroic charismatics'. The focus here is on formally and informally acknowledged leaders acting in unison to build and enact leadership culture, i.e. leadership as an all-embracing and far-reaching social influence process (Parry, 1998). Indeed, the central proposition is that leaders, in their demonstration of a peculiar brand of personal values–based leadership behavior, are more likely to be able to produce a distinctive 'fit for purpose' organizational culture(s). Thus, leaders' talk becomes implicitly and explicitly connected to the walk, enabling concerted organization culture role modeling and distinct cues for followers about what is expected of them within their own spheres of culture influence.

What is 'leadership culture'?

Previous excursions into defining 'leadership culture' are rare (Alban-Metcalfe & Alimo-Metcalfe, 2003 – extrapolated from studies of individual leadership), as are empirical papers investigating the nature and specific business effects of the relationships between leadership-culture constructs (Block, 2003; Parry & Proctor-Thompson, 2003). The prevailing literature generally indicates that personal leadership mainly impacts organizational culture and perhaps vice versa (as exemplified by Schein, 1992), although we are left unsure about the exact part leaders play, particularly through conversion of their personal values (Schwartz, 1994) into everyday collective leadership behavior.

As Crossan (2003) records from an interview with Chris Argyris, academics tend to concentrate on the internal and external validity of constructs, with theory running ahead of real-world application. Consequently, 'implemental' validity and usability is potentially overlooked. Here, we set out to investigate the makeup and potential research/business value of the concept 'leadership culture', leaning heavily on the transformational-transactional leadership 'by the team' school (Bass & Avolio, 1990), as opposed to leadership proffered by a designated sole leader. The term 'by the team' is used here to signify the collection and combined efforts of formal and informal leaders operating throughout an organization. As Block (2003) demonstrated, immediate supervisors can have a greater influence on employee perceptions of culture than all other leadership levels. To begin, we offer a research model (Figure 5.1) that places leaders' culture role modeling as the natural, albeit inadequately explored, 'implemental' link between 'leadership culture' and organization culture(s).

The model in Figure 5.1 above starts by positioning leadership 'by the team' as a collective leadership phenomenon made up of formal and informal leaders acting in concert. Bate (1994, p. 242) expressed the need to 'depersonalise and decentre the leadership concept, so that we begin to perceive leadership as a co-operative

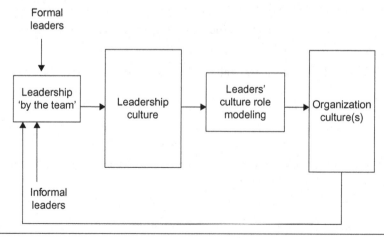

Figure 5.1 A model of 'Leadership Culture' within the context of organization culture(s).

or collective enterprise'. Here, leaders are classified as a combination of officially designated leaders, both 'near' and 'far' (Shamir, 1995) and 'emergent' leaders, encompassing those who have been granted this label by followers. Although we agree with the sentiments of Burns (1996) and Bass (1998) that all team members contribute toward transformational leadership (that includes the development of culture change capability), observation of practising leadership teams suggests this is often aspirational, with much effort required to forge such a leadership alliance.

As a case in point, a recently privatized New Zealand government agency senior executive team, after launching a series of change initiatives, undertook an analysis of their leadership culture using the Leadership Culture Display measure described in Chapter 8.

The MOST frequent Leadership Culture transformational behaviors they practiced were:

- Emphasize the importance of being committed to our beliefs
- Emphasize the importance of having a collective sense of mission
- Recognize member and/or team accomplishments
- Articulate a compelling vision of the future
- Set high standards

However, the LEAST frequent Leadership Culture transformational behaviors discovered were:

- Specify for each other what are the expected levels of performance
- Spend time teaching and coaching each other
- Encourage each other to rethink ideas that had never been questioned before
- Listen attentively to each other's concerns
- Provide useful advice for each other's development

So, what the senior management team (SMT) decided to do was:

- Celebrate that staff were engaging in the new business strategy and values
- Offer leadership support to one of the Divisional Managers (where the current span of control was too large)
- Each to bring a leadership problem to the SMT meeting
- Each to make a presentation on a leadership success story
- Set up leadership role swaps for themselves and shadowing for emerging leaders
- Set up a leadership 'walk the talk' program (culture role modeling)

Leadership culture is defined as 'that amalgam of lived purpose, critical behaviors and essential personal values, identified and agreed by the leaders as authentic and functional for their organization culture (whole or part), which the leaders (formal and emergent) role model through their everyday communications and actions'. Some attempts by business to match business brand with style of leadership culture are portrayed below.

'The power of all of us' – collaborative leadership is key.

'Connecting people' – leaders who can connect people through their community-building skills and contacts.

'Refresh the world in body, mind and spirit' – leaders who refresh inside are innovative, lifetime learners, looking for new ways to do things.

Other descriptions of well-known leadership cultures, how to create one and then ensure it is producing leadership culture, rather than consuming it, can be found in Ulrich and Smallwood (2007).

As Harris (2005, p.80) notes about distributed leadership, 'Effective leaders must have the ability to read and adjust to the particular context they face. In this respect, their leadership behaviour is contingent on context and situation. The choices that they make relate directly to their own beliefs, values and leadership style'. In this mode, leaders become a 'psychological group', consisting of people who interact with one another, are psychologically aware of one another and who perceive themselves to be a group (Schein, 1992). The group psychosocial traits present refer to shared understandings, unconscious group processes, group cognitive style and group emotional tone (Cohen & Bailey, 1997). Central to the idea of leadership culture is this coming together of consistent and authentic leadership behavior – with authenticity a product of personal values aligned with their behavioral counterparts (an idea illustrated later with some results from an empirical study of leadership team culture (Aitken, 2004)) – forming the bedrock on which an appropriate leadership culture and the form of authentic workplace culture role modeling subsequently employed by leaders can be founded.

An ill-defined leadership culture means a fuzzy and shaky platform for leaders' culture role modeling, resulting in inconspicuous and/or unclear cues for what is important (purpose and task focus) and how we should act around here, i.e. organization culture(s). As Kluckhohn (1951, p. 86) wrote, 'Culture consists of patterned ways of thinking, feeling and reacting, acquired and transmitted mainly by symbols, constituting the distinct achievements of human groups, including their embodiments in artefacts; the essential core of culture consists of traditional (i.e. historically derived and selected) ideas and especially their attached values'. In this way, creation and management of meaning through leadership culture becomes a continuous process whereby leaders, through words and deeds, communicate 'integrating ethos' (Selznick, 1957) in order to focus energy toward collective identity and joint purpose.

The argument outlined here is that without sufficient time and energy devoted to understanding what this guiding ethos looks and feels like, and then consciously attempting to role model it, leaders are unlikely to create sufficient critical mass to wield any salient directional social influence on organization culture(s). We suggest therefore that leaders need to talk in-depth about the exact nature of their walk, before they attempt to enact it. As Mumford states in Pearn (2002, p. 210–211), unless theories in use are surfaced and discrepancies acknowledged, learning at different levels of depth will not occur. In this sense, leadership culture learning should enable change leaders to close the gap between 'espoused theory' and 'theory in use' (Argyris & Schon, 1974). But, first of all, what might the components of a leadership culture be?

Components of leadership culture

To answer the above question, a recent study (Aitken, 2004) attempted to discover whether the match between leaders' specific personal values and the leadership behavior they actually observed in their teams (23 leadership teams from organizations across New Zealand and the UK, containing a total of 191 team members – 80% operating in the public sector), i.e. the type and strength of the leadership culture present, bore any relation to their evaluation of the leadership functioning within those teams, as measured by their satisfaction with the leadership 'by the team' abilities and perceived team effectiveness, i.e. two leadership culture outcomes. In part, this work was a ready response to Lord and Brown (2004, p. 7) who stated that, 'We maintain that articulating the connections between leaders and subordinates' self-concepts will provide leadership researchers with a platform to move beyond the study of leader behaviour to the study of leadership'; and directly addressed their resulting Hypothesis 5.5 (p. 212): 'Leader behaviour has its greatest effect when it activates coherent patterns of values'.

RESEARCH APPROACH

An extensive literature review (Aitken, 2003) had concluded with evidence of a theoretical association between specific types of personal values and leadership behavior constructs. In broad terms, this was reflected in a possible conceptual relationship between 'transformational' type personal values and transformational leadership behavior (i.e. people and future focused values and behavior – likely to facilitate the capability required for anticipatory business change) and also between 'status quo' type personal values and transactional leadership behavior (i.e. present and task focused values and behavior – likely to resist change by sticking with what is known and important today).

As Baker and Jenkins (1993, p. 2) note, 'The value concept is often used to identify unknown or underlying variables in individual actions. It is this ostensible uncovering of the cognitive path between personal values and behaviour which gives values' research its significance to management researchers'. Moreover, Hambrick & Brandon (1988), in the context of a general model of executive values and action, suggest that values first of all influence the perception of stimuli and thereby shape information gathering, and secondly values guide behavior in order to uphold established terminal values. This is the essence of investigating the influence of 'alignment' on the perception of leadership team culture, i.e. the unconscious alignment of personal values with the conscious perception of behavior that either reflects or does not match these values. As a reminder, this is why we explored the personal values that change leaders and those they interact with may hold, in the previous chapter.

In order to provide definition for the personal values and leadership behavior constructs being matched, a factor analysis of the Schwartz Value Survey (SVS) (Schwartz, 1994) and the Team Multifactor Leadership Questionnaire (TMLQ) (Bass & Avolio, 2001) revealed the factor structures listed in Figure 5.2. Tjosvold, Hui, Ding and Hu (2003) had already revealed support for values impacting on team effectiveness through team relationships. The approach taken was consistent with the emerging understanding that values have their impact through team member interaction (Morris et al., 1998). Influenced by 'Path-Goal' and 'Expectancy' theory (reported in Yukl, 1989) and using the research model in Figure 5.2 below, whose production was guided by the Hackman & Morris (1979) modeling framework, the practical proposition was that as alignment between team members' personal values and their perception of values-matched leadership 'by the team' behavior strengthens, they will expect the latter to continue to remain in line with the former, thereby

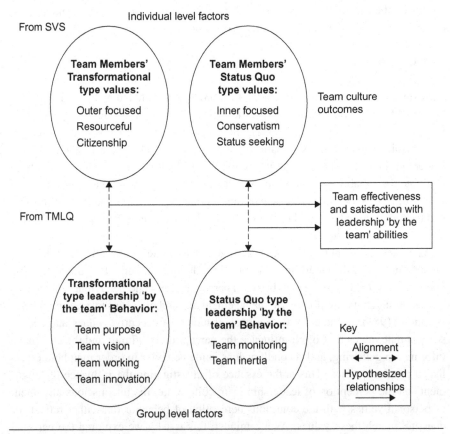

Figure 5.2   Research Model for link between Leadership Culture (executive's behaviours and values) and Team Outcomes.

maintaining their motivation for the team interaction, resulting in a positive assessment of leadership culture, as represented by measures of perceptions of team effectiveness and satisfaction with leadership 'by the team' abilities.

The idea tested here argued that alignment between a team member's personal values strength (for either transformational or status quo types of values) and their perception of the strength of the presence of team leadership behavior (which respectively mirrors either transformational or status quo types of values) leads to a perception of high team effectiveness and high satisfaction with leadership 'by the team' abilities. As the gap between a team member's personal values strength (for either transformational or status quo types of values) and their perception of the presence of team leadership behavior (which respectively mirrors either transformational or status quo types of values) grows, such that there is more of the behavior than is required by the strength of the values, then the subsequent perception of each of the two team outcome measures will be heightened.

However, if there is less team behavior present than is required by the personal values strength, then the same measures will be suppressed. The effect will be reversed if team member's transformational-type personal values are strong and the status quo–type leadership behavior present is perceived as not strong. In this case, as the gap becomes larger, i.e. the presence of status quo–type leadership behavior is perceived to be less (a situation considered to be positive by those holding transformational-type values), this will be associated with perceptions of high team effectiveness and satisfaction with leadership 'by the team' abilities.

FINDINGS

Analysis of the results relating to the examination of the central idea revealed the following. All alignment associate relationships for transformational-type values and transformational-type leadership 'by the team' behavior indicated a negative relationship with perceptions of team outcomes, as the gap between them increases. A positive relationship was found, if there is more transformational-type leadership 'by the team' behavior perceived, than the strength of transformational-type values held. Therefore, provisional support was evidenced for the central idea of the beneficial effects of a leader's personal values alignment with the appropriate demonstrable leadership action within the leadership culture they belong to, when considering transformational-type alignment associates. The relationship is stronger for Team Effectiveness when the associates are Citizenship and Resourceful, whilst the Outer Focused associates reveal a stronger relationship with Satisfaction with Leadership 'by the team' Abilities. As predicted by previously theorized associates (Aitken, 2004, p. 169), 'Resourceful' appears to show the highest overall impact and provides the highest and second-highest single impact through its association with Team Working and Team Innovation, respectively. Inspection of the items making up the factor 'Resourceful' indicate the possibility of motivational values elements that may underpin striving for team working and team effectiveness (e.g. capable, wisdom, intelligent, successful), and team working and team innovation (e.g. freedom, creativity, broad-minded), in a general sense.

However, this suggestion remains tentative given that the result only provides approximately 25% of the explained variance for these alignment associates. Interestingly, the relationship with Satisfaction with Leadership 'by the team' Abilities reverses and slightly reduces the relative impact of the Resourceful-Team Working and Resourceful-Team Innovation alignment associates, with the latter now in front of the former. Perhaps, in this research subject population, the perception of satisfaction with leadership 'by the team' abilities depends more on the climate for innovation (West, 1990) than team working. Further evidence of support for the differential effect of Resourceful-Team Working and Resourceful-Team Innovation alignment on the relationship with the team outcome measures was found in the results from the regression analysis. The Resourceful-Team Working alignment associate accounted for 26% of the variance in the assessment of team effectiveness, whilst the Resourceful-Team Innovation alignment associate accounted for 22% of the variance in the assessment of satisfaction with leadership 'by the team' abilities.

There is some limited support for the suggestion that Conservatism may be perceived as a transformational-type personal value within a predominately public sector workforce, recently subjected to social entrepreneur–type interventions. In a general sense, Waddock and Post (1991) stressed that the social entrepreneur generates follower commitment to public good projects by framing them in terms of important social values, rather than in economic terms, whilst Egri and Herman (2000) observe that nonprofit organizations can be viewed as altruistically driven and motivated to improve the society. Once again, inspection of the items making up Conservatism (e.g. helpful, self-discipline, responsible, obedient, respect for tradition) raises the possibility that such values may fit this view, whilst Status Seeking might be viewed as an entrepreneurial personal value, when attached to a social cause.

Further evidence of support for the differential effect of Conservatism (when considered as a transformational-type personal value) with transformational-type leadership 'by the team' behaviors (Team Vision and Team Working) alignments on the relationship with the team outcome measures is found in the results. The Conservatism-Team Vision alignment associate accounted for an increase of 6% of the total variance in the assessment of team effectiveness (i.e. the second and final significant model predictor), whilst the Conservatism-Team Working alignment associate accounted for an increase of 4% of the variance in the assessment of satisfaction with leadership 'by the team' abilities (once again, the second and final significant model predictor). What might be witnessed here is the presence of a public service ethos (vision and way of working) impacting on perceptions of the specified team outcomes.

Finally, once all personal values were treated as transformational types, analysis revealed that the combination of the relative alignment associate contributions – listed in order of their strength: Resourceful-Team Working, Conservatism-Team Vision, Resourceful-Team Innovation and Conservatism-Team Innovation – accounted for 31% of the variance in the Team Effectiveness scores, whilst Resourceful-Team Innovation, Conservatism-Team Vision, Resourceful-Team Working and Conservatism-Team Working accounted for 26% of the variance in the Satisfaction with Leadership 'by the team' Abilities scores.

As an illustration of identifying the prevailing leader's values and leadership culture, a UK Council wanted to move forward through encouraging their leaders to bring about cultural change by:

■ 'Facilitating continuous improvement contributions from all employees'.

■ 'Ensuring that individuals are becoming more effective, creative and entrepreneurial in their performance'.

■ 'Building a culture that recognises and values personal difference and development'.

■ 'Developing standards of behaviour, which support the organisation's values'.

In order to establish their current position, over 100 managers from across the organization completed earlier versions of the Leadership Culture Display (see Figure 5.3) and PBV assessment (see Chapter 4) to reveal the following.

MOST frequent leadership culture behaviors:

■ Set high standards

■ Recognize member and/or team accomplishments

■ Clearly communicate what each member needs to do to complete assignments

LEAST frequent leadership culture behaviors:

■ Spend time teaching and coaching each other

■ Motivate each other to do more than they thought they could do

■ Focus on developing each other's strengths

MOST important personal values:

■ Family security (safety for loved ones)

■ Healthy (not being sick physically/mentally)

■ Honesty (genuine, sincere)

LEAST important personal values:

■ Social power (control over others, dominance)

■ Devout (holding to religious faith and belief)

■ Accepting my portion in life (submitting to life's circumstances)

Given the need to change from a silo-based, output-driven organization to a collaborative, community outcome focus, the results confirmed a concentration on the former, but also showed a paucity of active leadership capability building. As a result, a series of cross-departmental team development exercises were designed so that leaders could learn to do joined-up work together. The predominant values indicated a good fit to the purpose of the organization, i.e. public service ethos for a deprived community, although highlighted a potential culture clash with a highly religious and significant immigrant population, whilst also revealing a possible, non 'can do' attitude.

DISCUSSION

The research approach laid out above demonstrated that alignment between two critical facets of leadership culture, namely leaders' personal values and leadership team behavior, does indeed influence team members' perception of the functionality of their team culture. The closer the gap between personal values and actual leadership behavior, the more positively participants regard their team culture. The role for leaders then is to make explicit the implicit culture through role modeling, so that leadership team members can begin to understand the pattern and strength of one another's transformational values and how these might be either facilitating or blocking values congruent behavioral responses to leadership culture change. As West and Altink (1996) point out, these factors do not occur simply because teams are put together. The degree of task and social reflexivity required to develop, maintain and enhance these norms of behavior will only bear fruit if (leadership) teams are trained and developed in how to recognize and utilize these values and behaviors.

In terms of wider research implications, the results also have important implications for work motivation theory. Work motivation can generally be defined as 'a set of energetic forces that originates both within and beyond an individual's being, to initiate work-related behavior, and to determine its form, direction, intensity and duration' (Pinder, 1998, p. 11). Need theories (e.g. McClelland, 1961), which focus on the role of psychological needs or values in motivation, still appear to have relevance for organizational development research. Indeed, the evidence suggesting the most significant impact in the research model of the personal value 'Resourceful', when one inspects the items comprising it, is in line with the import of McClelland's (1961) notion of the 'Need for Achievement' motive and McCrae & Costa's (1989) 'Big 5' personality 'Conscientiousness' trait, i.e. the latter contains the subscales of Competence, Order, Dutifulness, Achievement Striving, Self-discipline and Deliberation.

Along similar lines, Ashkanasy and O'Connor (1997) reported a stronger relationship between Schwartz and Bilsky's (1987) 'Achievement' value and high-quality leader-member exchange, when compared to other personal values. Thus, a worthwhile literature meta-analysis could usefully identify the theoretical and empirical strands between values, motives and personality traits, which in turn may possibly represent universal dimensions of human expression. This may address a concern in science known as the 'jangle fallacy' (Kelley, 1927), where near-identical constructs are often given different names and talked about as if they are distinct, and may be highlighting what Allport (1937) called a person's 'cardinal dispositions', or be indicative of Apter's (2001) 'reversal' theory propositions.

So, the pervasiveness of personal values and leadership behavior as influential phenomena in business leadership team social influence process appears profound. Results from the study above do indeed suggest that linking talking with walking, through role modeling a particular brand of leadership culture within leadership teams first, may hold some promise as a practical change leadership tool for organization culture(s) development. Whilst we have alluded to a leadership culture that may foster change, organizational development or renewal requires a particular brand of leadership culture called 'transformational'.

What is transformational leadership culture

Executive life is becoming evermore unpredictable and complex. Managers and professionals reaching influential positions usually have a full grasp of one remit and environment: accountancy, sales, operations, HRM, business unit/technical/ international experience etc. Leadership 'of' the business rather than leadership 'in' the business requires a different mentality and skills set. Whilst heroes can carry the day in times of crisis, building a sustainable culture of innovation, excellence and achievement requires a collective and distributed, as opposed to an individualised and hierarchical, leadership mind-set and approach. Creating leadership teams across the business achieves two things simultaneously. First, it encourages joined up, whole system operations, rather than badly stitched–together silos, and consequently may improve the utilization of resources and the customer experience. Second, reaching some critical mass by connecting all parts of the leadership will enable much stronger signals to be sent to the stakeholder community about the direction of business and accompanying culture change. The development of leadership usually entails dealing to the top team or high potentials as individuals, where the learning and networking remains. Constructing learning that reaches all the leadership components of a business system releases considerably more impact from the investment and facilitates wider exposure to the shifting levers of change. First, using Table 5.1 below, ask yourself if you are operating as a leadership team or a management group.

Business transformation is a common buzzword, but who could tell you what it looks like or how to assess how much your own organization has at its disposal? A study by Aitken (2004) revealed what executives believe this critical set of leadership behaviors

Table 5.1 Leadership team versus management group

Management group (transactional)	Leadership team (transformational)
Business units focus, drawing on 'silo' thinking and individual accountability for line performance	Focus on stakeholder environment, across business systems and leadership/management functioning – driven by strategy and improvement
Appears energized by competition for resources, results and sometimes favor	Energized by commitment to common purpose, goals and complementary and/or integrated ways of working
Contributions usually based on formal organization structure, seniority and meeting process	Variety of inputs from SMT, other leadership teams, individual initiatives and external insights
Essentially provides for the roundtable input of expert and/or functional reporting	Uses the diversity of know-hows, experience bases and business insights to build leadership team culture and capability
Process encourages relationships based mainly on contractual obligation	Process builds trust and capacity for shared learning and problem solving
Direction and motivation provided by, or sought from, single leader, e.g. the chief executive	Leadership shifts relevant to subteams, specialist tasks and as a possible leader-learning opportunity

Source: Concordia International Ltd © 2006.

business consists of. Following on from above, this framework is a first in considering transformational leadership as a collective responsibility and concentrates on what and how much behavior is actually displayed by groups of leaders within and across six clusters of behavior. When present, the combined transformational leadership behavior seeks to constantly review, refresh and reinforce the momentum of the business. By doing so, it sends out a clear and comprehensive message to all staff and stakeholders, expecting collegiate focus, ideas and investment for making the business fit for its current and emerging purpose, starting with role modeling by directors and executives.

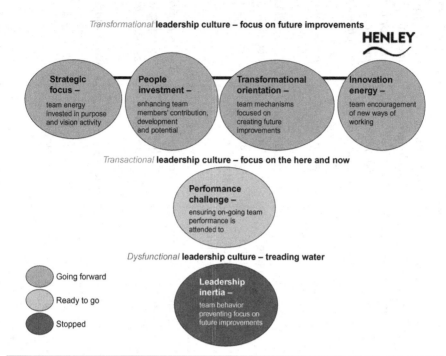

Figure 5.3 The Leadership Culture Display factors.
Source: Concordia International Ltd © 2006.

The framework is composed of four transformational dimensions (necessary for continuous step changes in business performance): 'People Investment' and 'Innovation Energy' being the most important, plus 'Strategic Focus' and 'Transformational Orientation'. Additionally, there is one transactional factor (showing if the everyday business engine is being attended to – the transactional element), called 'Performance Challenge', and one dysfunctional 'Leadership Inertia' set of behaviors (holding back any attempts to progress the organization). Figure 5.3 and Table 5.2 below provide more detail about the respective behaviors.

In the example below (Figure 5.4), the results indicate some marked differences in how the collective leadership is currently perceived by members of that same collective (represented by different colored lines). For development purposes, deep dialog about why executive colleagues view their leadership in this way will generate new ideas and activities for how best to focus and deploy the total leadership resource, both in formal gatherings and informal conversations, with one another, with staff and with critical stakeholders. By itself, the 'People Investment' assessment immediately draws attention to the current emphasis being placed on leadership development per se. Crucially, exploring the results reminds leaders to spend their

Table 5.2 Transformational leadership culture

Strategic focus energy divested in purpose and vision activity	People investment contribution to a culture that enhances people performance, development and potential	Innovation energy developing a collective culture for encouraging improved ways of working	Transformational orientation investment in team mechanisms that support the improvement leadership role	Performance challenge activity ensuring that ongoing team performance is attended to	Leadership inertia behavior that prevents effective responses to improvement change
Members of my team…..					
Articulate a compelling vision of the future	Encourage each other to build on their contribution	Encourage each other to rethink ideas that have never been questioned before	Agree that our meeting agenda items add value to our leadership work	Bring attention to failure to meet agreed standards	Avoid making decisions
Concentrate on strategic conversation	Pay attention to developing each other's strengths	Have radical ideas about the future	Make decisions stick	Alert each other to individual performance dips	Fail to respond to requests for assistance
Set future-oriented goals	Attend to each other's concerns	Create options for making strategic choices	Delegate operational matters to others	Closely monitor overall team performance	Avoid addressing problems as they arise

Source: Concordia International Ltd © 2006

energy on matters of collective and distributed leadership, being different from managers remaining preoccupied with their own business portfolios.

The power of role modeling in change leadership

Having identified the key components of leadership culture (including the transformational culture required for change to occur) and their potential usefulness as a leaders' culture modeling technique, attention turns to that part of the model in Figure 5.1 that remains to be explored – the exact nature of leadership culture transmission mechanisms used by change leaders with the intention of shaping and strengthening specific and optimal organization culture(s), i.e. after making the implicit culture explicit for themselves, converting the talk now matched with the walk into attempts to change organization culture(s). The principle alluded to is that unless leaders are fully aware of their own leadership culture, they are unlikely to be able to control the impact of their role as the modeling archetypes of organizational culture change. Organizational culture in this sense has been conceptualized as a complex web of norms, values, assumptions and beliefs, which are characteristic of a particular group, reinforced and perpetuated through training, rewards, sanctions and 'socialization' (Lytle, Brett, Barsness, Tinsley & Janssens, 1995).

The rest of this chapter positions leaders' culture role modeling as a prime candidate for study within this socialization process. We have established that a leader's personal values, when explored and made tangible through behavior, can prescribe a preferred state of organizational affairs. As already shown, in the presence of strong values-behavior congruence, leaders and followers are more likely to form

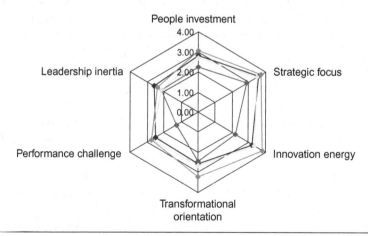

Figure 5.4 An example Leadership Culture Display readout.
Source: Concordia International Ltd.

a positive appraisal of the people in question. But what happens if leaders engage in values-incongruent behavior? Not only might this result in cognitive dissonance for the leadership team concerned (Festinger, 1964), but other employees also are unlikely to respond to leadership culture role modeling that is dissociated in this way, thereby confounding attempts to change employees values/behavior in line with the requirements of a new organizational culture, talked about but clearly not walked by leaders. But what are the role modeling delivery mechanisms through which culture can be channeled and can role modeling work in the context of organizational culture creation and development?

Unfortunately, the underlying processes and mechanisms by which transformational leaders exert their influence on followers have not been fully explored (Kark, Shamir & Chen, 2003). As one example of a culture transfer mechanism that sounds like indirect role modeling, Shamir, House and Arthur (1993) argued that transformational leaders (those leaders charged with forging organizational culture) may raise the salience of the collective identity in followers' self-concepts by emphasizing shared values, both directly and indirectly, through references to the symbolic actions of founders and former leaders/members. Indeed, the literature abounds with assumptions about the power of leaders to shape organizational culture, summed up by Thomas and Ramaswamy (1996), who suggested efforts that examine the impact of top managers on firm performance implicitly assume that the characteristics, biases or values of these managers are reflected in the resource allocation priorities. As a prime example, Miles and Snow (1978), in their seminal work examining the link between top management beliefs and company strategy, structure and process, found that firms led by managers who focused on effectiveness competed on the basis of innovation, whilst those led by managers focused on efficiency competed using cost control. However, uncertainty remains about the leadership into business culture social-psychological conversion processes, and this is not helped by the predominance of cross-sectional quantitative questionnaire research, itself often reliant on indirect and often distant reports of everyday leadership behavior.

Schein (1992) lists a number of culture change mechanisms, including role modeling, that leaders might use to influence organizational culture: directing attention to critical incidents/priorities, reacting to crises, formal statements of intent, telling stories, legends and myths, symbolic actions, design of work facilities/systems/processes, rewards and sanctions, methods of problem solving/decision making etc. We have generic results that indicate indirect and direct effects of transformational leadership on perceived organizational effectiveness through its influence on transformational/transactional culture (Parry & Proctor-Thompson, 2003). However, what leaders (and researchers and business consultants) really need to know for their culture change intervention resource investment decisions is which of these mechanisms works best in what situations and why? For example, what might be the best blend of leadership activities, in what order of delivery and over what timeframe, to produce a transformational leadership culture leading to successful organizational culture(s)? Indeed, there appear to be no studies to date that even explore the frequency of use of such leadership culture change mechanisms across organizational change environments. Hence, perhaps belated calls for comparative inter-pretations and sense making by leaders – how do leaders interpret their roles, think and act in different contexts (Storey, 2005).

Half a century ago, McGregor (1960) noted how difficult it would be to see Theory X supplanted by Theory Y as the basic model underlying organizational processes, especially if the people holding such beliefs constantly observe behaviors that rein-force them. People become socialized by leaders, either intentionally or unintention-ally, to those practices with which they are most familiar – old habits die hard. Both the cognitive-perceptual and learning models of human behavior (Levy, 1970 and Skinner, 1974, respectively) infer specific reactions to the environmental events cre-ated by others. More recently, House (1977, p. 194) implores leaders to 'express, by their actions, a set of values and beliefs to which they want their followers to sub-scribe'; Conger and Kanungo (1998) relay that effective leaders engage in exemplary acts worthy of imitation, whilst for Kouzes and Posner (1999), 'modeling the way' is positioned as a worthwhile leadership practice. Whilst theory and anecdote is plentiful, Ashforth and Saks (1994) appear to be unique in testing whether conscious attempts to socialize employees as intended bear results. They found that common institution-alized tactics conducted in a fixed sequence of steps and with a fixed timetable for completion – rather than a series of idiosyncratic or individual experiences – related to lower levels of innovation (i.e. higher levels of compliance) by new employees.

However, Bandura (1986) noted that complex behavior can occur without the time and ongoing personal experiences of behavior shaping. The primary social learning process here is identification – we watch others and learn from them, e.g. shadowing effective change leaders. He identified three primary modeling mech-anisms: imitation (merely copying others), cued (an existing repertoire prompted by the behavior of others such as formal or informal leaders) and vicarious (see-ing others being reinforced for behaving in certain ways), with research indicating that people are more likely to imitate models who are high in prestige or expertise (Craighead, Kazdin & Mahoney, 1976). In this sense, leadership culture sense mak-ing is 'simply, familiar structures that are seeds from which people develop a larger sense of what may be occurring' (Weick, 1995, p. 50). And, as Pye (2005) notes, it is here that leadership has its dual role, helping to extract appropriate cues and pro-viding a crucial cue for others to extract.

So, how can leaders be proactive in the way they set out to impact culture and performance? 'Walking the talk' (practising what you preach) has become a com-mon phrase in the language of leadership, and rightly so. Table 5.3 lists five main signals for change leaders to use.

To date, the empirical work on role modeling appears in three work settings. Rich (1998) found a positive (though indirect) association between role modeling and overall salesperson performance, with sales managers suggesting the following seven categories of role modeling behavior: personally demonstrating proper selling

Table 5.3 Walking the talk: everyday signals for shifting business culture and performance

Signal	Example
Physical symbols	A new chief executive may choose to turn his/her large office, with the inspiring view, into the staff rest area.
Reward and recognition focus	Reinforcement of the newly required values can be done through pay and benefits as well as specific personal acknowledgments.
Repeated attention paid to priorities	At every turn, delegation of a task can be explained as connected to a part of the strategy.
Behaviour in crisis situations	An emergency gives leaders the spotlight where a message or response has immediate emotional resonance and is therefore remembered, for good or bad.
Time devoted to role modelling culture	How much personal time and energy does the leader put aside to demonstrate the culture change priorities he/she has set for others?

Source: Based on Argyris (1985).

techniques to salespeople, showing up on time to meetings and appointments, conducting oneself in an honest moral manner, presenting a professional image through appropriate dress and grooming, listening to salespeople (so, salespeople will in turn listen to customers), being a team player and finally never asking salespeople to do things that the manager would not do him or herself. Orpen (1985) assessed the effects of an insurance company behavior modeling program containing eight modeling modules, designed to improve managers' skills in dealing with their subordinates. A year later, trainees subjected to the training received substantially higher performance ratings and branch profits when compared to managers in the control condition.

Finally, in the banking sector, the use of video-based behavior modeling combined with associated role play (Bell, 1992) resulted in improved levels of employees' understanding, attitude and behavior, including a perceived improvement in the level of service and customer care. However, Bell concludes by noting that sustainable skill development using these training methods (alerting the viewers to what they are about to see, and what the behavior seeks to achieve; showing the behavior in an organized and structured way and isolating the distinctive and sequential stages of the process – codified into learning points) can only happen where there is an opportunity for real practice, including high-quality feedback. This suggests similar research techniques are required for studying the impact of leadership culture role modeling on organizational culture(s).

Transformational leadership is essentially open ended, enabling organizations not only to cope with change, but also to be proactive in shaping their future. However, the role of the Board and senior executive team in creating the conditions for business transformation can be problematic because:

Frequently, in top teams, competitiveness, suspicion and departmentalism replace trust, the ability to take risks and to be open with one another. In order to enhance the quality of its strategic management processes and for transformation to take place, there is a need to get beneath 'ritualistic discussion, the appearance of substance and interest' and develop 'feeling as a team'.

(Vaill, 1989)

A precondition for generating a culture of sustained excellence and achievement is establishing an ethical culture on the basis of doing the right thing by stakeholders, whatever the conflicts of desire to perform or pressures to do so. This requires deep dialog amongst senior executives and the Board about what is – and is not – acceptable behavior, and an understanding that it is the norm to challenge openly or whistle-blow. Unethical behavior presents a number of tangible and intangible risks, including fraud, health and safety violations and workplace dysfunction such as bullying, harassment and unlawful discrimination. The response by governments and regulators to these ethical breaches is to impose increasingly onerous legislation, such as corporate governance codes, workplace directives (e.g. from the EU), as well as desperate internal and external media messages to rebuild tarnished reputations. However, an ethical culture is not created by imposing a set of rules or demanding employees sign a code; it is evident when leaders do what they say they value (walk the talk) in ethical terms.

Executives whose perceptual-emotional makeup recognizes there are multiple ways of framing reality are more likely to succeed in business transformation. To create wealth in this way is to combine values that are not easily joined together, and are therefore scarce and of greater intangible value. The propensity to reconcile such dilemmas also correlates with bottom-line performance, and women have been found to be better reconcilers (Hampden-Turner & Trompenaars, 2002). Also, supervisors rated high in transformational leadership behaviors have been shown to be associated by staff with higher perceived levels of mission, adaptability, involvement and consistency when compared with their transactional counterparts (Block, 2003). Block found that immediate supervisors have a greater influence on employee perceptions of culture than all other leadership levels within the organization. Leaders wanting some pragmatic means to shape culture quickly would therefore be advised to follow the recipe outlined in Figure 5.5.

WHAT QUESTIONS DOES THIS RAISE FOR THE CHANGE LEADER?

There are a number of critical questions change leaders should ask themselves as a result of this chapter.

1. Do you have a business culture development plan that would enable delivery of your strategy and business plan through your leadership culture?

    Creating a culture development plan (i.e. converting mission and values into directly observable and measurable behaviors) to connect the corporate vision with the business plan is rare, but well worth the effort for leaders working and developing cooperatively to reinforce a new or changing business direction. For example, in creating a culture development plan for a company that considers personal development as a primary mechanism to improve business innovation, all the means at its disposal could be used to reinforce its presence, via coaching for example. Leaders can also make decisions at this point about whether to stay on or get off the company journey, depending on the fit with their own values

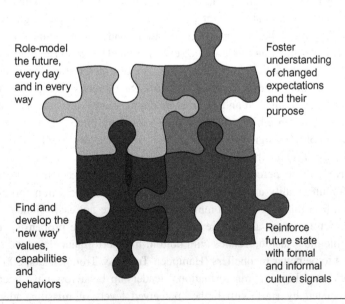

Figure 5.5   Shifting business and performance fast without a blueprint.
Source: Copyright Concordia International Ltd.

and priorities. Acting otherwise is unsustainable both for the individual and the company in the long run.

2. What does your leadership and workplace culture look like – how do others see and evaluate it?

3. Are your espoused organizational values and behavior aligned with your actual personal values and actions?

4. Have you discussed the potential impact of your different personal values on your individual and collective leadership behavior and working practices?

5. What are the critical signals you need to send to the workplace for focusing behavior and energy on the things that matter today and tomorrow?

6. By what means do you intend to shape business culture and which behaviors and activities stand the best chance of making a difference?

7. Are you talking about and agreeing the components and ways of conducting your individual and collective walks before you step out into the working environment?

8. How transformational is your leadership culture and/or does it need to be?

Finally, are you seeking out and developing change leaders and followers who hold the 'Move forward' personal value in good measure (see Chapter 4) whilst continuing to build change leadership capability and release innovation together? Combined and nurtured, these may be the magic ingredients for creating a culture of sustained (and preferably sustainable) business innovation, excellence and achievement.

This chapter addressed the challenge laid down by Collinson and Grint (2005, p. 6), 'to develop more nuanced and complex (leadership) models that, for example, recognise the "embeddedness" of leadership practice in the economic, technological and social relations of organisation and society'. For the leadership social influence process to bear fruit as intended, leaders must know the exact look of their walk and its precise link to the values origin of their talk, before they begin attempts to influence their followers together.

Additionally, they need to know which behavior change influence mechanisms are likely to have the most impact on organizational culture(s). This is consistent with the leader's current views. For example, a content analysis of the views of 10 senior women across the Queensland, Australia public service (Limerick & Field, 2003) revealed the importance of role modeling where ethical behavior is concerned. Leaders are advised to select and practice the role modeling and other activities that demonstrate and convert commitment to a particular cultural paradigm, and continually monitor the gap between their espoused and actual values and behavior (current state of leadership culture) by receiving feedback on their progress from those they are attempting to influence (those within the executive/emergent leaders collective and the recipients of their leadership actions).

As Thomas (1999) notes, creating an effective leadership team requires, amongst other things, managing complex operations, issues and strategies seamlessly, i.e. speaking with one voice, and modeling the behaviors they want people to emulate. Thus, this chapter positions leaders' culture role modeling as a start point for investigating how to convert leadership culture into organizational culture. Bearing in mind that some 50–70% of change management initiatives fail to make any lasting impact on the organizations they purport to reform (LaClair & Rao, 2002), this is not a trivial matter.

A final case study shows change leaders taking this seriously. A global pharmaceutical company wanted its research and development leaders to collaborate more effectively, responding to Morten Hensen's challenge that 'whilst most managers acknowledge the value of a "collaborative culture", few know how to build one'. Achieving success, like so many aspects of organizational life, is dependent on having an appropriate leadership culture. Traditionally, changing leadership culture has been seen as very difficult and slow to achieve. The emphasis had been on the leader rather than shared leadership across the group. A facilitated experiential workshop was employed to create a rapid approach (using the Leadership Culture Display detailed in Chapter 8) to measure and share perceptions on behaviors expected in a transformational leadership team, as opposed to a management group.

It has been shown that the behaviors of key individuals can be transformed by experiential workshops that build trust in a safe environment, where handling the balance and the ambiguity between role complexity and organizational turmoil is key. The methodology works with and on the knowledge of the 'leadership team'. The content generated is an articulation of what is known and how it can be utilized. Overlaid on this are the values and the behaviors representing the leadership environment within which the substantive issue will be worked on. This social and political emersion, together with the use of real data about current leadership behavior, caused the participants to question whether they needed to be a team at all, and consequently new communication intents and arrangements were put in place to share knowledge without the constraints of organizational structure or business process (see Green & Aitken, 2006).

Change leadership consultants and researchers could add value by using methodologies that can capture and assess the relative power of leader-induced organizational culture(s) influence mechanisms, used either singly or in combination, for organizational culture creation and development. This is likely to require studies that include experimental, case study and real-life observation of leadership in business. Indeed, a W. K. Kellogg Foundation–funded review by Russon & Reinelt (2004) of 55 leadership development programs found that few programs have an explicit program theory (or theory of change) explaining how and why a set of activities is expected to lead to outcomes and impacts, whilst the evaluation type and scope were often constrained by the funding organization's requirement for immediate feedback. We address evaluation measures more fully in Chapter 8.

This chapter has offered change leadership and organization development research and practice professionals a rationale, framework, measures and way forward (including detail of what a transformational leadership culture looks like in terms of change leadership action or inaction) for change leaders who wish to create their own leadership culture and then discuss its likely impact on their workplace culture(s), within the context of change. We now build on this in Chapter 6 by turning our attention to the life-long learning and development of change leaders, including the identification of specific, research derived, change leadership capabilities, types of development process and related activities.

References

Aitken, P. (2002). An investigation of the relationships between Leader and Team Member personal values, their alignment and Team Transformational Leadership – an emergent research model. *Henley Working Paper Series* (0222).

Aitken, P. (2003). Exploring the measurement properties of and theoretical associates between the Team Multifactor Leadership Questionnaire (TMLQ) and the Schwartz Value Survey (SVS), using original research and a recent team leadership and personal values study. *Henley Working Paper Series* (0310).

Aitken, P. (2004). The relationships between personal values, leadership behaviour and team functioning. *Doctor of Business Administration Thesis*, Henley Management College/ Brunel University.

Alban-Metcalfe, R. J., & Alban-Metcalfe, B. (October 2003). Leadership culture and change inventory – an organisational 360 feedback instrument. *Selection & Development Review*, *19*(5).

Allport, G. (1937). *Personality: a psychological interpretation*. New York: Holt.

Apter, M. J. (Ed.), (2001). *Motivational styles in everyday life: A guide to reversal theory*. Washington, DC: American Psychological Association.

Argyris, C. (1985). Interventions for Improving Leadership Effectiveness Bradford, 30 (21 pages). *The Journal of Management Development*, *4*(5).

Argyris, C., & Schon, D. A. (1974). *Theory in practice: Increasing professional effectiveness*. San Francisco, CA: Jossey-Bass.

Ashforth, B. E., & Saks, A. M. (August 1994). Socialisation tactics: Dimensionality and longitudinal effects of newcomer adjustment. *Paper presented at the annual meeting of the Academy of Management*, Dallas, TX.

Ashkanasy, N. M., & O'Connor, C. (1997). Value congruence in leader-member exchange. *The Journal of Social Psychology*, *137*, 647–662.

Baker, S., & Jenkins, M. (1993). The role of values in the design and conduct of management research: perspectives on managerial and consumer Ccgnition. *Working Paper, SWP* 4/93, Cranfield School of Management.

Bandura, A. (1986). *Social foundations of thought and action: A social cognitive theory*. Englewood Cliffs, NJ: Prentice Hall.

Bass, B. M. (August 1998). *Current developments in transformational leadership: Research and applications*. San Francisco, CA: Invited address to the American Psychological Association.

Bass, B. M., & Avolio, B. J. (1990). The implications of transactional and transformational leadership for individual, team and organisational development. *Research in Organisational Change and Development, 4*, 231–272.

Bass, B. M., & Avolio, B. J. (2001). *Permission set for the multifactor leadership questionnaire for teams*. California: Mind Garden.

Bate, E. L. (1994). *Strategies for culture change*. Oxford: Butterworth-Heinemann.

Bell, R. (1992). Using video-based behaviour modeling training to improve performance at work. *Training & Management Development Methods, 6*(1–4), 501–506.

Block, L. (2003). The leadership-culture connection: An exploratory investigation. *Leadership & Organisation Development Journal, 24*(5/6), 318–334.

Burns, J. M. (1996). *Empowerment for change*. University of Maryland Unpublished manuscript, Kellogg Leadership Studies Project.

Cohen, S. G., & Bailey, D. E. (1997). What makes teams work: Group effectiveness research from the shop floor to the executive suite. *Journal of Management, 23*(3), 239–290.

Collinson, D., & Grint, K. (2005). Editorial: The leadership agenda. *Leadership, 1*(1), 5–9.

Conger, J. A., & Kanungo, R. N. (1998). *Charismatic leadership in organisations*. Thousand Oaks, CA: Sage.

Craighead, W. E., Kazdin, A. E., & Mahoney, M. J. (1976). *Behaviour modification*. Boston, MA: Houghton Mifflin.

Crossan, M. (2003). There is no silver bullet. *Academy of Management Executive, 17*(2), 38.

Egri, C. P., & Herman, S. (August 2000). Leadership in the North American environmental sector: Values, leadership styles, and contexts of environmental leaders and their organizations. *Academy of Management Journal, 43*(4), 571–604.

Festinger, L. (1964). *Conflict, decision and dissonance*. Stanford, CA: Stanford University Press.

Green, J., & Aitken, P. (2006). Creating a leadership culture for knowledge utilisation. *Journal of Medical Marketing, 6*(2), 94–104.

Hackman, J. R., & Morris, C. G. (1975). Group tasks, group interaction process and group performance effectiveness: A review and proposed integration. In L. Barkowicz (Ed.), *Advances in Experimental Social Psychology: Vol. 8 .* New York: Academic press.

Hambrick, D. C., & Brandon, G. L. (1988). Executive values. In D. C. Hambrick (Ed.), *The executive effect: Concepts and methods for studying top managers* (pp. 3–34). Greenwich, CT: JAI Press.

Harris, A. (2005). Leading from the chalk-face: An overview of school leadership. *Leadership, 1*(1), 73–87.

House, R. J. (1977). A 1976 theory of charismatic leadership. In J. G. Hunt & L. L. Larson (Eds.), *Leadership: The cutting edge*. Carbondale, IL: Southern Illinois University Press.

Kark, R., Shamir, B., & Chen, G. (2003). The two faces of transformational leadership: Empowerment and dependency. *Journal of Applied Psychology, 88*, 246–255.

Kelly, E. L. (1927). *Interpretation of educational measurements*. Yonkers, NY: World.

Kluckhohn, C. C. (1951). The study of culture. In D. Lerner & H. D. Laswell (Eds.), *The policy sciences*. Stanford, CA: Stanford University Press.

Kotter, J. P., & Heskett, J. L. (1992). *Corporate culture and performance*. New York: The Free Press.

Kouzes, J., & Posner, B. (1999). *Encouraging the heart*. San Francisco, CA: Jossey-Bass.

LaClair, J., & Rao, R. (2002). Helping employees embrace change. *The McKinsey Quarterly, 4.*

Levy, L. H. (1970). *Conceptions of personality.* New York: Random House.

Limerick, B., & Field, T. (2003). Women's voices on developing an ethical public service. *Women in Management Review, 8*(8), 398–405.

Lord, R. G., & Brown, D. J. (2004). *Leadership processes and follower self-identity.* Mahwah, NJ: Lawrence Erlbaum Associates.

Lytle, A. L., Brett, J. M., Barsness, Z. I., Tinsley, C. H., & Janssens, M. (1995). A paradigm for confirmatory cross-cultural research in organisational behaviour. *Research in Organisational Behaviour, 17,* 167–214.

McClelland, D. C. (1961). *The achieving society.* Princeton, NJ: Van Nostrand Reinhold.

McCrae, R. R., & Costa, P. T., Jr. (1989) The structure of interpersonal traits: Wiggin's circumplex and the five-factor model. *Journal of Personality and Social Psychology, 56,* 586–595.

McGregor, D. M. (1960). *The human side of enterprise.* New York: McGraw-Hill.

Miles, R. E., & Snow, C. C. (1978). *Organisation strategy, structure, process.* New York: McGraw-Hill.

Miller, D. (2002). Successful change leaders: What makes them? What do they do that is different? *Journal of Change Management, 2*(4), 359–368.

Morris, M. W., Williams, K., Leung, K., Larrick, R., Mendoza, M. T., Bhatnagar, D. Li. J., Kondo, M., Luo, J. L., & Hu, J. C. (1998). Conflict management style: accounting for cross-national differences. *Journal of International Business Studies, 29,* 729–748.

Orpen, C. (1985). The effects of behaviour modelling training on managerial attitudes and performance: A field experiment. *International Journal of Manpower, 6*(4), 21–24.

Parry, K. W. (1998). Grounded theory and social process: A new direction for leadership research. *Leadership Quarterly, 9*(1), 85–105.

Parry, K. W., & Proctor-Thompson, S. B. (2003). Leadership, culture and performance: the case of the New Zealand public sector. *Journal of Change Management, 3*(4), 376–390.

Pearn, M. (Ed.), (2002). *Individual differences and development in organisations.* Wiley.

Pinder, C. C. (1998). *Work motivation in organisational behaviour.* Englewood Cliffs, NJ: Prentice-Hall.

Pye, A. (2005). Leadership and organising: Sensemaking in action. *Leadership, 1*(1), 31–48.

Rich, G. A. (1998). The constructs of sales coaching: Supervisory feedback, role modelling and trust. *The Journal of Personal Selling & Sales Management, 18*(1), 53–63.

Russon, C., & Reinelt, C. (2004). The results of an evaluation scan of 55 leadership development programmes. *Journal of Leadership and Organisational Studies, 10*(3), 104–107.

Schein, E. H. (1992). *Organisational culture and leadership.* San Francisco, CA: Jossey-Bass.

Schwartz, S. H. (1994). Are there universal aspects in the structure and contents of human values? *Journal of Social Issues, 50*(4), 19–45.

Schwartz, S. H., & Bilsky, W. (1987). Toward a psychological structure of human values. *Journal of Personality and Social Psychology, 53,* 550–562.

Selznick, P. (1957). *Leadership in administration.* New York: Harper & Row.

Shamir, B. (1995). Social distance and charisma: theoretical notes and an exploratory study. *Leadership Quarterly, 6,* 19–47.

Shamir, B., House, R. J., & Arthur, M. B. (1993). The motivational effect of charismatic leadership: A self-concept based theory. *Organisation Science, 4,* 577–594.

Skinner, B. F. (1974). *About behaviourism.* New York: Knopf.

Storey, J. (2005). What next for strategic-level leadership research. *Leadership, 1*(1), 89–104.

Taylor, C. (2005). *Walking the talk – building a culture for success*. Random House, New Zealand.

Thomas, R. J. (1999). Leading as a team. *Strategy and Leadership, 27*(6), 10–14.

Trompennars, F., & Hampden-Turner, C. (2002). *21 Leaders for the 21st Century – How innovative leaders manage in the digital age*. NY: McGraw-Hill.

Thomas, A. S., & Ramaswamy, K. (1996). Matching managers to strategy: Further tests of the miles and snow typology. *British Journal of Management, 7*, 247–261.

Tjosvold, D., Hui, C., Ding, D. Z., & Hu, J. (2003). Conflict values and team relationships: Conflict's contribution to team effectiveness in China. *Journal of Organisational Behaviour, 24*, 69–88.

Ulrich, Dave, & Smallwood, Norm (Jul/Aug 2007). Building A Leadership Brand Boston. *Harvard Business Review, 85*(7,8), 92.

Waddock, S. A., & Post, J. E. (September/October 1991). Social entrepreneurs and catalytic change. *Public Administration Review, 51*(5), 393–401.

Weick, K. E. (1995). *Sensemaking*. London: Sage.

West, M. A. (1990). The social psychology of innovation in groups. In M. A. West & L. J. Farr (Eds.), *Innovation and creativity at work*. Chichester: John Wiley and Sons.

West, M. A., & Altink, W. M. M. (1996). Innovation at work: Individual, group, organisational and socio-historical perspectives. *European Journal of Work and Organisational Psychology, 5*(1), 3–11.

Yukl, G. A. (1989). *Leadership in organisations* (2nd ed.). Englewood Cliffs, NJ: Prentice Hall.

Chapter 6

The Evolution of a Change Leader

If a man will begin with certainties, he shall end in doubts; but if he will be content to begin with doubts, he shall end in certainties.

Francis Bacon (1561–1626), Essays of Great Place

Introduction

The year 2009 is the 150th anniversary of *On the Origin of the Species* by Charles Darwin. Just as in species evolution, becoming an effective change leader takes time and requires changes within the leader themselves, making them ever more adaptable to the shifting environments within which they operate. In this chapter we look at the nature of the change leader's learning journey and provide examples of development focus which reflect this by:

1. Considering the business contexts within which change leaders learn.
2. Commenting on the nature of the learning process and developmental stages.
3. Identifying the 10 dynamic capabilities for change leaders to develop over time.

The context for learning

Learning to become a change leader is itself a change journey. Shaped by what work, formal/informal learning and life throws their way, it is the conscious reflection on personal responses to these episodes, which provides the core ingredients of judgment; subsequently used as a guide for selecting the most appropriate leadership actions, when faced with ever-changing circumstances.

The main focus of change leaders, as opposed to change managers, and ultimately the end game for the journey of change leadership development itself, is to solve what Grint calls 'wicked problems' (Grint, 2005). At a time when the sustainability of financially driven market capitalism and the nature of the leadership accompanying it, which seeks continuous economic growth and short-term shareholder value gains, is being challenged for the first time in living memory, 'wickedness' in all its guises stares back at us through the crestfallen faces of much glamorized turnaround CEO's. However, as Grint explains, wicked problems have no simple solution because they:

1. Are novel (responding to vu jade rather than déjà vu – which managers can deal with).
2. Have no stopping rule and thus no definition of success.
3. May be intransigent in nature such that we have to learn to live with them (some problems are so complex that you have to be highly intelligent and well informed just to be undecided about them).
4. Are often embedded in other problems where a proposed solution often generates another problem.
5. Have no right or wrong solutions, merely better or worse developments.
6. Often include stakeholders who may have a different approach and understanding.
7. Involve developing understanding through construction of the 'solution'.
8. Mean securing collective consent rather than providing the 'right' answer.
9. Suggest collaborative, non-authoritarian processes are more suitable.

10. Are problems for leadership not management – where the leadership role is to ask the appropriate questions to address the wicked problem (see the 10 critical capabilities described later on in this chapter).

Grint (2005) notes the irony is that while leadership (through questioning and reflection) may be the most appropriate way of coping with intractable problems, this is often perceived as indecisive or weak by others, although the only real need for 'command' authoritarian-type decision making comes when there is an immediate and critical crisis to be resolved. After all, as we discussed in Chapter 4, leader's values, beliefs and mindsets, and the anticipated perceptions of followers, clearly influence their behavior, judgments and choices of action (Aitken, 2004). Case studies of transformational change have identified a number of challenges related to the context:

- **Divisions and boundaries:** the presence of internal barriers and silos
- **Complexity:** the number of stakeholders and interested parties proliferates as areas of business become more inter-dependent for success
- **Low expectations:** large-scale change can be more energizing than incessant incremental change causing weariness
- **Approach as important than end goal:** employees having an opportunity to shape the how of change
- **Pilots work:** for example Tesco's 'living service programme' trial which engaged employees before larger implementation
- **Speed is of the essence:** bring parties together early to hammer out agreements, orchestrate activity and relay quick wins
- **One size doesn't fit all:** each operating unit may require a different approach related to its fitness for purpose past and future culture

The answer to the question what works best then is 'it depends', because raising conscious and effective change leaders requires developing flexibility in leadership style and activity to match the prevailing business conditions and culture; past, current and desired. An adaptation of the work by Goleman, Boyatzis, and McKee (2004) on different types of emotional intelligence required for a variety of leadership scenarios illustrates this well in Table 6.1.

Another similar example of matching change leaders to what the business needs to do next to thrive provided by Stace & Dunphy (2001) suggests: 'Coaches' are required for developmental transitions, 'Captains' work best with task-focused transitions, 'Charismatics' are well placed to deal with transformations and 'Commanders' suit turnarounds. As we already know, Higgs and Rowland (2005) discovered that in all change leadership instances, use of top–down positional power by leaders was shown to impair attempts to change the business. In high-magnitude whole system change, 'Emergent' combined with 'Framing Change' leadership behavior is the most effective,

Table 6.1 Leadership styles and their situational impact

	Coercive/ Commanding	Authoritative/ Visionary	Affiliative	Democratic	Pacesetting	Coaching
The leader's modus operandi	Demands immediate compliance	Mobilizes people toward a vision	Creates harmony and builds emotional bonds	Forges consensus through participation	Sets high standards for performance	Develops people for the future
The style in a phrase	'Do what I tell you'	'Come with me'	'People come first'	'What do you think?'	'Do as I do, now.'	'I believe in you'
Underlying emotional intelligence competencies	Drive to achieve, initiative, self-control	Self-confidence, empathy, change catalyst	Empathy, building relationships, communication	Collaboration, team leadership, communication	Conscientiousness drive to achieve initiative	Conscientiousness drive to achieve initiative
When the style works best	In a crisis, to kick start a turnaround, or with problem employees	When changes require a new vision, or when a clear direction is needed	To heal rifts in a team or to motivate people during stressful circumstances	To build buy-in or consensus, or to get input from valuable employees	To get quick results from a highly motivated and competent team	To help an employee improve performance or develop long-term strengths
Overall impact on emotional climate	Negative if it strays beyond the immediate crisis	Most strongly positive	Positive	Positive if the consensus seeking is genuine	Negative if prolonged	Positive in all circumstances

as is the latter in short-term change horizons (implementation within 12 months). In longer-term initiatives (more than 18 months) a 'Master' approach combined with 'Creating Capacity' emerged as the best strategy, reinforcing the idea that leaders should not attempt to go it alone. Follow-up research discovered that a combination of the factors described below explained nearly 50% of the variance in change success.

Change conditions exist in three diverse rich spheres: the inner world of the change leader; their organization's stage of development, particularly its people and culture; and the wider community (local and global) in which the leader, their people and organization operate. This suggests evolving flexi-change leaders should be exposed to development events that enable them to become wise about the connections between themselves, business, society and the world, having learnt first from their personal handling of peculiar, local and simple change instances. To make this development goal realistic, manageable and less overwhelming for a single leader, the change leadership behaviors already identified by Higgs and Rowland (2005) are worth developing, i.e. they have proven potential to increase the chance of successful change implementation. These are the ability to conceptualize and communicate a macro change framework, rather than a detailed project plan, called 'Framing', and a leader's inclination, wherewithal and skills for 'Creating Capacity' for change responsiveness in the business system, focused on nurturing others individual and collective capabilities, alongside making and communicating connections across stakeholders.

At this juncture, although we should recognize the influence leadership power has on strategic change through making change happen, it is more useful to conceive this as 'power to' rather than 'power over', since the former highlights the productive side of power that allows leaders to achieve outcomes working together with their followers. Extreme use of 'power over' is often found in narcissistic leaders (who are pseudo-transformational) as recognized using the following criteria:

1. Sense of grandiosity and self-importance
2. Fantasizes about being great
3. Believes they are special, only understood by special people
4. Demands constant admiration
5. Feel that things are their due and automatic acceptance guaranteed
6. Is exploitative and ignores the rights of others
7. Lacks empathy and does not see others needs
8. Often envies others and thinks others envy them
9. Subject to strong feelings of anger, shame, humiliation and emptiness
10. Won't recognize any of the above and therefore has zero self-awareness.

The opposite of narcissistic leadership is 'servant leadership', the type of leadership to work toward developing given three essential attributes for well-functioning organizations are contained within it; the ability to forge trust, appreciating others and becoming comfortable with empowerment. Too much 'charisma' becomes the undoing of leaders, making them inflexible, convinced of their own infallibility and unwilling to change. As Stacy (1993) summarized, the link between power and the way in which it is used provide very important boundaries around the group learning process from which new strategic directions emerge. The application of power in particular forms has fairly predictable consequences for group dynamics. Where power is applied as force and consented to out of fear, the group dynamic will be one of submission, or where such power is not consented to, the group dynamic will be one of rebellion, either covert or overt. Power may be applied as authority and the predictable group dynamic here is one in which members of the group suspend their critical faculties and accept instructions from those above them. Groups in states of submission, rebellion or conformity are incapable of complex learning; i.e. the development of new perspectives and new mental models, required for effective change leadership.

The learning process and developmental stages

Living consciously is a state of being mentally active rather than passive. It is the ability to look at the world through fresh eyes. It is intelligence taking joy in its own function. Living consciously is seeking to be aware of everything that bears on our interests, actions, values, purposes and goals. It is the willingness to confront facts, pleasant or unpleasant. It is the desire to discover our mistakes and correct them. It is the quest to keep expanding our awareness and understanding, both of the world external to self and of the world within
Branden (1999)

This quote suggests leaders consider their own and others human condition, values, intent and modus operandi as a first port of call when confronting change. Unfortunately, only when you interview leaders about the influences on their leadership learning, do they discover that their understanding of leadership has been shaped by causes they were not previously conscious of (Kempster, 2006; McCall, Lombardo, & Morrison, 1988; McCauley & Brutus, 1998). For a development model of 'Becoming' a change conscious leader see Kempster (2006, p.16). From interviews, five ways of enhancing and accelerating leadership development were discovered, almost entirely based on observational and opportunistic learning, as opposed to formal development through pre-arranged interventions:

1. Impact of watching notable leaders, and critical episodes where they are validated as a leader by these significant people in confronting a difficult, emotionally charged, confrontational leadership situation.

2. Securing self-identity as a leader, through successful transitions from being a professional contributor and/or by building a strong sense of conviction of what leadership entails by observing role models.
3. First-hand experience of the use/misuse of power over people that remains memorable.
4. Daily interactions with and active participation in acts of leadership and 'followership', with an increasingly diverse range of people and more complex tasks and decisions.
5. Facilitated reflection on the lived experience of self and others as leaders.

All of the above speaks to 'The Discipline of Building Character' (Badarraco, 1998). As Badarraco (1998) explains, all of us have experienced situations where our professional responsibilities unexpectedly come into conflict with our deepest values, e.g. a budget crisis forces us to dismiss a loyal, hardworking employee. Here we often have conflict between right and right and it is through these defining moments that we learn how managers become leaders by translating their personal values into calculated action, where self-enquiry must lead to shrewd, persuasive and self-confident action, when managers need to determine if their ethical vision will be supported by their colleagues and employees, which is then negotiated with shareholders and customers; and ultimately where astute executives can use these defining moments as an opportunity to redefine their company's role in society. The development path is to continually explore the 'Who' questions; 'Who am I?' as an individual executive, 'Who are we?' as leaders of followers and 'Who is the company?' as a leadership representative of the enterprise. This is developed in the following table and can be actioned using the PBV dialogue explained in chapter 4.

Who am I?	Who are we?	Who is the company?
What feelings and intuitions are coming into conflict here?	What are the other strong, persuasive interpretations of the ethics of this situation?	Have I done all I can to consider and secure my leadership position and the strength of my organization given the chosen direction?
Which of the values that are in conflict are most deeply rooted in me?	What point of view is most likely to win a contest of interpretations inside my organization and influence the thinking of other	Have I thought creatively and boldly about my organizations role in society and its relationship to shareholders?

(Continued)

Who am I?	Who are we?	Who is the company?
What combination of expediency and shrewdness, coupled with imagination and boldness will help me implement my personal understanding of what is right?	Have I orchestrated a process that can manifest the values that are held within my organization?	What combination of shrewdness, creativity and tenacity will help me transform my vision into reality?

If this is the case, then more reflection-enhancing processes like coaching and mentoring, provided at the early phases of growth as a change leader, may prove beneficial in increasing the change capability of leaders and hence their attunement to leadership learning as they grow. This may also encourage a shift in taking more self-responsibility for personal development goals and outcomes. In the life cycle of a change leader this becomes especially poignant at the 'midlife crisis' juncture (Webb, 2006), where executive career derailment can occur from internal conflict caused by the search for a more authentic self. We look at this in more detail later. Here, the coaching process can alert leaders to their own and others deeper sense of meaning in life by exploring the executive's view of their environment, behavior, values, character formation and personal narrative.

Taking the idea of coaching one stage further, leaders might also coach others to help them sustain their own growth and effectiveness in demanding times. The demanding nature of change leadership can lead to psycho-physiological damage which can be ameliorated through experiencing the compassion generated by developing other people (Boyatzis, Smith, & Blaize, 2006). As can the positive psychology approach of playing to the strengths of the leader, where a strength can be defined as 'a natural capacity for behaving, thinking or feeling in a way that allows optimal functioning and performance in the pursuit of valued outcomes' (Linley & Harrington, 2006), who list character strengths which are clearly applicable for developing post-capitalist change leaders, under the headings; 'Wisdom & Knowledge' (cognitive strengths that entail the acquisition and use of knowledge), 'Courage' (emotional strengths that involve the exercise of the will to accomplish goals), 'Humanity' (interpersonal strengths that involve tending and befriending others), 'Justice' (civic strengths that underlie healthy community life), 'Temperance' (strengths that protect against excess) and 'Transcendence' (strengths that forge connections to the larger universe and provide meaning).

To allow any of the above to happen change leaders must first of all be able to overcome blocks to their own learning (adapted from Boydell & Temporel, 1981) such as: PERCEPTUAL – not seeing a problem that exists, CULTURAL – the way things are here prevents me, EMOTIONAL – fear or insecurity about exploring new ground, MOTIVATIONAL – no drive to do anything different, COGNITIVE – outmoded mental models of how the world is, INTELLECTUAL – capacity to acquire new understanding, EXPRESSIVE & ABSORBATIVE – communication capability, SITUATIONAL – lack of appropriate opportunity to grow, PHYSICAL – inadequate time or facility and LOCAL CONDITIONS – insufficient support for transfer and application of learning to the business. A diagnostic is available to measure the latter (see Concordia's LTE in Chapter 8). As Argyris (1993) and Revans (1982) note, an effective leading–learning experience should include a real problem that requires solution generation and implementation of the selected solution, a description of the problem that includes actual or proposed conversations from those for whom the problem matters, and an accompanying scenario of the espoused theories and theories in action, including thoughts and feelings that are not normally discussed.

Turning to developmental stages, two classic works by Jaques (1989) and Bennis (2004) provide change leadership role complexity and personal growth windows respectively. Their propositions have been adapted and summarized in Table 6.2. These are useful for change leaders who want to identify where they are on their developmental journey and what to pay attention to at each stage. Of course, they could also be used to assess the strike rate of change leadership development initiatives. Indicative stages of the leadership development 'pipeline' focus are also included.

Whilst it is useful to be able to predict how a change leader's journey may map out, Porter, Lorsch and Nohria (2004) remind us of potential learning surprises for the first time senior executive brought in to instigate change:

1. You can't run the company – too engrossed in many tactical meetings to use your change leadership time wisely.

2. Giving orders is very costly – everyone consults you before acting or uses you as an indirect endorsement.

3. It is hard to know what is really going on – you learn about events after the fact and dissent comes to you indirectly.

4. You are always sending a signal – stories about you become magnified and people act by trying to anticipate your mood, interests and priorities.

5. You are not the boss – board and executive respective roles and responsibilities are rarely transparent, consistent and clear.

6. Pleasing shareholders is not the goal – analysts who don't understand the business push for high-risk strategies, and management incentives become distorted when share price moves up, but not down.

Table 6.2 Change leadership role complexity and personal growth windows

Jaques – Transitions to leadership	Bennis – Seven ages of the leader
1st transition ■ Hands on ■ Observe, monitor and record events ■ Adhere to defined procedures ■ Report anomalies Role – react to and eliminate variation in day-to-day operations Performance evaluated using task measures	The Infant Executive – recruit a team of guides/mentors who will support you as you grow Pipeline Focus: meeting professional standards and on technical skill
2nd transition ■ Diagnose observations ■ Draw conclusions ■ Examine trends ■ Identify potential problems and obstacles ■ Improve and implement ■ Eliminate common cause variation	The Schoolboy, with Shining face – your image, words and deeds in both your work and personal life will be scrutinized for the first time – obtain an accurate picture of the gap between your identity (who you think you are) and your developing reputation (how others perceive and judge you) Pipeline Focus: getting work done through others and helping others perform effectively The Lover, with a Woeful Ballad – you begin to separate from your peer pack, now sometimes managing or even removing former colleagues. You learn what to pay attention to as the problems come across your path and how to delegate effectively so you can move from working in to working on the business Pipeline Focus: identifying and supporting people to become managers

Role – continually monitor progress Performance evaluated using process measures 3rd transition ■ Build paths from existing to future state ■ Design processes to achieve the required system dynamic ■ Use direct judgment and analysis ■ Pre-plan alternate paths and minimize impact of variations Role – operate processes that achieve the required system dynamic Performance evaluated using output measures	The Bearded Soldier – comfort in the leadership role brings confidence and conviction and followers may begin to act on your every word, becoming reluctant to challenge and possibly not tell what needs to be heard. Check your ego and become wiling to hire people who are more talented than you Pipeline Focus: blending function and business strategy and penetrating other managers to understand what is going on at grass roots to develop managers own performance tracking
4th transition ■ Design and integrate dynamic systems to deliver value ■ Co-ordinate several pathways, their parallel processes and interactions ■ Balance resource needs, trade off tasks to achieve future states	The General, Full of Wise Saws – allow people to speak the truth and listen to their stories. Here your mandate will be to bring about change and your actions will be judged on their potential impact on long-term fortunes. However, you need to understand the mood and the motivations of your people before acting; to understand history, current context and gain support. Only then move to focus all stakeholders on what is truly important going forward Pipeline Focus: integrating disciplines and function strategy and developing across business leaders

(Continued)

Table 6.2 Continued

Jaques – Transitions to leadership	Bennis – Seven ages of the leader
Role – operate a system of value delivery with the required dynamics Performance evaluated using outcome measures Final transition ■ Envision future states ■ Sense and integrate interconnections between factors in the organization and its environment – adjusting as needs must ■ Identify the value the organization delivers to its customers and stakeholders Role – deliver value through strategy Performance evaluated using value measures	The Statesman, with Spectacles on Nose – the values drivers of early ambition and the navigation of the politics which often accompany advancement are put aside, with wisdom provided through interim 'mentoring' roles with the organization, sector or future leaders Pipeline Focus: coaching future CEO's The Sage, Second Childishness – when you mentor your achievements will not be lost. Instead you're leaving a legacy for future generations. Others watch your adaptive capacity to respond to personal changes in your own life. They learn from your ability to use your past experience and future curiosity to make nimble decisions that continue to bring success Pipeline Focus: coaching future board chairs and directors

7. You are only still human – the company is in danger of becoming too much about you and vice versa whilst gaps widen between your and other's rewards.

So, given what we know from our review of change leader's capabilities, we have identified what we think would be the top 10 capabilities to invest in over the life span of becoming an effective change leader. We offer these up as research proven 'dynamic capabilities' (Ambrosini & Bowman, 2009; Ambrosini, Bowman, & Collier, 2009) which, when blended together, underpin effective change leadership.

Ten dynamic capabilities for change leaders

In times of change, the learners will inherit the Earth while those attached to their old certainties will find themselves beautifully equipped to deal with a world that no longer exists.

Eric Hoffer (in Kofman, 2006)

It is important to have a capability-based approach to developing change leadership talent and there is a good business reason for doing so. Results of a McKinsey study (in Workman & Duncan, 2006) indicate that companies scoring in the top quintile of talent-management practices outperform their industry mean return to shareholders by 22%. Moreover, the classic study by Collins and Porras (2005) revealed from 1700 years of combined history in visionary companies that were 'built to last' only four individual cases of an outsider coming directly into the role of CEO; it was the continuity of the quality of the internal leadership talent pipeline that made the difference through preserving the 'core'. Below we offer our ten capabilities for the change leader's development portfolio.

These can be developed through embarking on a series of challenging job assignments which present diversity, adversity, variety and intensity, as recommended by Workman and Duncan (2006). The latter suggest self-managed development against a clear backcloth of what constitutes evidence of success with interventions across three areas; establishing a work experience sequence that combines five major development opportunities (starting something from scratch, fixit or turnaround, project/task forces, change in scope and scale, and line/support switch); helping managers confront the psychological transitions required by job and level changes; and providing evidence of personal leadership impact on others and events to help managers deepen their learning.

Indeed, expanding self-awareness is crucial to growth such that low self-awareness accuracy is found to be part of a more general inability to correctly gauge the reactions and feelings of others, often resulting from a failure to actively seek feedback leading to an inability to adapt or modify behavior and failure to learn from experience (particularly problematic in a rapidly changing environment); whereas high self-awareness produces high self-monitoring and higher role functioning job retention, and managers who are assessed by others are seen as more tolerant, patient, co-operative and trusting (Fletcher, 1997). Accurate and informed self-awareness therefore is the essential base ingredient for all the other capabilities outlined below. We have already highlighted the importance of accessing personal values in Chapter 4. We expand on how self-awareness could be developed in our coverage of the emotional intelligence capability, included as one of our ten capabilities described below.

CAPABILITY 1 – DEVELOP MINDFULNESS, USING THREE CAPACITIES FOR LEADERSHIP OF CHANGE DECISION MAKING

> *The rhetoric of management requires managers to pretend that things are clear and that everything is straightforward. Often (they) know that managerial life is more ambiguous and contradictory than that but they can't say it. They see their role as relieving people of ambiguities and uncertainties.*
>
> *Coutu (2006)*

Three 'thinking' capacities (adapted from McKenzie et al., 2007), frequently under-represented in development experiences, would help overcome the debilitating position implicit in the quote above.

Capacity one – wait and see

Delaying sense-making and postponing framing the problem would increase flexibility in the interpretation of events, which usually continue to evolve. This discourages closure on understanding ill-defined problems, caused by reverting to frames of thinking that have worked before in similar, but not the same, circumstances.

Capacity two – keep an open mind

Forestalling closure on interpreting what the event means allows multiple options to be developed for the variety of conditions the problem generates. Dialogue about multiple meanings helps create a shared understanding of the complexity and can lead to joined-up thinking for systemic implementation.

Capacity three – be comfortable with contradictions

Holding on to several meanings at once creates tension, but this in turn can lead to overarching solutions which can satisfy multiple stakeholders and thus facilitate implementation.

Inquiry requires a genuine willingness to hold an open mind, to question and challenge in order to build understanding. In addition it is the ability to accept that you as a leader are not the expert. Someone in your team may indeed have a better insight into a problem or challenge than you do. The ability to inquire is an important capability that can support a leader's attempts to make sense of the challenges that face them in implementing change in their part of the organization.

CAPABILITY 2 – ACCESS BROADBAND 'CAPABILITY' FROM ACROSS THE LEADERSHIP MEMBERSHIP

Studies of change leaders (Mant, 1999) indicate they were all 'bright' (logical thought, clearly expressed), but also had a feel for materials, movement, people and the physical world (often incorporating most of Gardner's repertoire of seven 'intelligences' – linguistic, logical, spatial, musical, kinesthetic, interpersonal and intrapersonal; Gardner (1993)).

Having access to these within a leadership team yields four advantages; 'versatility' (connections between ideas, people, events, etc. are made easier because of access to every possible way of thinking or doing – as Jacob Bronowski said: 'Every act of imagination is the discovery of likenesses between two things which we thought unlike'), 'social light-footedness' (can relate to all kinds of people and understand what they are trying to say and contribute, leading to an ability to differentially motivate – of considerable value in multi-disciplinary and international contexts), 'systems awareness' (the intellectual firepower to consider simultaneously the prevailing conditions and options for, and impacts, trade-offs and consequences of, acting in a particular way – or rapid judgment when you don't, or can't, know what to do) and 'dilemma resolution' (conflicts within a person created by concerns about opposing internal drives – treat as interpersonal conflicts by giving each concern its own voice, presenting its arguments, inquiring into the other's argument and engaging in dialogue; once all the parts have had their say, deeper interests will be revealed and a solution can be sought to serve every part).

A team of all the talents is worth building because it enables three things: the ability to make joint and considered decisions about across-organization challenges and together see them through to resolution, the management of complex operations, issues and strategies seamlessly, and role modeling collaborative behaviors leaders want others to emulate, which we covered in depth in Chapter 5. The broader and deeper the leadership cohort within a business the greater the breadth of 'improvement change' insights generated and the stronger the leadership voice, thus reducing the possibility that purpose and direction becomes lost in translation as the business grows and becomes more dispersed.

CAPABILITY 3 – BECOME A CO-CREATOR OF A LEARNING CULTURE

Do you send any of the following leadership learning blocking signals to your workplace? (Kofman, 2006):

- Keep others informed, but hide mistakes.
- Tell the truth, but don't bring bad news.
- Take risks, but don't fail.
- Beat everybody else, but make it look as if nobody lost.

- Be a team player, but what really matters is your individual performance.
- Express your independent ideas, but don't contradict your boss.
- Be creative, but don't deviate from the rules.
- Promise only what you can do, but never say 'no' to your boss's requests.
- Ask questions, but never admit ignorance.
- Think about the global system, but you'd better optimize your own sub-system.
- Think long term, but you'd better deliver immediate results.
- Follow all these rules, but act as if none of them exist.

Learning is concerned with why and how we change and the facilitation of learning among all members of a business for continuous transformation. De Geus (1997, p.63), from his work within Shell, advocates 'learning to play and playing to learn' as a way to enhance the speed, openness, inventiveness and courage of decision makers, i.e. learning how to change and becoming capable of making the decision to change. This involves acquiring learning processes, as well as knowing how to establish preconditions for learning, summarized in the following table (Frey, 2008), should you want to know more.

Approaches to studying organizational learning and learning organizations

	Learning process	Preconditions for learning (favorable learning context)
Individual level	<ul><li>Argyris and Schön 1978 (shifting theories-in-use)</li><li>Coopey 1995 (political process)</li><li>Dewey 1933 (interrelated processes)</li><li>Kolb 1984 (cyclic learning)</li><li>Nonaka 1994 (spiral)</li><li>Senge 1997 (ladder)</li></ul>	<ul><li>Argyris 1990 (removal of defenses)</li><li>Senge 1990a (trust in leader)</li><li>Starkey 1996 (removal of barriers)</li></ul>
Organizational level	<ul><li>Dixon 1994 (cyclical collective learning)</li><li>Dunphy et al., 1997 (creation of corporate competencies)</li></ul>	<ul><li>Fiol and Lyles 1985 (four contextual factors)</li><li>Garvin 1993 (giving time, developing skills, opening up boundaries)</li></ul>

(Continued)

Learning process	Preconditions for learning (favorable learning context)
▪ Dutton and Duncan 1981 (development of knowledge about the action–outcome of relations) ▪ Fiol and Lyles 1985 (development of insights, knowledge and association) ▪ Hedberg 1981 (development of new norms and mental maps) ▪ Nystrom and Starbuck 1984 (unlearning) ▪ Stata 1989 (shared learning processes of individuals) ▪ Change management scholars like Pettigrew 1985 and Tichy 1983 (OD process toward new organizational culture)	▪ McGill, Slocum and Lei 1993 (several supportive factors) ▪ Nevis, DiBella and Gould 1995 (10 facilitating factors) ▪ Pedler et al., 1991 (11 structural characteristics) ▪ Senge 1990a (five main disciplines) ▪ Tannenbaum 1997 (12 learning environment factors)

Source: Adapted from Lahteenmaki, Tovonen, and Mattila, 2001, p. 115. Note: Full reference details listed in the table can be sourced in Frey (2008).

And different forms of learning can also facilitate the holy grail of full employee engagement with organizational change (Hersovitch & Meyer, 2002). They found training, participation, reciprocation and empowerment increased involvement, value identification and learning capacity for change. Examples of successful change efforts in organizations which included the above were captured by Pascale, Millemann, and Gioja (1997).

CAPABILITY 4 – FUTURE SENSE-MAKING COMBINED WITH STRATEGIC THINKING

This requires being able to recognize, understand and address what is going on within the whole system in which change leaders operate. In essence, the ability to recognize those specific events that need to be addressed may well be a part of a broader pattern. However, all too often, responding to events and even patterns fails to solve problems. Leaders need to be able to dig deeper and understand that behaviors that result in problematic outcomes may be the result of the structures that underpin their area of operation. For example, leaders responsible for a sales force need to understand the structures that underpin the behaviors of the sales people (e.g. reward structures, reporting, recruitment, relation and induction processes, and sales management structures). However, in order to achieve real change it is important that leaders are able to identify the assumptions and mindsets that underpin and feed in to these structures. For the sales example above these assumptions may relate to beliefs about the motivational drivers, commitment and work ethic of individuals who work in sales.

Sense-making is about the capability to see what is happening on the surface and to understand what is causing this to happen before attempting to solve a problem or bring about change. Most change processes don't generate the depth of understanding and awareness for sustaining change in very demanding contexts, where different people need to align in complex settings with shifting conditions (Pye, 2005). Theory U (Senge, Scharmer, Jaworski, and Flower, 2006) distinguishes different depths of perceiving reality allied to different levels of action. Essentially learning to sense-make involves three elements; 'observe, observe, observe' (sense becoming one with the world), 'retreat and reflect' (allow presence for inner knowledge to emerge) and 'realize' (act swiftly with a natural flow), alongside developing six capacities: suspending, re-directing, letting go and letting come (presencing), crystallizing, prototyping and institutionalizing. Reading widely, joining future analyst clubs and accessing related websites will also promote this capability and, in line with our focus on change leadership in the post-financial crash era, books such as those by Avery (2005) and Dixon (2007) will considerably enhance system awareness. It is essential for a change leader to have a clear understanding of the business they are working in. They need to understand the core business models and their interaction with the dynamics of the business context. This is not to say that they have to be experts. It is more about the ability to see their role and how the changes they make relate to the business strategy and to understand why this strategy is being pursued. An excellent resource for developing strategic thinking is De Kluyver (2000).

CAPABILITY 5 – DEVELOP 'TOTAL' LEADERSHIP

To be an effective leader of change requires attunement and application to all facets of life where leadership is released (Friedman, 2006). Leaders at all levels require authenticity, integrity and experimentation in parallel leadership at work, family life, community engagement and most importantly their own personal growth. According to Higgs (2003), unique, authentic, high-performing leadership role models ('being yourself with skill') can bring about business change by changing the hearts and minds of stakeholders and customers, whose new, 'sustainability' informed values will demand a different vision of business and measures of its success. The change leadership role will increasingly focus on how to equip yourself and other leaders with the internal and external antennae, wherewithal, mindset, powers of persuasion and application to face up to, balance and sometimes rework the competing local–global business realities and self, business and societal values, as we outlined in Chapter 4.

'Authentic' leadership is behaving in alignment with one's deep-seated personal values. Acting otherwise can be done either unconsciously (self-betrayal) or consciously (disrespect for truth). Whilst early life and current circumstance clearly affect the presence and expression of authenticity, the likely development path is through raised self-awareness, facilitated self-regulation via coaching and habit breaking/formation. A classic example of a breakdown in business authenticity is claiming to support teamwork, whilst having all rewards and recognitions attached to individual contributions, especially when it is mainly channeled through the salary of the CEO. Becoming confident in setting an example for others to follow requires reflection and brave, ego-free conversation with your leadership colleagues, on how, as collective leaders, you will enact your truth together.

At the heart of leadership we are dealing with the dilemmas and choices created by potential breakdowns in three forms of alignment.

■ First, considering yourself in your own particular business context, translating your analysis of the situation (Thinking) into an appropriate strategy, your personal values into workplace culture through role modeling (Being), and your (and others') capabilities (Acting) into how best to run the organization. We return to this in Chapter 10.

■ Second, making judgments about final selection from the range of leadership action options available to you, from the mixture of what you think is the best way forward, with what you feel and believe is right and proper, and what you (and others) can actually do. Here we can contrast 'authentic' leadership – a creative response to the paradox between being 'true to oneself' and 'true to the organization', where personal convictions and organizational goals are attuned; with 'defiant leadership', which is true to the individual but unresponsive to the organization, 'compliant leadership', where the leader suppresses their own imperatives by doing what they are told and 'pseudo-leadership', pretending to act for the organization whilst only fulfilling personal desires.

■ Third, in so doing, remaining acutely aware that what you believe you represent to the world (your identity) is matched by what others see you demonstrate (your reputation). Note that the opportunities for misalignment are multiplied when making decisions in Board and senior executive teams, explaining why deep dialogue about 'walking the talk' is essential in these interactions (see Chapter 5).

Why do we need 'total' leadership now?

- Labor market dynamics and competitive pressures are forcing a war for change leader talent.
- Workforce values are changing – the prospect of leading a full life and meaningful work is much sought after by talented people.
- As organizations become less hierarchical and status driven, developing local and global distributed leadership by seeking and connecting leadership from any walk of life is a competitive advantage.
- Alliances and partnerships need to tap into diverse informal leadership.
- Credibility in the wake of media magnified management scandals demands scrupulous attention to the way leaders live.
- Impacts of family and personal care responsibilities need to be built into leadership thinking.
- Care for the world in general is generating significant interest in how leaders contribute to sustainability across all dimensions of self, business and society (see Chapters 4 and 5).

CAPABILITY 6 – DEVELOP 'TRANSCULTURAL' COMPETENCE

Before outlining what constitutes 'transcultural' competence, it is crucial for change leaders to consider three possible mindsets of how culture might be perceived (Peck, Towell, & Gulliver, 2001). The commonest, but least realistic, approach in the corporate world is 'integration' where cultural change entails an organization-wide attempt to shift attitudes or beliefs toward a common view, usually manipulated by senior managers. 'Differentiation' on the other hand emphasizes that culture is invariably made up of a collection of values and beliefs, some of which may be contradictory and held by identifiable and disparate sub-cultures. Here, cultural change will be localized and incremental and will be influenced by a range of internal and external factors. Finally, 'Ambiguity' recognizes that individuals may share some views of the world, disagree about some and are ignorant and indifferent to others. Using this view culture is continually changing as the interpretations form and reform. A change leader must therefore learn to work with a diversity of cultural forms even as they search for and move beyond producing an organizational credo which attempts to unite. A critical change leader's personal value is to 'value values diversity' and this is required even more when leaders work in international contexts.

Indeed, Trompennars and Hampden-Turner (2002) identified seven dimensions of potential national culture difference which change leaders should be aware of. They are:

Rule making (universalism)	Exception finding (particularism)
Self-interest and personal fulfillment (individualism)	Group interest and social concern (communitarianism)
Preference for precise, singular 'hard' standards (specificity)	Preference for pervasive, patterned 'soft' processes (diffusion)
Emotions inhibited (neutral)	Emotions expressed (affective)
Status earned through success and track record (achievement)	Status ascribed to person's potential, e.g. age, family, education (ascription)
Control and effective direction from within (inner-directed)	Control and effective direction from outside (outer-directed)
Time conceived of as a 'race' with passing increments (sequential)	Time conceived of as a 'dance' with circular iterations (synchronous)

Change leaders who make change appealing to the prevailing ends of the continuum are more likely to gain traction for the change. In terms of specific competencies to develop over time Schneider and Barsoux (2003) differentiate between competencies for managing differences abroad or at home.

Operating abroad (as expatriates)	Operating from home (as internationalists)
Interpersonal (relationship) skills	Understand business inter-dependencies
Linguistic ability	
Cultural curiosity	Respond to multiple cultures simultaneously
Tolerance for uncertainty and ambiguity	Recognize the influence of culture 'at home'
Flexibility	
Patience and respect	Be willing to share power
Cultural empathy	Demonstrate cognitive complexity
Strong sense of self (or ego strength)	Adopt a 'cultural–general' approach
Sense of humor	Rapidly learn and unlearn

However, the concept of a global mindset incorporates an assumption that such knowledge and relationships are dynamic, and the cognitive, behavioral and emotional structures organizing them must evolve alongside the changes taking place in the peculiar cultures, in order to maintain and improve global business effectiveness. For an excellent exposition of the cultural roots of different forms of leadership, viewed as inter-relationship diagrams with followers, see Lewis (2007). To test your current level of 'cultural intelligence' obtain the questionnaire from Earley and Mosakowski (2004).

CAPABILITY 7 – DEVELOP 1:1 RELATIONAL SKILLS: COACHING

The importance of change leaders acquiring a coaching skills set is apparent in the following definition. Coaching could be described as (Stewart, O'Riordan, & Palmer, 2008)

> *a collaborative and egalitarian relationship between a coach, who is not necessarily a domain-specific specialist, and coachee, which involves a systematic process that focuses on collaborative goal setting to construct solutions and employs goal attainment processes, with the aim of fostering the on-going self-directed learning and personal growth of the coachee.*

The myriad of micro-skills which make up effective coaching practice, e.g. building rapport, active listening, reflective attention (or mindfulness), interpersonal sensitivity, and so on, are the same subset of skills required to forge relationship and communication connections so vital for the change leader's skillful engagement and dialogue with willing or unwilling followers of change. For a fuller description of these communication micro-skills and how to employ them in coaching conversations see Nelson-Jones (2003;2005). Indeed, a 'coaching' leadership style has been shown to be the most consistently effective style for improving business climate and performance, (Goleman, 2000).

The mutuality of skill development for the parties to coaching can be viewed through seven potential layers of deep dialogue, this depth of engagement being critical to foster change: 'social dialogue' (providing support, encouragement and care); 'technical dialogue' (meeting learning needs associated with work processes, policies and systems); 'tactical dialogue' (generating practical ways of dealing with work or personal issues such as time management or dealing with recalcitrant colleagues); 'strategic dialogue' (putting problems, opportunities and ambitions into context and envisioning different future states); 'self-insight dialogue' (reaching deeper understanding of values, drives, emotions, thinking processes); 'behavioral change dialogue' (melding insight, strategy and tactics into a coherent programme of personal adaptation); and 'integrative dialogue' (to enable clarity on who they are, what they contribute and how they fit in for exploring their personal place in the world as it is and as it could become). As important is the finding that coaching can increase individual, organizational and public service reputation leadership performance

(Cortvriend, Harris, & Alexander, 2008). For a comprehensive and up-to-date coverage of coaching and leadership see the *International Coaching Psychology Review*, Special Issue, March 2009. For those interested in the differences between coaching, mentoring and counseling skills see Stone (2007); and for a person-centred coaching model and set of people guidance techniques view Egan (2002).

CAPABILITY 8 – DEVELOP 1: MANY DIALOGUE SKILLS; ACTION LEARNING, FACILITATION AND PROCESS CONSULTING

The lived experience of leadership is that it is all about relationships and genuine dialogue and the key is making these meaningful and productive. If leaders surround themselves with sycophants dialogue is stifled and the leadership environment is likely to create destructive consent instead of constructive dissent.

It is common for organizations and leaders to use programmed or habitual knowledge rather than developing the skill of revealing insights from the reality of the world of work which is unfolding around them. So, finding the right questions to ask, such as what are we trying to do, what is stopping us from doing it and what can we do about it, are part of a conversation repertoire that change leaders need to develop. 'Action Learning' (Revans, 1982) comprises a way of involving people in problem solving and solution generating through work on real-time change challenges. As Revans (1980, p.226) explains, 'the action learning process is founded on the concept that the leader cannot change the organization unless every individual in the organization is changed in the process'. The skills and their origins are summarized in Table 6.3 (Frey, 2008).

A change leader also needs to master the technique of facilitation (an extension of chairperson skills) as is obvious from the role of the facilitator described in Table 6.4.

They also need to be able to recognize and deal with the defensive routines commonly associated with change environments, as laid out in Table 6.5.

One of the major dilemmas facing change leaders is do they lead the change all by themselves or bring in a change consultant? One way out of this, or to identify the right type of consultant, is to learn about process consultation. Whilst it is not our intention to describe this in full, see Schein (1969), some extracts will demonstrate its importance. Process consultation is defined as a set of activities on the part of the consultant (or change leader) that helps the client organization to perceive, understand and act upon the change process events unfolding in the change environment. It is based on the following premises:

1. The client or client organization is hurting somehow but does not know the source of the pain or what to do about it.

2. The same (client or client organisation) does not know what kind of help may be available and which consultant can provide the kind of help that is needed in the right way.

Table 6.3 Comparison of different types of action learning

Point of comparison	Scientific school	Experiential school	Critical reflection school
Framing of the encounter by learning coach	Grist for the mill of situation analysis	Opportunity to learn from a mistake and grow personally in choices and skills	Focus on deep values and beliefs in individuals and system
Interventions with the team before the team meeting	Reflect on steps the team has to take and suggest they look at gaps or needed data	Reflect on situation; encourage action to test understanding with manager; plan and role play	Help probe organizational assumptions; encourage questions regarding empowerment; plan and role play
Interventions with the team during the team meeting	(1) No interventions (2) Ask the manager to join team in situation analysis	(1) No interventions (2) Ask everyone to think together about situation so they can learn from this	(1) No interventions (2) Put difficult issues on the table; raise questions about system; share views
Interventions with the team and/or system after the team meeting	Re-frame the problem and consider next steps for data collection in light of what was learned	Examine behavior and implications for personal growth and for understanding system; re-frame the problem, next steps	Analyze data from team analysis of forces shaping own behavior and system's culture; re-frame problem, next steps

Source:: Adapted from Marsick and O'Neill, 1999, p. 166.

Table 6.4 The content and process of facilitation

Content	Process
Guiding agenda and contracting	Set up – right people and right relationships, clarifying aim and participation roles and responsibilities
Keeping discussion on topic	Time keeping with objectives kept in sight, pacing the flow
Testing for agreement	Monitoring group response, identifying and naming communication problems, managing conflict, equalizing participation
Deconstructing and reformulating the problem	Clarifying and re-phrasing
Synthesizing – themes and alignment	Arriving at agreements and disagreements
Defining success	Soliciting feedback and ownership

Table 6.5 Defensive routines in change conversations

Type of defensive routine	How to recognize routine?	What to do?
Competition/ forcing	Trying to get own ideas through, get own way	■ Paraphrase oppositions view ■ Why so important to get this view across? ■ Create room for others ■ Referee dominators
Avoiding, diverting	Avoids the issue at hand by deflecting attention to others (which may be interesting in itself)	■ Broken record ■ Recognize 'did you realize' feedback ■ Focus on task/purpose ■ Is this helpful to get us where we need to go?

(Continued)

Table 6.5 Continued

Type of defensive routine	How to recognize routine?	What to do?
Confronting	Sets up situation to produce anger, dissent or hurt – relies on brute strength – does not consider validity of other's view	■ Back to basics – seek common ground ■ Don't get hooked into emotion ■ Remain fact based ■ Depersonalize
Denial	Strong desire to hang on to existing world view – down playing real issues – avoidance of any chance of seeing alternatives	■ Explore resistance (outside group discussion if necessary) ■ What would have to change in order for things to be different? ■ Is this a valid view?
Protecting others	Attempting to stand in for others or speak on their behalf	■ Encourage 'I' statements ■ Contract with parties ■ Silence ■ Check out with protectee
Going for the easy option	Seeking consensus to avoid conflict, save time or seek an end – produces inferior result or watered down solution	■ Does this meet needs/outcome? ■ Time out ■ Is this going for the easy option to avoid conflict? ■ Consequences of declaring victory too soon ■ What is required to reach a more robust solution?
Withdrawal	Taking your bat and ball and going home – seeking to manipulate the process by manipulating how others feel	■ Identify 'uninvolved' early and bring in ■ Explicit reflection ■ Original needs ■ Acknowledge fear/loss ■ Discuss impact on group

(Continued)

Table 6.5 Continued

Type of defensive routine	How to recognize routine?	What to do?
Court jester	Joking or acting the fool to manipulate the process	■ Utilise group feedback ■ Ignore first time ■ Focus on task ■ Time out for person
Smoothing	Avoiding conflict or disagreement at all cost – seeks to bury issues and ensure harmony at the cost of honesty, openness and seeking an objective view	■ Open-ended questions focused on stage of agreement/disagreement ■ Focus on data and outcome ■ Consequences of compliance ■ Explore emotional neutrality

3. The nature of the problem is such that the same not only needs help in figuring out what is wrong but would benefit from participation in the process of making a diagnosis.

4. The same has 'constructive intent', and is motivated by goals and values that the consultant can accept, and has some capacity to enter into a helping relationship.

5. The same is ultimately the only one who knows what form of intervention will work in the situation.

It is often the case that ineffective change leaders abdicate the last responsibility, leading to a shift of ownership of the problem and the solution and losing the chance for them and the organization to learn for next time. Process consulting is of course also linked to action learning, facilitation skill and emotional intelligence development as outlined in the table below.

CAPABILITY 9 – EMOTIONAL INTELLIGENCE

Whilst the importance and make-up of emotional intelligence was covered in Chapter 3, here we outline how each facet may be developed.

Emotional intelligence element	Ideas for development

Self-awareness	■ Reflect on specific situations/problems you have faced:
	  – How did you feel?
	  – What concerned you?
	  – What excited you?
	  – How did the reactions of others affect your feelings?
	■ How did you decide on your actions?
	■ How consciously did you take account of your feelings and emotions?
	■ How would your responses and actions have been different if you had been more aware of them?
	■ Based on this reflection, how can you improve your reactions/decision making/solutions for the future?

Emotional resilience	■ Reflect on how you adapt your behaviors to deal with different situations ■ Develop an understanding of how decisions are made and the balance between objective certainty and the need to arrive at judgments based on a balance of probabilities ■ Identify situations presenting difficult decision–options and reflect on behaviors you adopted in such situations which led to successful outcomes ■ When faced with challenge spend time openly exploring the reason for it and seek opportunities to learn from such discussions ■ Actively seek opportunities to involve others in exploring solutions to difficult problems or situations
Motivation	■ Develop a clear understanding of results and goals relating to the work situations and problems you find ■ Analyze potential for personal satisfaction and benefits which would flow from effective resolution of problems

(Continued)

Emotional intelligence element	Ideas for development
	■ Reflect on situations in which you have felt a high degree of personal motivation and reveal the personal values driving this (see Chapter 4) and identify how this may be transferred to other situations or work behaviors ■ Identify/build a clear picture of your personal goals/aims and establish ways in which work situations may support their achievement – discuss with an uninvolved third party
Interpersonal sensitivity	■ Spend time discussing problems or solutions with team members, invite their comments and spend time reflecting on how their contributions throw light and feeling on the problem ■ Spend time reflecting on how your ideas may be perceived by those involved with or supported by the action ■ Identify situations when you feel you have obtained real 'buy-in' and identify ways in which you can generalize the behaviors which brought this about ■ Spend time listening to others responses to hypotheses you have about a problem ■ Count how much time you spend identifying with your co-workers and the priority you give to bringing their reactions to bear on understanding your own motives and actions
Influence	■ Spend time understanding and developing the perspectives of others ■ Examine issues, problems and situations and hypothesize how this would come across by putting yourself in their shoes ■ What do others need from their job, relationships with me, etc. ■ How well do I know the 'hot buttons' of those I need to bring to my side

(Continued)

Emotional intelligence element	Ideas for development
Intuitiveness	■ Develop an understanding of how you can assess and manage risks in decision making ■ How might alternative decisions you could have made in past events have played out ■ Spend time discussing complex decisions with others involved with or impacted by them ■ How would additional insights have impacted on past decisions ■ When faced with difficult decisions reflect on options and potential improvements resulting from further analysis before undertaking the analysis ■ Develop awareness of your method of decision making in all spheres of your life
Conscientiousness	■ Obtain feedback from others to see how consistent you are in practicing what you preach ■ Only openly commit to goals and decisions that you feel are important and can be delivered ■ Identify how others judge your commitment to decisions and actions ■ Establish a clear and rigorous approach to establishing priorities and ensure that you apply this in practice ■ Ensure you create time to deliver your contribution to high-priority publicly announced actions

A significant amount of leadership practice is habitual, so attempts to change yourself must include rehearsal and practice of new behaviour, a means of tracking the change and the involvement of an interested albeit neutral party, for example a coach, in keeping you honest with yourself.

Capability 10 – High-Quality Performance Challenge Culture and Dialogue

Change leadership invariably involves some form of feedback on progress to those embarked on the change within the context of performance. And this cannot be left to the appraisal cycle alone. So, change leaders need a method of establishing how much and what type of performance culture they are creating and then some evaluation of how skillful they are in having discussions which will enable people to build their capacity to contribute to change.

A performance culture assessment, together with an effective dialogue process is set out below.

To what extent does your leader...?	To a great extent	To some extent	To a limited extent	Insufficiently	Not at all
Provide you with regular feedback					
Provide feedback which challenges you to improve your contribution					
Converse with you in a way which helps you personally grow and develop					
Discuss ways in which you may be stretched to achieve goals beyond your current remit					
Facilitate innovative thinking by you					
Encourage you to contribute to building the capability of others					
Encourage you to contribute to delivering business priorities					
Encourage you to contribute to across-sector priorities					
Build an everyday performance culture where people help one another to perform to the best of their abilities					

Source: Reproduced with the permission of the National School of Government (Paul Aitken) and AKT Productions (Graham Haynes).

The GROW model for performance challenge dialogue

The aim of any 'performance challenge' dialogue, whether a formal interim or annual review or a short interaction 'on the job' is to:

- Raise the person's awareness of what is really going on, and what impact they are actually having (so they gain insights).
- Ensure that they take responsibility for doing something about those insights (with support from the organization, their manager and other colleagues where appropriate).

The secret of using GROW (Figure 6.1) is to support the person in exploring and clarifying what they really need to achieve (GOALS), to ensure they fully understand where they are at present (REALITY) and take responsibility for closing the gap between their current reality and the organization's expectations (OPTIONS for change). Time should be taken to go through all the options available, to test the validity of each option and to jointly establish which option is the very best for them at that point in time. Finally, their (WILL) to carry out the necessary change actions must be tested and confirmed. There is no point identifying what the

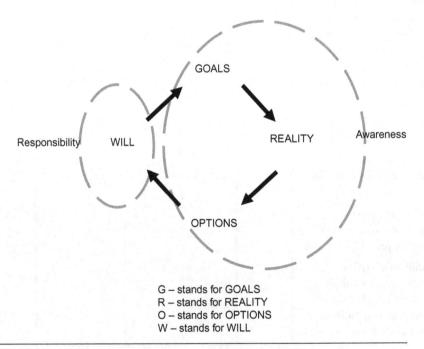

G – stands for GOALS
R – stands for REALITY
O – stands for OPTIONS
W – stands for WILL

Figure 6.1   Adapted from G.R.O.W. (Whitmore, 1996).

specific goal is, explore all the options to find a way forward and then having no motivation to follow through.

The approach outlined below can be applied effectively in a broad range of situations and conversations from a formal review to a 5-minute performance affirmation and/or problem-solving exercise.

G – Goal

Take time to fully establish exactly what the person needs and wants to achieve. Check the realism of the goal. If what he/she is trying to achieve is beyond their capabilities, not relevant to the needs of the organization or outside budgets, then think again about a more realistic and appropriate target.

Do	Don't
■ Agree the purpose of the conversation at the outset ■ Ask if there is anything they want to put on the agenda ■ Focus on what must and can be changed – name the performance problem or performance affirmation ■ Focus on the critical aspects ■ Raise longer-term goals as well as short-term fixes ■ Try and set learning goals rather than improvement targets ■ Ensure change goals are SMART	■ Come with a closed purpose and position ■ Take ownership of the problem, goals or solutions

R – Reality

This is probably where most of the value from a dialogue lies. The objective is to raise the awareness of the other person so that they gain insights about their impact on others and on business and/or job goals. Check exactly where they are at present in relation to their goals or objectives. Be prepared to challenge and to give feedback where necessary here. There are some people whose grasp of reality in relation to their performance is suspect! Some people actually need to be told they are maybe not as good as they think they are. Others are actually further ahead than they think they are. Out of this part of the dialogue should flow some pointers to development and/or strength stretch areas. These could be in skills or knowledge, but you should also look out for behavioral issues which might need to be addressed.

Therefore this part of the dialogue should work at more than one level. For instance the person might say, 'I think I am getting all my reports and deliverables completed on time so what else matters?' This response may prompt the manager to pause the conversation and say 'It is true that you are meeting those targets, but what impact do you think your style is having on your colleagues and on the people you work with?' If this is an issue that has come up before, some specific feedback and observations could now be fed in. Failing that, the manager could observe 'right now you seem to be rather defensive and abrupt which is making me feel uncomfortable. I wonder if this is how your colleagues and customers sometimes feel'. The result of this will hopefully be an increase in the person's self-awareness that can be the first step in improving their performance.

Do	Don't
■ Consider strengths and development needs in the context of their current role, development and career stage ■ Ask for their view of their performance first ■ 'Own' the feedback that you give ■ Have the optimal 5:1 positive comments to negative ones in mind to generate deeper listening ■ Raise questions and hypotheses ■ Explore differences ■ Focus on observed behavior connected with the role requirements ■ Give concrete examples	■ Dive in on the back of your strongest feelings ■ Begin with your list ■ Deflect responsibility onto your sources of information ■ Avoid the 'feedback sandwich' – use the feedback bridge instead – positive comment and suggestion for improvement because change will be beneficial in the following ways ■ Introduce unsubstantiated opinion ■ Get drawn into irrelevant content ■ Respond to deflection which will take you off track ■ Use emotive language ■ Position yourself as a 'know-all' ■ Criticize performance – critique it instead ■ Focus on the person or personality ■ Make global judgments

O – Options

This is the part of the conversation where options are explored for closing identified gaps between goals and reality. Explore, explore, explore. Offer support to come up with a few options and then test each option by taking time to investigate the pros and cons of each. Then get them to make a decision – if possible THEIR decision – as to which is best for THEM taking into account the needs of the department, business, sector, etc.

Do	Don't
■ Explore possibilities ■ Seek to raise development ideas ■ Ask 'what could you do as a first step?' ■ Ask 'what else could you do?' ■ Ask 'what would happen if you did nothing?' ■ Establish evaluation criteria ■ Help them to evaluate each option	■ Settle for the first option

W – Will

In this phase of the conversation, the manager's role is to check that their direct report's motivation to act differently is really what it needs to be in order to achieve the new goal. Has he/she identified how the achievement of this goal will benefit them personally as well as the organization? How confident is he/she in achieving their goal? Do they have a clear plan and progress-tracking mechanism for making this happen?

Do	Don't
■ Be sure and clear what your expectations of them are going forward ■ Retain the sense of an ongoing development partnership ■ Check understanding – ask them to do the final summary of your expectations of them	■ Assume the messages have been received and will be acted upon

Throughout the conversation there are some other aspects of your approach, language and behavior that you may wish to consider. Most importantly apply the 20:80 rule – 20% of the time ask powerful questions which generate high-quality and challenging dialogue and 80% of the time actively listen to what's happening verbally and emotionally between the two of you and respond accordingly.

Do	Don't
▓ Ensure it is a two-way discussion ▓ Describe, don't judge ▓ Speak plainly ▓ Be clear ▓ Be specific ▓ Limit volume of information ▓ Consider value of your data and words for its impact on the most critical change you require ▓ Summarize as you go ▓ Emphasize development throughout ▓ Focus on helping ▓ Listen attentively to words and reactions ▓ Give time to think ▓ Let silence help shift the ownership ▓ Be firm, fair and assertive – verbally and non-verbally ▓ Check understanding before you proceed	▓ Do all the talking

Remember, it may not be appropriate to work through the whole of GROW, or proceed in a linear way. You need to remain agile in the dialogue as new information and emotion emerges. Consider what is achievable in the time you have and given the preparation you have undertaken. Don't rush to conclude and ensure you and the other person are in the right psychological and physical 'space' to make the dialogue as productive as possible. Rehearse thoroughly for those particularly challenging conversations. Supporting approaches and skills can be found in the following references; Whitmore (1996), Scott (2002), Egan (2002) and Nelson-Jones (2005; 2003).

Of course, none of the above will be much use unless you can find yourself a leader–builder organization which values such conversation. The following criteria (Yearout, Miles, & Koonce, 2000), identifying effective leader–builder companies should help you find one.

- Have an unusually strong vision of their futures.
- Their executives and managers display remarkably consistent behaviors, regardless of their level in the organization (strong leadership culture).
- A strong emphasis on continuous development and replenishment of the leadership talent pool and pipeline will be found.

- Identification of specific leadership competencies to support current and emerging mission and strategy will be evident.
- Strategy-culture alignment will be obvious to all stakeholders.
- The senior leadership team will display public and private unity.
- Everywhere there will be evidence of continuous organizational renewal.

Having identified some critical change leadership learning and development processes and ten must-have capabilities in Chapter 6, in Chapter 7 we now outline development tools, techniques and example cases which can be drawn from to create your own change leader development approach, design and content.

References

Aitken, P. (2004). *The relationships between personal values, leadership behaviour and team functioning*, Doctor of Business Administration Thesis. London: Henley Management College/Brunel University.

Ambrosini, V., & Bowman, C. (2009). What are dynamic capabilities and are they a useful construct in strategic management. *International Journal of Management Reviews*, *11*(1), 29–49.

Ambrosini, V., Bowman, C., & Collier, N. (2009). Dynamic capabilities: an exploration of how firms renew their resource base. *British Journal of Management*, *20*, S9–S24.

Argyris, Chris (Winter 1993). Education for leaing-learning New York, 14 pages. *Organizational Dynamics*, *21*(3), 5.

Avery, G. C. (2005). *Leadership for sustainable futures*. Northampton, MA: Edward Elgar.

Badarraco, J. L. (1998). The discipline of building character. *Harvard Business Review*, *6*, 115–124.

Bennis, W. G. (2004). The seven ages of the leader. *Harvard Business Review*, *January*, 46–53.

Boydell, T., & Temporel, P. (1981). *Helping managers to learn*. Sheffield, UK: Sheffield Polytechnic.

Branden, N. (1999). *The art of living consciously: the power of awareness to transform daily life*. New York: Fireside.

Collins, J., & Porras, J. I. (2005). *Built to last – successful habits of visionary companies*. London: Random House.

Cortvriend, P., Harris, C., & Alexander, E. (2008, July). Evaluating the links between leadership development coaching and performance. *International Coaching Psychology Review*, *3*(2), 164–179.

Coutu, D. (2006). Ideas as art. The HBR interview with James G. *March, HBR*, 83–89.

De Geus, A. B. (1997). *The living company: habits for survival in a turbulent business environment*. Boston, MA: Harvard Business School Press.

De Kluyver, C. A. (2000). *Strategic thinking – an executive perspective*. Upper Saddle River, NJ: Prentice Hall.

Dixon, P. (2007). *Futurewise – six faces of global change*. London: Profile Books.

Earley, P. C., & Mosakowski, E. (2004). Cultural intelligence. *Harvard Business Review*, *October*, 1–8.

Education for leading-learning Argyris, Chris. Organizational Dynamics. New York: Winter 1993. Vol. 21, Iss. 3; p. 5 (14 pages)

Egan, G. (2002). *The Skilled Helper: A Problem-management and Opportunity Development Approach* (7th Edition). Pacific Groove, CA: BROOKS/COLE.

Fletcher, C. (1997). Self-Awareness – a neglected attribute in selection and assessment. *International Journal of Selection and Assessment, 5*(3), 183–187.

Frey, C. (2008). Action learning intervention in a change context and commitment to organisational change. Unpublished Henley Working Paper, Henley Management College.

Friedman, S. D. (2006). Learning to lead in all domains of life. *The American Behavioural Scientist, 49*(Issue 9), 1270–1297.

Gardner, H. (1993). *Frames of mind, the theory of multiple intelligences*. New York: Basic Books.

Goleman, D. (2000). Leadership that gets results, Harvard Business Review, March-April.

Goleman, D., Boyatzis, R., & McKee, A. (2004). *Primal leadership: realising the power of emotional intelligence*. Boston, MA: Harvard Business School Press.

Grint, K. (2005). Problems, problems, problems: the social construction of 'leadership' [Sage: The Tavistock Institute]. *Human Relations, 58*(11), 1467–1494.

Hersovitch, L., & Meyer, J. P. (2002). Commitment to organizational change: extension of the three-component model. *Journal of Applied Psychology, 87*(3), 474–487.

Higgs, M. J., & Rowland, D. (2005). All changes great and small. *Journal of Change Management, 5*(2), 121–135.

Jaques, E. (1989). *Requisite organisation*. Arlington, VA: Cason Hall.

Kempster, S. (2006). Leadership learning through lived experience: a process of apprenticeship? *Journal of Management and Organisation, 12*, 4–22.

Kofman, F. (2006). Conscious business, Sounds True Inc., U.S.

Lahteenmaki, S., Tovonen, J., & Mattila, M. (2001). Critical aspects of organizational learning research and proposals for its measurement. *British Journal of Management, 12*, 13–129.

Lewis, R. D. (2007). *When cultures collide: leading across cultures* (3rd edition). Boston, MA: Nicholas Brearley International.

Linley, P. A., & Harrington, S. (2006). Playing to your strengths. *The Psychologist, 19*(2), 86–89.

Mant, A. (1999). *Intelligent leadership*. Sydney: Allen and Unwin.

Marsick, V. J., & O'Neill, J. (1999). *The many faces of action learning, management learning*. London: Sage.

McCall, M. W., Lombardo, M. M., & Morrison, A. (1988). *The lessons of experience*. Lexington, MA: Lexington Books.

McCauley, C. D., & Brutus, S. (1998). *Management development through job experience: an annotated bibliography*. Greensboro, NC: Centre for Creative Leadership.

McKenzie, J., Woolf, N., van Winkelen, C., & Morgan, C. (2007). Critical mental capacities for effective strategic decision making in complex and unpredictable business conditions. In: *Knowledge Management Forum 7th Annual Conference, Foresight and Organisational Becoming Track*, Henley Management College.

Nelson-Jones, R. (2003). *Basic counselling skills*. London: Sage.

Nelson-Jones, R. (2005). *Practical Helping and Counselling Skills (5th edition)*. Sage.

Pascale, R. T., Millemann, M., & Gioja, L. (1997). Changing the way we change. *Harvard Business Review, 75*(6), 126–139.

Peck, E., Towell, D., & Gulliver, P. (2001). The meanings of 'culture' in health and social care: a case study of the combined trust in Somerset. *Journal of Interprofessional Care, 15*(4), 319–327.

Porter, M. E., Lorsch, J. W., & Nohria, N. (2004). Seven surprises for new CEO's. *Harvard Business Review, October*, 62–72.

Pye, A. (2005). Leadership and organising: sensemaking in action. *Leadership, 1*(1), 31–48.

Revans, R. W. (1980). *Action learning: new techniques for managers.* London: Blond and Biggs.

Revans, R. W. (1982). *The origin and growth of action learning.* London: Chartwell Bratt.

Richard, E. B., Melvin, L. S., & Blaize, N. (Mar 2006). Developing Sustainable Leaders Through Coaching and Compassion Briarcliff Manor. *Academy of Management Learning & Education, 5*(1), 8.

Schein, E. H. (1969). Process Consultation: Its Role in Organization Development. Reading, MA: Addison-Wesley, p. 120.

Schneider, S. C., & Barsoux, J. L. (2003). *Managing across cultures* (2nd edition). London: Prentice Hall.

Scott, S. (2002) Fierce conversations: achieving Success at work and in life one conversation at a time; Viking Books.

Senge, P., Scharmer, C. O., Jaworski, J., & Flowers, B. S. (2006). *Presence: exploring profound change in people, organizations and society.* London: Nicholas Brearley Publishing.

Stace, D., & Dunphy, D. (2001). *Beyond the boundaries* (2nd Edition). Sydney: McGraw-Hill.

Stacy, R. (1993). Strategy as order emerging from chaos. *Long Range Planning, 26*(1), 10–17.

Stewart, L. J., O'Riordan, S., & Palmer, S. (2008). Before we know what we've done, we need to know what we're doing: operationalising coaching to provide a foundation for coaching evaluation. *The Coaching Psychologist, 4*(3), 127–133.

Stone, F. M. (2007) Coaching, Counselling & Mentoring: How to Choose & Use the Right Technique to Boost Employee Performance: How to Choose and Use the Right Technique to Boost Employee Performance (2nd Edition), Amacom.

The Australian Psychological Society Interest Group in Coaching Psychology. (2009). Coaching and leadership [Special issue]. *International Coaching Psychology Review, 4*(1).

Trompennars, F., & Hampden-Turner, C. (2002). *21 leaders for the 21st century.* New York: McGraw-Hill.

Webb, P. J. (2006, November). Back on track: the coaching journey in executive career derailment. *International Coaching Psychology Review, 1*(2), 68–73.

Whitmore, J. (1996) Coaching for performance: Growing human potential and purpose – the principles and practice of coaching and leadership (people skills for professionals); Nicholas Brearley Publishing.

Workman, D., & Duncan, J. (2006). The economic impact of competencies. *Human Resources, April*, 20–21.

Yearout, S., Miles, G. and Koonce, R. (2000). Wanted: leader-builders, training and development. *American Society for Training and Development*, Leadership Special, March.

Chapter 7

Development
Approaches

*Leadership is a dance, in which leaders and followers jointly respond to the
rhythm and call of a particular social context, within which leaders draw
from deep wells of collective experience and energy, to engage followers
around transforming visions of change and lead them in the collective creation of compelling futures.*

Cammock (2003, p.17)

Introduction

What is clear from the quote above is that learning to lead and implement change requires continued attunement to the change context, where leadership is singular as well as plural, and depends for its existence on forging deep connections with the change players, and deep reflection within the leader's own sense of self, both responding to and undergoing change. Coupled with the finding that the role of leaders and accompanying behavior is the root cause of many business change problems and provides the seeds for success, is the reason why we looked at the evolution and adaptability of a change (or changing) leader in Chapter 6.

To date, the responsibility for change leadership has mostly been considered as the province of one person, normally residing near the top of a hierarchy. For example, a very uncommon longitudinal study of successful executives found two vital qualities (Collins, 2001):

1. HUMILITY (being self-effacing and arrogance free) – high profile, larger-than-life CEOs, where the business was entirely bound up in their persona, correlated negatively with the progression from 'good to great' (only 11 out of 1,435 Fortune 500 listed companies from 1965 who outperformed companies in their sector made the shift).

2. WILL – individual and collective persistence in the pursuit of business goals.

The findings indicated that 'quiet leadership' was the norm for these good-to-great CEOs, leaders dedicated to building the organization rather than their CVs, with an emphasis on starting with the right team rather than the right project, product or even industry. Paraphrasing Collins, good-to-great leaders first get the right people on the bus, the wrong people off it, and the right people in the right seats, and then together they figure out where and how to drive it. First consider who, and then focus on what. Build the superior executive team before vision, strategy and organizational structure, on the basis of three simple truths:

- If you begin with who, rather than what, you can more easily adapt to a changing world (people will not have joined for a specific reason).
- The problem of motivation and professional loyalty largely goes away.
- With the wrong people and everything else OK, you will still not create a great organization.

For change leaders who would like to sustain company performance in this way, the development questions in Table 7.1 are worth asking inside your organization.

This switch away from individual (leader-centric) to relational aspects of collective change leadership is captured by Boydell (2005) whose three stances on leadership

Table 7.1 Questions to facilitate moving from 'good to great'

Companies (good to great) key factors identified	Development questions
Level 5 leadership – an executive in whom genuine personal humility blends with intense professional will	How would you describe the personal qualities that have made the difference to your continued successful performance as a manager?
Attending to the people first and strategy second – got the right people on the bus, moved the wrong people off, ushered the right people to the right seats and then figured out what to do together	How have you approached executive team selection, ways of working with other leaders across the business, leadership development and performance management?
Confronted the most brutal facts of their current reality, yet maintained absolute faith that they would prevail in the end – held up faith and facts together all the time	How do you approach the challenges you face in continually improving performance over time?
Good-to-great transformations do not happen overnight or in one big leap – comparison companies that could not sustain performance lurched back and forth with radical change programs, reactionary moves and restructuring	How do you build for future success at this organization?
Performance breakthroughs require a simple, hedgehog-like (the hedgehog knows only one thing very well – unlike the fox) understanding of three intersecting things: What a company can be best in the world at? How its economics work best? What best ignites the passion of its people?	What are the critical factors that have contributed to business success to date?

(*Continued*)

Table 7.1   Continued

Pioneers in the investment in and application of carefully selected technologies that directly linked to their hedgehog concept	What technology techniques have made the difference to outstanding performance?
	Where does the challenge to the continued relevance of your existing business model come • from?
Consistently display three forms of discipline: disciplined people (you do not therefore need a hierarchy), thought (no bureaucracy required) and action (excessive controls unnecessary). Combine this with an ethic of entrepreneurship and you have the magic alchemy of great performance	How have you maintained and extended the performance levels of key people throughout the organization?

indicate a movement from 'doing things well' and 'doing things better' (the remit for management and continuous improvement) to 'doing better things' (the province of change leadership). Table 7.2 provides a flavor of the environment, process and content for development that will foster this switch.

Capabilities and techniques

Historical perspective argues that the problems central to effective leadership – motivation, inspiration, sensitivity and communication – have changed little in 3,000 years. Focus on the human side is important.

Clemens and Meyer

To create a forward-facing curriculum, we need to draw on studies that have attempted to project what generic leadership capabilities will be required for the future. The following list, provided by Bolden and Gosling (2003) and McIntyre (1999), is indicative for the next 10 years, although on the face of it seem timeless. We have added example development activities for each capability. We have also matched these to our top 10 change leadership capabilities listed in the previous chapter. The activities were selected to provide personal 'change' development challenges and are enumerated in Table 7.3.

Table 7.2 Change leadership development approaches

	Stance 3 – relational – doing better things
Leadership style	Making meaning together
Leaders and leadership	Leaders as social architects create conditions for all to practice leadership in the sense of relational dialogue, having conversations across boundaries, and between different world views
Assumptions about organization context	Complexity and ambiguity, needs and problems are interconnected so that tackling one impacts on the others, social fragmentation – between individuals, groups, organizations, professions – gets in the way of collective action Turbulence, many more voices wanting to be heard, no longer willing to accept the position they are put in, many alternative purposes and courses of action becoming visible Joined-up working, multiagency alliances, partnerships, use of networks Situations arise that cannot be handled simply by doing better than what is already done
Organization metaphor	Network of conversations to explore a mystery and create a story of the future together
Organization structure	Comprises different structures for specific purposes – meeting legal regulations, doing some things well and others better within the overall context of doing better things; supports the cooperation of communities of practice/interest etc. Structure may take any number of forms – hierarchy, matrix, flexible network of local organizations, groups and teams, rapidly forming and dissolving around fast-changing business needs and corporate relationships
Picture of people	Resourceful, knowledgeable, purposeful humans
Mission, vision and strategy	Continuously evolving through active engagement of many stakeholders Mission, vision and strategy of overall community defined to support the diverse versions from multiple stakeholders

(Continued)

Table 7.2 Continued

	Stance 3 – relational – doing better things
Distribution of purpose	Appreciation that people want to achieve things together, to participate in creating an unknown future – while recognizing that multiple stakeholders have their own legitimate purposes and aspirations
Distribution of power	Appreciation that diverse stakeholders have legitimate power within the overall community and can use this to make things happen as well as not happen
Distribution of risk	Appreciation that we are all in this together – joint risk taking, support and endeavor to move on and do better things
Distribution of knowledge	Much knowledge in and between stakeholder groups Appreciation that different views, opinions and beliefs are valid to those who hold them
Organization change and development programs	Multistakeholder meetings Relational action learning Large group (open space events) Future search exercises Relational practice (dialogue and bonding) Whole systems development
Focus of training and development	Individual and collective competence plus cross-boundary multistakeholder working
Underpinning learning disciplines	Social constructionism (making sense of the situation with other people), linguistics, adult development

Adapted from Boydell (2005).

As we have already discovered, the 'emotional' and 'relational' aspects of change leader development are often overlooked because they are less tangible and open to discussion. Goleman, Boyatzis and McKee (2001) set out a coaching process that they suggest is designed to rewire the brain toward more emotionally intelligent behaviors. The change leader self-talk proceeds as follows:

1. Who do I want to be? Prompts a picture of what life would look like if everything were going right, highlighting missing emotional and relational elements as well as strengths to run with.

Leadership capabilities	Suggested development activities
Integrity and moral courage: (headings provided by Bolden & Gosling, 2003) Capability 5 – develop 'total' leadership Capability 9 – emotional intelligence Capability 10 – high-quality performance challenge culture and dialog	■ Review the stories of Mandela, Ghandi, Pankhurst, Bhutto etc. ■ Shadow practitioners dealing daily with clients/customers experiencing severe personal distress ■ Give messages to people where distress will be generated ■ Become an advocate or mediator ■ Confront difficult people
Self-awareness and humility: Capability 6 – develop 'transcultural' competence Capability 7 – develop 1:1 relational skills; coaching Capability 8 – develop 1: many dialog skills; action-learning, facilitation and process consulting Capability 9 – emotional intelligence	■ Spend time in cultures and communities that are different from your own socioeconomic experience ■ Seek out negative feedback on your 'emotional' and 'relational' skills ■ Obtain clinical psychology insights on your 'emotional' and 'relational' skills ■ Become a customer of the environment you have shaped ■ Reflective writing
Empathy and emotional engagement: Capability 6 – develop 'transcultural' competence Capability 7 – develop 1:1 relational skills; coaching Capability 8 – develop 1: many dialog skills; action-learning, facilitation and process consulting Capability 9 – emotional intelligence	■ Work within autism care ■ Volunteer for the Samaritans ■ Spend time in a hospice ■ Become an executive coach ■ Become a Citizen Advice Bureaux volunteer ■ Work in one-to-one relationships where there is a formal and recognized difference in the power of the players and you have least power ■ Work with people who have different temperaments from you ■ Read about other people's cultures and how to interact with them

(Continued)

Table 7.3 Continued

Leadership capabilities	Suggested development activities
Transparency and openness: Capability 5 – develop 'total' leadership Capability 8 – develop 1: many dialog skills; action-learning, facilitation and process consulting Capability 9 – emotional intelligence Capability 10 – high-quality performance challenge culture and dialog	▪ Expose all your thinking on a subject for scrutiny and challenge ▪ Have your ideas/actions/decisions reviewed by experts ▪ Review peer review processes in medicine, science etc. ▪ Learn to be candid with respect ▪ Create a leadership learning blog
Clarity of vision: Capability 4 – future sense-make combined with strategic thinking	▪ Read the stories of successful entrepreneurs ▪ Set up a business with others ▪ Receive career coaching ▪ Read science fiction ▪ Join a futurists club
Adaptability and flexibility: Capability 6 – develop 'transcultural' competence Capability 8 – develop 1: many dialog skills; action-learning, facilitation and process consulting	▪ Work in a foreign culture ▪ Become self-employed ▪ Move between jobs, sectors or countries ▪ Join a community that you have never experienced ▪ Become a follower in your area of the business for a while ▪ Creative writing ▪ Virtual world games

Energy and resilience:
Capability 7 – develop 1:1 relational skills; coaching
Capability 9 – emotional intelligence

- Take part in physical, emotional and thinking conditioning activity, e.g. mind-gyms
- Discover the secrets of Olympic gold medal winner preparation
- Take part in an activity that you find difficult or you are afraid of
- Practice self-regulation and self-control through the Eastern religions and practices
- Review stories of people who have overcome profound difficulty

Decisiveness in the face of uncertainty:
Capability 1 – develop mindfulness, using three capacities for leadership of change decision making

- Practice in a flight or other simulator
- Review stories of leaders in crisis situations
- Work as a special assistant to a senior executive faced with difficult and novel challenges requiring closure

Judgement, consistency and fairness:
Capability 5 – develop 'total' leadership
Capability 8 – develop 1:many dialog skills; action-learning, facilitation and process consulting

- Jury service
- Shadow an arbitrator
- Observe the exercise of power in people decisions with a 'firm and fair' role model
- Manage an employment tribunal case
- Take part in key role internal selection processes
- Become a special constable

Ability to inspire, motivate and listen:
Capability 6 – develop 'transcultural' competence
Capability 8 – develop 1:many dialog skills; action-learning, facilitation and process consulting

- Mentor vulnerable young people or adults
- Work with the speech impaired
- Act as an adult literacy coach
- Work with challenging behavior
- Teach adult literacy or numeracy
- Coach someone in your pastime

(Continued)

Table 7.3 Continued

Leadership capabilities	Suggested development activities
Capability 9 – emotional intelligence Capability 10 – high-quality performance challenge culture and dialog	■ Take part in drama ■ Create and sell an idea, product or service ■ Learn counseling skills ■ Learn facilitation skills ■ Work across the demographics and generations
Respect and trust: Capability 5 – develop 'total' leadership Capability 6 – develop 'transcultural' competence	■ Look at the 'respect' agendas ■ Create your own respect and trust agenda with your work colleagues ■ Consider who approaches you and for what reasons ■ Rely on a stranger to support you in a challenging situation ■ Practice remote leadership ■ Lead/assist organizational facet/culture assessment and organizational health check ■ Allocate time and energy to critical organizational communication issues and by doing so highlight what is important for this organization ■ Facilitate collective responsibility ■ Demonstrate your trust in others ■ Create opportunities for people outside your culture to comment on what they see ■ Lead certain relationships, such as:

Knowledge and expertise:
Capability 2 – access broad-band 'capability' from across the leadership membership
Capability 3 – become a co-creator of a learning culture
Capability 8 – develop 1:many dialog skills; action-learning, facilitation and process consulting

Delivering results:
Capability 10 – high-quality performance challenge culture and dialog

consultation exercises with different cultures
a collective agreement negotiating team

- Obtain or commission a systematic review of the literature related to your subject expertise to use for evidence-based decision making
- Teach or train others in your specialist field
- Write a book about your topic
- Lead in a function/business unit/specialism that is unfamiliar to you
- E-learning for bite-size knowledge/skill acquisition
- Read newspapers regularly
- Read *The Economist, New Scientist* etc.

- Set goals for the short term and long term using measures of 'sustainable' performance
- Be coached to deliver on your priorities
- Shadow a renowned deliverer
- Action learning to address live business challenges
- Build some business entity, taking responsibility for delivering its current and future capability requirements

(Continued)

Table 7.3 Continued

Leadership capabilities	Suggested development activities
And in addition to the above, we include how to build leadership team capabilities (adapted from McIntyre, 1999) for: Strategic goal setting: Capability 2 – access broad-band 'capability' from across the leadership memebership Capability 4 – future sense-make combined with strategic thinking:	■ Monitoring trends in the external environment ■ Communication across the leadership-management community about critical priorities for success, which are then reinforced through actions and words ■ Determine measures of organization-wide intellectual, people and social capital ■ Take part in strategy planning in own department ■ Leadership of a strategic project including implementation ■ Participate in interdepartmental work ■ Participation in/leadership of cross-functional working parties ■ Evaluation and review of strategic initiatives ■ Participation in exercises collecting stakeholder feedback ■ Analyze themes from a range of strategic planning documents ■ Secondment to a strategic role ■ Assist in strategic planning for voluntary/community organizations ■ Become a director/board member in voluntary/community organizations ■ Shadow another leader involved in strategy ■ Read books on strategic leadership

Network building:
Capability 5 – develop 'total' leadership

■ Share current networks

■ Set networking goals for all team members
■ Assess networking effectiveness as a team
■ Create a 'Yellow Pages', detailing the capabilities of team members
■ Set aside time for knowledge sharing about their areas of operation, company, industry, profession

■ Promote ongoing two-way communication with employees, customers, suppliers, stakeholders and local community
■ Participate in relevant industry, sector, civic or professional bodies
■ Seek involvement in media activity and contingency planning
■ Present to a variety of audiences on a variety of topics
■ Lead project on internal/external communications
■ Shadow a PR person
■ Seek representative roles/opportunities
■ Seek out challenging public situations where attention is focused
■ Hold social/networking events
■ Facilitate social/networking events
■ Develop maps of key stakeholders
■ Describe stakeholders issues/ideas
■ Poll/survey attitudes/perceptions
■ Use processes for policy development that engage communities/ stakeholders

■ Establish/support professional and peer networks
■ Develop communication plans for key initiatives
■ Take regular opportunities to communicate with staff

(Continued)

Table 7.3 Continued

Leadership capabilities	Suggested development activities
Collaboration: Capability 2 – access broad-band 'capability' from across the leadership membership Capability 3 – become a cocreator of a learning culture Capability 5 – develop 'total' leadership Capability 6 – develop 'transcultural' competence Capability 8 – develop 1:many dialog skills; action-learning, facilitation and process consulting	■ Dialog about common purpose, objectives and goals ■ Establish contracts for reciprocal support and evaluate their performance ■ Define trust and respect together in behavioral terms ■ Train members in conflict-resolution techniques ■ Assess the relationship and leadership effectiveness performance of the team ■ Work and play together outside of the organization periodically ■ Learn leadership together
Information processing: Capability 4 – future sense-make combined with strategic thinking Capability 8 – develop 1:many dialog skills; action-learning, facilitation and process consulting	■ Have the right people with the right information present for the nature of the decision making or problem solving ■ Train members in running effective and productive meetings ■ Always test team decisions against their ability to reinforce corporate objectives ■ Commit members publicly to responsibility and action ■ Critique intellectual/professional output ■ Have project experience with other professionals from different disciplines ■ Assist in leading a complex project – taskforce ■ Second to a 'problem' area

- Secondment to CE's office
- More peer discussion/reflection
- Seek out people with new and challenging ideas
- Practice boiling down complex issues to simple and clear pragmatic application points
- Find out how other people do your job
- Practice using images as well as words
- Encourage/participate in group problem solving
- Ask questions/be asked questions of
- Seek peer feedback from the best people in your field
- Discuss how your employees and customers would define business success
- Evaluating internal operations
- For every input/output measure have a related outcome measure
- Simplify the action list (bearing in mind that humans can only hold a maximum of seven items in their short-term memory)
- Identify synergies between 'change' initiatives for business system change
- Create action-impact feedback loops

Focused action:
Capability 7 – develop 1:1 relational skills; coaching
Capability 10 – high-quality performance challenge culture and dialog

2. Who am I now? Knowing where your real self overlaps with your ideal self will give you positive albeit moderated energy to move to the next step.

3. How do I get from here to there? Developing a realistic action plan to change ingrained habits one at a time and use situations as a cue to break the cycle by recognizing the normal reaction and then rehearsing/trying something new.

4. How do I make change stick? Making change stick requires scenario visualization and then repeated practice of the real thing so that the learning becomes tacit.

5. Who can help me? Create a community of supporters and reality checkers for confirmation and affirmation of the desired change.

There are always two sides to a change leader's capability coin; so they might use the self-reflection above to avoid the flipside of personal qualities that have the potential to undermine a change leader's development and business change implementation – see below.

Change Leader's Personal Qualities – Facilitators and Derailers (Catherine Hayes Partnership)

Confidence
- Makes a stand, and won't take 'No' for an answer
- Willing to say sorry and own up to their mistakes and misjudgments
- Changes their position after receiving input and feedback from others
- Perceived as assertive and decisive

Too much confidence = Arrogance
- 'It's my way or the high way'
- 'I am right and everyone else is wrong'
- 'It's not my fault that I didn't deliver'
- 'What do you mean "I" need to change?'
- Perceived as 'they think they are better/cleverer than everyone else'

Emotion
- Has presence
- Generates enthusiasm in their interactions with others
- Adapts their style to match their audience
- Perceived as passionate

Too much emotion = Melodrama
- The nonstop speaker
- Interrupting and talking over others
- Seeking/demanding attention
- Speaks before thinking
- Perceived as flamboyant and dramatic

(Continued)

Energy
- Motivates and inspires
- 'What you see is what you get' people know where they stand
- Engages others and generates energy for action
- Perceived as positive and inspiring

Too much energy = Volatility
- Short temper
- Mood swings (expressive and withdrawn)
- Others not sure how to take this person
- Distant and difficult to relate to
- Perceived as 'high maintenance'

Caution
- Analytical
- Gathers the views, opinions and knowledge of others before making decisions
- Willing to say 'No' when required
- Perceived as thorough and diligent

Too much caution = Risk averse
- Procrastinates
- Fearful of making the wrong decision
- Slow decision maker
- Obsesses about what could go wrong
- Resistant to the new/different/unfamiliar
- Perceived as difficult/awkward/reluctant

Scepticism
- Assesses a situation from multiple angles before making a decision for action
- Politically aware
- Actively seeks feedback from others
- Perceived as fair

Too much scepticism = Distrust
- Focuses on the downside
- Says 'No' without hearing the whole story and considering options and alternatives
- Difficult to relate to
- Constantly critical/distrusting of others
- Perceived as defensive/cynical

Reserve
- Listens before speaking
- Clear headed and calm in emotional situations

(Continued)

- Connects with people and situations when appropriate
- Perceived as thoughtful and considerate

Too much reserve = Aloofness
- Difficult to get to know
- Rarely expresses emotions or feelings
- Keeps themselves to themselves
- Avoids conflict
- Perceived as a loner

Light-hearted
- Challenges the thoughts and views of others
- Risk taker
- Uses humor to generate energy
- Initiates and encourages difference
- Perceived as 'fun' and sociable

Too much light-hearted = Mischievousness
- Breaks the rules for the fun of it
- Impulsive – acts before thinking of the consequences
- Flies by the seat of their pants
- Perceived as a trouble maker
- Says what they think without considering the impact on others

Imagination
- Continuously looks for something new/different
- Ideas and options generator
- Spontaneous and unpredictable
- Turns ideas into tangible results
- Perceived as different/unique

Too much imagination = Eccentricity
- Generates lots of ideas that rarely get executed/turned into practice
- Has difficulty prioritizing
- Others find them difficult to take seriously
- Perceived as being odd and unfocused

Politically aware
- Will engage in conflict with the aim to resolve it
- Has an open agenda that others understand
- Adapts their style to the situation
- Perceived as astute and trustworthy

(Continued)

Too political = Passive resistance
- Inconsistent – says one thing and does something else
- Has their own agenda
- Avoids conflict and difficult conversations
- Difficult to trust – people do not know where they stand or how they are perceived
- Perceived as 'slippery' and untrustworthy

Should we become saturated with details of 'hard' and 'soft' capabilities, it is worth revisiting a much simpler role development formula provided by Drucker (2004), whose legacy includes wisdom extrapolated from 65 years of observing executives in action. Learn these eight simple practices and you will have the foundations to be an effective change leader:

1. They asked, 'What needs to be done?'

2. They asked, 'What is right for the enterprise?'

3. They developed action plans.

4. They took responsibility for decisions.

5. They took responsibility for communication.

6. They were focused on opportunities rather than problems.

7. They ran productive meetings.

8. They thought and said (and did) 'we' rather than 'I'.

As Drucker (2004) explains, Numbers 1 and 2 give executives the knowledge they need to take a business forward. The next four help them convert this knowledge into effective action, whilst 7 and 8 ensure that the whole business feels responsible and accountable.

Staying with the emphasis on role development, a longitudinal study of the impact of business tools and techniques (Total Quality Management, Customer Relationship Management and Supply Chain Management), Nohria, Joyce and Roberson (2003) concluded that none of these techniques had a direct impact on competitor's comparative business performance; 'Without exception, companies that outperformed their industry peers excelled at what we call the four primary management practices – strategy, execution, culture and structure. And they supplemented their great skill in those areas with a mastery of any two of four secondary management practices – talent, innovation, leadership, and mergers and partnerships,

(Nohria et al., 2003, p. 43). For strategy communication, a change leader will need to know the general trends in their external environment, available for example from *The Economist* New Year special edition.

Here are some illustrations (adapted by the authors from the 2008 edition).

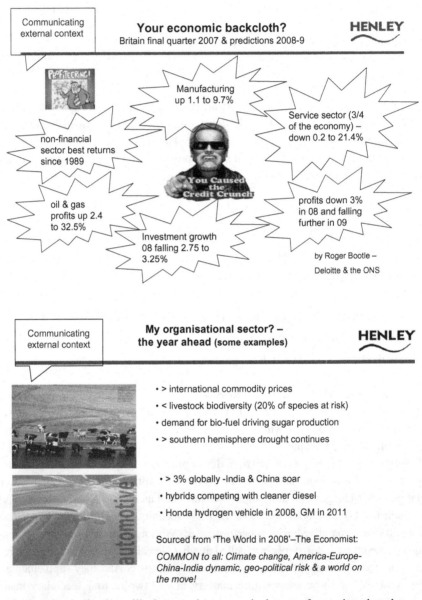

And a change leader will also require a practical way of ensuring that they use their change leadership time intelligently. The UK IOD survey results below suggest where priorities should lie.

Are you operating as a 21stC Leader? HENLEY
(adapted from 2005 UK IOD survey of 800 leaders)

1. Continually develop a vision of the future and constantly align business purpose, values, strategy and delivery to it.

2. Adapt leadership style to the situation and proactively identify and meet people's motivational requirements.

3. Harness the passion, strength and potential of everyone to achieve, improve and aim higher.

4. Be a visible role model and interact successfully with your critical stakeholders (service investors) and clients (service recipients).

5. Be commercially/socially astute –fully understand the sector you are operating in and identify its current and future performance drivers.

Ask yourself the question, if you are not using your own finite resources for activity across these change leadership priorities what are you using it for and could someone else relieve you of those activities which do not contribute to your change leadership role? After all, research by Mankins (2004) suggests that:

■ Top management teams spend relatively little time together (on average only 21 hours per month are spent in leadership teams).

■ Agenda setting is unfocused and undisciplined (<5% had a process for ensuring consideration of priorities for the leadership team).

■ Too little attention is paid to strategy (three hours per month – 80% spent on matters that account for only 20% of an organization's long-term value).

■ Meetings are not structured to produce decisions (>65% are not even called for this purpose).

A review of the extensive literature on a change leader's role focus offers up the following key development goals provided by Frey (2008).

■ Challenging the status quo and creating a readiness for change: confronting and challenging the current reality and its fitness for future purpose. Leading a dialog in the organization that tests out options for change.

■ Communicating a shared and urgent vision: communicating the future direction. Not only must all employees in the organization find the goal emotionally compelling, they must also clearly understand how they will contribute to achieving that goal.

■ Building coalitions: creating additional sponsors at different levels of the organization, involving as many people as possible to build commitment. Change leaders need the involvement of people who have the resources, the knowledge and the political clout to make things happen.

(Continued)

■ Enabling others to act: by energizing, empowering, building teams, providing tangible support with appropriate resources and putting in place the appropriate systems and structures.

■ Rewarding and recognizing: using rewards and recognition to gain support; recognizing short-term gains or success stories to emphasize recognition of the new behavior and taking action in identifying and addressing resistance.

■ Modeling the way: enacting the new behaviors in deeds as well as in words; personally demonstrating senior management involvement and commitment. This is seen as fundamental to the success of the   . transformation process. Successful implementation occurs where executives teach new behaviors by example.

Projecting ahead, Parry and Bryman (2006) have suggested that we should now be developing post-charismatic and post-transformational leadership perhaps based around embedded learning, truly distributed leadership in teams and learning from experience and failure (Fullan, 2001). In this way, change leadership development and its practice is more open to public scrutiny and challenge by those who are impacted by it, including the effects on the leader(s) themselves. What might constitute appropriate development here? In Jackson and Parry (2008), several novel approaches are considered which we have adapted and built upon:

■ Consider the life and achievements of Benjamin Franklin (or other leaders who have been shown over time to have moral authenticity), as explored by Mumford and Van Doorn (2001), who, based on the biographical analysis, proposed a theory of pragmatic leadership that involves: identifying and communicating solutions to significant social problems, meeting the practical needs of followers, working through elites in solution generation and demonstrating the feasibility and tangible benefits of these solutions.

■ Grint (2001) suggests that effective leaders need to embrace a panoply of arts for their development. For example, from philosophy change leaders can learn to create a sense of organizational identity that makes sense for the future (who are we to be now?), from fine art memorable visions can be created (what will our next journey look like?); consider the martial arts for enacting fast and calm tactical responses to rapidly changing conditions that threaten, or the performing arts for developing dialog and discursive techniques, wordsmithing, narrative (Boje, 2001), storytelling, use of metaphor and analogy (Michalko, 2001) and role modeling the priority values, behaviors and work focus actions that make up the requisite culture (Aitken, 2007).

■ For role modeling, the development of bodily knowledge and drama display is relevant if we consider change leaders to be social influencers through the way talk is walked and the signals this sends to the culture about priority business values, behaviors and goals. Works by Aitken (2007), Starratt (1993) and Gardner and Avolio (1998) have covered some of this territory.

■ An addition to the above is the challenge of developing and maintaining focus whilst all round you is constantly shifting. 'It's not that "mindfulness" is the answer to all life's problems. Rather, it is that all life's problems can be seen more clearly through the lens of a clear mind' (Kabat-Zinn, 1990, p. 25). In a study with Motorola, Barrios-Choplin, McCarty and Cryer (1997) found that in addition to physiological and emotional benefits, contentment, job satisfaction and communication significantly increased after mindfulness training. Segal, Williams and Teasdale (2002) suggest the following skills development: concentration – focusing full attention on one object or activity, awareness – the conscious knowledge that life is 'as is', acceptance – one must accept life as is and let go, decentering – seeing thoughts just as thoughts and not truths and 'Being' rather than 'doing' (we have no time to stop and stare, smell, taste, feel).

■ Finally, drawing out 'emotional' and 'relational' aspects of change leadership development, a real stretch into the realms of personal development outlined by Sanders, Hopkins and Geroy (2003) requires movement from transformational to transcendental leadership, built on the idea of Thompson (2000) who contends that good and effective leadership is a developmental process of growth and maturation that is fed by the leader's inner spirit more than his/her outer strivings, such that leaders become less concerned about the constraining realities of their external environment and more concerned about internal development that goes beyond current realities. They are then freer to consider and express new models of how the world should be and their own and organization's place within it.

In brief, this requires the development of three dimensions: consciousness – entailing movement toward more complexity, greater awareness and less egocentrism through deconstructing and reconstructing own meaning and reality; moral character – moving from the disposition of rewards and punishment, through meeting social obligations and adherence to norms; leading eventually to an internalized set of principles universally accepted as right or wrong. Thomas Aquinas provided a moral development model comprising three levels of virtues (Sandlin, 1992) – Intellectual (seeking rational truth using wisdom, science, understanding and prudence (the management domain), Moral (justice, fortitude and temperance), very similar to Collin's (2001) findings of humility and will and Theological (love, faith and hope) or like Kouzes and Posner's (1988) 'encouraging the heart', with the heart reflecting social responsibility and the promotion of fairness lying at the centre and seat of life and finally Faith – defined as a universal way of making sense of one's own existence (Fowler, 1981) where individuals become incarnates and actualizers of the spirit of the fulfilled human community (representing overtones of corporate social responsibility).

Parks (2000) describes the emotional development of faith as consisting of four stages. In the first stage, the leader depends on an outside authority for feelings of assurance, rightness, hope, loyalty and fear, moving progressively through inner-dependence to interdependent. This final stage involves a qualitative shift in the balance of vulnerability, trust and faith such that it becomes possible for leaders to depend on others without fear of losing the power of self, fostering a deeper trust of self and a profound awareness of relatedness to others.

In considering these emotional and relational aspects of organizational life, evolutionary psychology (Pinker, 1997) reminds us how hardwired human behavior can be. Here are some common people frames of mind together with ways in which change leaders can respond.

If people are hardwired to	Then the message for change leaders is
Use emotions as the first screen for all information received	■ Recognize that people hear bad news first and loudest
Avoid risky situations when feeling relatively secure and to fight frantically when feeling threatened	■ Understand that people will resist change except when they are dissatisfied ■ Realize that people will act and think creatively when given space, safety and support
Feel more self-confident than really justifies	■ Routinely question whether managers or their employees are understanding the difficulty of work-related challenges
Quickly classify people, situations and experiences into categories – good or bad, in or out – rather than engage in time-consuming and nuanced analysis	■ Be careful that identifying people potential and performance management processes have some independent objectivity built in ■ Realize that mixing disparate functions or teams means having to overcome deep-rooted propensity to stereotype strangers

(Continued)

If people are hardwired to	Then the message for change leaders is
Gossip	▦ Do not waste time trying to eradicate rumors but use your energy to plug into the grapevine and make sure it stays healthy, not malicious
Participate in public competitions for status and chest thumping about their successes	▦ Encourage employees to refrain from one-upmanship but understand you are fighting their natural programming
Feel most comfortable in communities with no more than 150 members	▦ Keep organizations from growing too large without breaking them into smaller units ▦ Refrain from asking people to identify with more than one group at a time
Seek superiority or security in hierarchical systems	▦ Recognize that hierarchy is a natural urge and that people will establish status distinctions even if the organization tries to remove them
Lead in different ways or not be leaders at all	▦ Accept that people cannot demonstrate particular leadership qualities they do not innately possess, even if the business situation demands it ▦ Understand that desire to lead is the most critical condition of a leader

As Anderson (2002) explains, the increasing speed of business operations and instability associated with technological change and globalization has magnified the importance of agility, flexibility and adaptation in change leaders. Recent studies conceive of organization as a continual process of meaning formation and development through discourse. This philosophy sees an organization as always changing, only momentarily fixed by members as they negotiate tensions between stability and change.

Analysis of the discussion processes that take place inside organizations by Anderson (2002) draws several conclusions about the language of team members as they struggle with organizational change. 'First, organizational members experience executive texts in contradictory ways, as they see executives acting as both a stabilizing and a destabilizing force. Members adopt a logic of team membership and conduct benchmarking as a method for negotiating organizational identity which allows them to 'try on' new discursive practices. Most significantly for the study of organizational change, Anderson argues that team members make translations between organizational practices and individual utterances through intertextual reports of prior, future and absent voices, and they textualize organizational change through writing practices. This suggests we alter how we view organizational change, demonstrating that change occurs when members temporarily stabilize the organization by textualizing current practices (in writing or in generic voices), alter these stabilized practices, and voice new utterances to hear how proposed practices might sound in the future. This conclusion underscores the role of language in the widespread view that change, not stability, is the normal state of contemporary organizational life'. As Jackson and Parry (2008) point out, we can envisage a move in the form of leadership development from exploring who is representative of a leader, through identifying what a leader is made up of, and what the leader does (leadership), to concentrating on discovering what is going on in the 'leadership space'.

The next port of call for research on developing change leaders will be considering what impact particular acts of leadership are having and how different displays of leadership can affect the leader's, follower's and organization's 'movements' in different ways. All this suggests much more use of experiential and reflective learning, including sampling, watching and recording/playing back change leaders acting individually and together in real time, alongside observed and analyzed reaction by the leaders themselves, their followers and other stakeholders. The art of change leadership development really should imitate life.

We now move on to look at some development cases that we are/have been involved in. These are not meant to be exemplars, because any development program has to be geared to the right context, given the resources at its disposal. Rather, we present them because in varying degrees they reflect some of our core philosophy and principles for developing change leaders, which we outline next.

Development cases

Leadership is not magnetic personality that can just as well be glib tongue. It is not 'making friends and influencing people', that is flattery.

Leadership is lifting a person's vision to higher sights, the raising of a person's performance to a higher standard, the building of a personality beyond its normal limitations.

Peter F. Drucker

INTRODUCTION

To lead change successfully, the developing leader has to apply Drucker's sentiments to himself/herself first. This principle sits at the heart of all our case studies.

The first few years of a leader's career is a critical proving ground for the development of baseline skills; understanding the technical aspects of the organization and how the business works; the basics of management and how it differs from professional work and the fundamentals of working with and through others. Major tests of leadership potential typically follow this initial phase and this period is often characterized by some grouping of five major development themes.

1. Starting something from scratch
2. Fix it or turnaround
3. Cross business projects or task forces
4. Significant increase in scope and scale of responsibility
5. Switching; line/support, front line/strategic leadership roles

Development richness can then be enhanced by:

■ Establishing a work experience sequence that combines variety with complexity of assignments

■ Helping managers confront the basic psychological transitions required by job and level changes

■ Providing regular feedback and coaching to help managers extend, reflect on and embed their learning

Below, we present four cases (Cases 1 and 2 with participants from single UK organizations, private and public sector respectively, and Cases 3 and 4 with customers from multiple organizations in the public sector – one within the UK and another from New Zealand) where these principles have been applied to real leadership development programs. Their development and implementation has been influenced by the authors, with a particular emphasis on facilitating participants to improve, in tandem, both personal and organizational effectiveness to lead change, combined with an emphasis on building whole of organization approaches, and for the last two cases, whole of sector leadership culture and capability. In effect, as our guide, we have used the 'double triangle' leader-organization learning framework, first presented in Chapter 1 and further developed in Chapter 10. Our intention in offering up these cases is to give readers some insights into how we have translated some of our ideas into practice. This is especially true of Case 4.

Case 1

Developing change leadership capability in a UK energy company

BACKGROUND

The organization was a significant player in the energy sector. As with many organizations in this sector, the company was facing volatility in its markets with high levels of competition. Responding to this context required a capability to implement significant changes rapidly and effectively. Historically, this was not a capability that was well developed within the organization. Indeed, a number of previous change initiatives had proved to be costly, disruptive and ultimately unsuccessful.

Within the organization's retail business, very significant competitive pressures were giving rise to need for significant changes in structures, processes and practices in order to sustain the market share and produce appropriate levels of profitability.

PURPOSE OF DEVELOPMENT PROGRAM

Against this background, the organization initiated a process for designing and implementing a program designed to build change leadership capability. However, there was a strong imperative to ensure that any investment in development should produce clear outcomes in terms of its impact on:

■ Individual participant's capabilities to lead change

■ Changes in business results

■ Development of change capability throughout the organization.

The specific outcomes required from the program are shown in more detail in Table 7.4.

PROGRAM DEVELOPMENT

The first step in developing a program to meet the above requirements was to identify the competencies required for effective change leadership. In order to do this, a project team was established. The team comprised a mixture of senior line leaders

Table 7.4   Desired outcomes for the change leadership programme (CLP)

1. Individual impact	The learning on the CLP should enable the participants to increase their own ability to lead and implement change through new tools, processes, mind-sets and behaviors (e.g. how to work with sponsors, how to anticipate and engage resistance, how to design and monitor change implementation plans, how to surface and transform assumptions and mental models, how to facilitate ownership in others).
2. Business impact	The learning on the CLP should enable participants to bring about a discernible shift in business results for their identified change work (e.g. revenue growth, profits, cost reductions, customer service improvements, process reconfiguration).
3. Organization impact	The learning on the CLP should enable participants to strengthen the capability of the organization around them to implement change (e.g. a sense of urgency, more aligned employees, committed stakeholders, energy and motivation to try out new ways of working, clarity of implementation plans and new roles, reallocation of priorities, increased change and transition skills, a more vigorous learning community).

and the development specialist. The team was supported by a consultant with specialist expertise in change management and change leadership. In order to develop a competency, the team began with a session in which they shared their own experiences and learning. This led to a very broad initial view of the key areas of change leadership competence. The consultant then undertook a series of interviews with individual managers who the project team had identified as being successful in implementing change projects. The data from these interviews was then analyzed to identify common patterns of competencies. The team reviewed this analysis, combined with their initial view of key areas of competence and desk-based research input provided by the consultants. From this meeting, an overall change leadership competency framework was established. This framework is shown in Table 7.5.

Table 7.5 Change management competencies

1. Change Initiation: ability to create the case for change and secure credible sponsorship.
2. Change Impact: ability to scope the breadth, depth, sustainability and returns of a change strategy.
3. Change Facilitation: ability to help others, through effective facilitation, to gain insight into the human dynamics of change and to develop the confidence to achieve the change goals.
4. Change Learning: ability to scan, reflect and identify learning and ensure insights are used to develop individual, group and organizational capabilities.
5. Change Execution: ability to formulate, and guide the implementation of a credible change plan with appropriate goals, resources, metrics and review mechanisms.
6. Change Presence: demonstrates high personal commitment to achievement of change goals through integrity and courage while maintaining objectivity and individual resilience ('a nonanxious presence in a sea of anxiety').
7. Change Technology: knowledge, generation and skillful appreciation of change theories, tools and processes.

PROGRAM DESIGN

In designing the program, the project team agreed that the development should be built around actual change work or projects. No one would be able to attend the program unless they had a specific change project or piece of change work for which they were accountable. Furthermore, to ensure that the change project was significant to the business, participants were required to have a line executive sponsor for the work.

Given this principle, the overall design for the program was as follows:

Step 1: Select the work line executives who act as sponsors. Identify the key areas of work and business impact required.

Step 2: Select the participants. Participants in the program agreed with the line executives. In broad terms, they were leaders acting as change agents in relation to the key areas of change required by the business.

Step 3: Building a support infrastructure. The overall design envisaged a combination of workshops and coaching during learning implementation. This required the identification and training of a group of coaches as an important part of the overall development infrastructure. It was also agreed that the line executive sponsors would play a role in the process (including contributing to final assessments) and therefore briefing of sponsors was an important aspect of infrastructure building.

Step 4: Establishing current reality and constructing outcomes. The existing change leadership competencies of participants were established using a 360° assessment against the competency framework outlined above. In addition, each participant developed an initial work plan for their change project and agreed this with their line executive sponsor.

Step 5: Module 1. This three-day module was designed to provide a range of impacts relating to change and its leadership (see Table 7.6 for details).

Step 6: Implementation and support. Each participant worked on the implementation of their change project. Support was provided by their allocated coach. In addition, the development delivery team provided ongoing support on a 'help line' basis.

Step 7: Module 2. This two-day module took place three months after Module 1. Prior to this module, a further 360° assessment of change leadership competencies was conducted. The feedback from this was used within the module. Further input on change tools was also provided (see Table 7.6 for details).

Step 8: Implementation and support (continued). Participants continued with work on their change projects with further support from coaches and the delivery team 'help line'.

Step 9: Evaluation and feedback. Three months after Module 2, participants attended a session with line executive sponsors. Each participant's project was reviewed in

Table 7.6 Module outlines

Module 1	Module 2
Exploring competency feedback with peers and coaches	Reviewing lessons from experience since Module 1
Theories of change	Capturing and using the learning from a change process
Making your change a business issue	Assessing and measuring progress
Advocating your case and securing sponsorship	Learning from other organizations
Handling the human response to change	Peer feedback on leadership behaviors
Building commitment and energy	Live practice – change facilitation
Designing workable implementation plans	Sustaining implementation

terms of individual business and organizational impact. This assessment was based on a combination of line sponsor assessment and a final 360° competence assessment. In the course of the review, ongoing development needs were agreed.

Step 10: Sustainment. Identification of next steps in participants' projects; implementation of actions to meet development needs; ongoing coaching on a reducing basis.

PROGRAM OUTCOMES

Some 100 participants went through this program over a two-year period. Analysis of the feedback and evaluation indicated that the program had succeeded in building capability in relation to significant improvements in all of the competence areas with the exception of change technology. Importantly, the line executive assessments indicated significant outcomes in terms of individual, business and organizational impact. Thus, overall, the program succeeded in building change capability into the organization. This was indeed reflected in their ability to sustain (and grow a little) the organization's market share during a period of fierce competition.

Case 2

'Future Leaders' at the UK Land Registry

With the world's largest online transactional database of over 21 million titles, Land Registry underpins the economy by safeguarding ownership of many billions of pounds worth of property. Around £1 million worth of property is processed every minute in England and Wales.

As a government department established in 1862, executive agency and trading fund responsible to the Secretary of State for Justice and Lord Chancellor, Land Registry keeps and maintains the Land Register for England and Wales. The Land Register has been an open document since 1990. For further information about Land Registry, please visit www.landregistry.gov.uk.

BACKGROUND

Purpose and key roles

A primary goal of 'Future Leaders' (FL) is to communicate and create a culture in which:

- Ambition is encouraged
- Management and education are seen as important
- Personal success is valued
- Broadening experience and the willingness to seize opportunity when it arises are accepted as key to rapid career progression

This case focuses on the CAM program, an up to three years involvement in a relatively unique learning vehicle, being entirely driven by the participant alongside their day job, within a 'completion model' framework (see below), and using end of year assessment (see the Presentation Protocol headings below) before progression to the following years, thus ensuring personal and organizational return on investment.

The participant is encouraged to utilize a network of developmental support and learning-work application integration throughout their stay, provided through the following key stakeholder roles:

- CAM Steering Group – oversees the CAM project and ROI for Land Registry. Conducts the end of each year assessment.

■ FL Manager – provides coordination and links between the Land Registry, CAM participants and the external learning partners (National School of Government and Henley Management College). Acts as a catalyst for generating across organization development placements and ensures that the 'completion model' is delivered in negotiation with the participant and their line manager.

■ Line Manager – cements the link between day job and program planning and performance, providing feedback on leadership capability application.

■ Personal Development Adviser (PDA) – acts as confidential support to participants throughout (ratio of approximately 1 PDA to 6 participants). Facilitates action learning in the PDA group and assists participants in leadership capability progression reflection and sense-making from their formal, informal and independent learning experiences (also using diagnostics).

■ Internal Mentor – assists with developing general business awareness and/or specialist learning. Provides advice on career pathway options and how best to convert them.

DESIGN FEATURES OF CAM

Stage 1 – attendance at the CAM assessment centre provides feedback on leadership capabilities and is the passport to entry.

Stage 2 – inaugural setup event, followed by a 'Learning to Learn' day, where a development goals action plan is drafted with the PDA and subsequently signed off by the FL director and line manager.

Stage 3 – delivery of a twice yearly 'Leadership Forum', where participants involve all the CAM stakeholders in analysis of and recommendations for live strategic leadership issues.

Stage 4 – end of year assessment presentation, detailing the ROI and development plan for the forthcoming year, which has to be passed to go forward to the next year.

Stages 3 and 4 are repeated each year, with new participant cohorts joining those still on the program and taking responsibility for delivering the 'Leadership Forum'.

Throughout the stages, participants organize their own learning delivery against their development goals, with the support of the key stakeholders.

MEASURES OF SUCCESS

A key measure of success for the program is an 'increase in the numbers and proportions of internal candidates getting to assessment centres for senior posts and increases in the numbers and proportions of internal candidates who are actually selected for senior posts'.

This was as a response to a business need to improve the performance of internal 'talent' during a period when many advertised posts had been filled with external candidates. Whilst Land Registry welcomed fresh ideas, it wanted to ensure that the business benefited from better use of internal skills and experience. Many of the individuals progressing through the program have contributed to an increase in business results for their teams as a result of these opportunities.

In terms of progressing internal talent in the direction of senior management, the program, from 34 participants, has produced: one Area Manager, two Deputy Area Managers and 14 people who have achieved temporary or permanent promotions in key roles such as Regional Team Leaders.

Others are developing from lateral development opportunities that are designed to broaden thinking and achieve a wider perspective of the public sector.

COMMENTS FROM FUTURE LEADERS REFLECTING THE CONTENT

'Since being accepted on to the CAM program last November, my working life has changed dramatically. Throughout this year I have been involved in a variety of activities that have stretched my capabilities, challenged my intellect and developed my business sense. These have included working with an outside consultant on a customer segmentation project, shadowing a senior manager at the Ministry of Defence and representing Land Registry at the Young Public Sector Programme where I delivered an argument on a controversial subject to a panel of judges and a cross-section of civil-service employees.'

'When I began my CAM journey I was a Customer Service Advisor at Croydon office. Shortly after my promotion to a position within ETG, a head office group, I found that the development work I was doing with CAM was invaluable in helping me settle into my new role. Skills I learned in presenting, writing and creating strong arguments improved my practical skills, while workshops on marketing and strategic thinking broadened my business outlook. The work I did on the Leadership Forums has informed me in the wider Land Registry picture and the issues our organisation faces, and this knowledge is integral to the decisions I make on a daily basis'.

'The Future Leaders Development Programme has provided outstanding opportunities for me to develop my leadership skills and experiences in ways that would not have been possible within the confines of the usual land registry appraisal/development process.

Having spent nearly all my LR career in an operational environment, with appropriate but necessarily limited leadership skills, I have undertaken development activities to widen my leadership experiences, including delivery of leadership training; assessment centre assessor; and legal consultation responses.

I have undertaken training workshops on a wide range of core leadership skills, including report writing; critical and strategic thinking; finance; project management; and image/impact; and have utilized these skills within the development activities undertaken.

The re-assessment process within the programme, together with self assessment tools and the 360° feedback process, provide useful means of measuring the success of the chosen development activities and overall growth as a leader'.

'What an amazing experience, challenging, scary and sometimes unpredictable but always rewarding! If you want to experience life outside of your comfort zone then future leaders is the best way to achieve it.

For me it has been a fast moving and undeniably beneficial experience. From an RE2 lower caseworker to an RE2 Upper district team leader and then onto a development opportunity as an SRE regional leader in Coventry office, all in 2 years! During this time I have also taken part in leadership forums, led a project looking at the future leaders programme itself and undertaken the first year of a management diploma at Henley Management College.

I have learnt a huge amount about myself and tested my abilities to the full. I have met and been able to learn from people in all areas of the Land Registry and have had unprecedented access to senior board members, all of who have helped me to develop into a more confident and mature leader.

After years of individuals "waiting in turn" to progress, The Future Leaders programme is challenging that culture by bringing through the talent with right the skills and attributes, at the right time, to facilitate changing business needs regardless of grade or time with the organisation. Overall, it is enabling much more effective succession planning based on current business needs rather than tradition'.

'Assessment Presentation Protocol headings' and 'Completion Model' (see the following table)

Presentation Protocol headings

Year 1

Overall impression and business impact made by the individual

Overall strength of the evidence presented

Planning – original aspirations and program choice

Implementing – formal learning, assignments postings, leadership forums etc., practical use of learning and people and relationship issues

Reviewing – significant learning points, significant achievements, benefits to the business, critical review

Intentions for Year 2

Year 2

Overall impression and business impact made by the individual

Overall strength of the evidence presented

(Continued)

Evidence of an emerging leader

Evidence of return on investment – specific, tangible, quantified

Evidence of final year business benefit – why should the individual continue?

Completion Model – CAM participants' activities

Scheme elements

General
Integrated support/appraisal by line manager
Mentor
Personal development adviser
Steering group feedback
Individual attention of future leaders manager
Development centre (not applicable to this period)
360 degree feedback (not applicable to this period)

Major events (attendance)
Inaugural event
Leadership forum 1
Leadership forum 2
Planning team member for a Leadership forum?

Learning modules (3 days maximum)
Day 1
Day 2
Day 3

Supporting portfolio (*at least two to be completed per year). Those asterisked must be included at some time in the three years)*
*Professional qualification
*Tour of duty Head Office or other contrasting internal location
*Action learning assignments set by Boards or designated others
Interchange (private sector and public secondments)
Shadowing (at least three)
Other temporary postings and detached duties
Leaders UK Development Program
'Preparing for Top Management'
The Whitehall and Industry Group
SPATS

The Programme continues to run, although with smaller numbers, as operational efficiencies are required across the business in response to the economic downturn.

Case 3

▌ Leaders UK (National School of Government)

BACKGROUND

The National School of Government is the business school for government, and provides high quality learning and development solutions to government organisations and individuals providing public services. National School of Government's Leader's UK learning consortium supported by Ashridge Business School and the University of Birmingham provides a learning environment that encourages participants to set and deliver stretch goals for change leadership, whilst also contributing to program peer's collective leadership development.

Leaders UK (LUK) is a unique leadership program designed to release and build individual and collective leadership talent that can make a difference to the lives of people in UK communities. By the end of the program, delegates will have received insights from public, private and third-sector leadership practitioners and academics, which will enable them to achieve this.

Collaborative leadership (a team of all the talents) lies at the heart of how we can best deliver public services. Working across organizational boundaries, coordinating networks and linking service delivery systems allow us to integrate inputs and outputs to achieve public value outcomes. However, such collaborative or systems leadership requires us to use our individual leadership wisely to cocreate with our colleagues. Some overarching questions for LUK participants are: how do we lead in complex public systems? Or in a congested and fragmented policy environment where there are no established lines of hierarchy? Or where there are competing priorities, policy frameworks and values to navigate? How best do we utilize our expensive and finite leadership resources for the benefit of those we serve?

The LUK program responds to such challenges. It aims to equip participants to be public service system leaders, to be able to shape the future purpose, strategy for, and delivery of public services. It facilitates building confidence and competence to engage with and shape the system to deliver better outcomes for consumers and citizens. Thinking, feeling and acting systemically, personally and collegially is a critical competence in the increasingly complex and turbulent world of public life.

The core program and successful graduation requires your best commitment to 22 contact days spread over two years (see the Learning Journey Schedule in Figure 7.1 below). In between, delegates will need to allocate additional time for working on delivering a Personal Leadership Development Plan and Learning Group–Leadership Project Plan.

Throughout the program, participants have a Leaders UK Faculty Learning Facilitator who will take a special interest in personal and group development.

An example program schedule is shown below. The dates are set for the Learning Modules (some of which will also include a Case Study Visit). Learning Group dates are negotiated with allocated Leaders UK Faculty Learning Facilitators.

LEARNING JOURNEY SCHEDULE

At the Launch, delegates are introduced to the program design, learning principles, mechanisms and responsibilities and meet members of core Faculty, as well as getting to know learning peers, who will be supporting each other's development throughout the program (Figure 7.1).

This is directly followed by the first Learning Module entitled 'Personal Leadership Skills', where participants engage with leadership practitioners and academics with the intention of raising awareness of the leader you currently are, alongside building a personal vision of the leader you would like to become.

The journey continues with insights into the other half of LUK's leadership proposition, which is the collective as opposed to individual leadership required for 'Leading Collaboration and Partnership'. An example of this modules aim and objectives is:

Aim: To explore the different uses, requirements and impacts of 'collective' as opposed to individual leadership, (the latter covered in 'Personal Leadership Skills') Objectives:

- To review how collaborative and partnership leadership can positively impact organizational outcomes

- To consider approaches to embedding collaborative working as our preferred way of working in the public sector (for example through stakeholder management)

- To identify the characteristics of collective leadership and how it can applied to shaping organizational culture and performance

- To experience collaborative leadership and reflect/give feedback on own/other's capabilities

- To identify leadership action points and priorities for participant's own leadership and organizational development.

This is followed by aspects of organizational leadership that relate to creating new directions, through 'Leading the Business (Strategy and Entrepreneurship)'. Before the final learning module, there is a reminder of what the purpose of public service through 'Leading with Consumers and Citizens', before pulling all the above together at 'Leading the Public Service System'. An example of this module's aim and objectives is:

Aim: To apply the principles and practices of systems leadership by working with a senior management team of a public sector organization in their review of current leadership approaches and in particular partnership working.

Objectives:

■ To reflect on systems leadership research and practice in a real world context

■ To practice process consulting methodology (including a 'coaching' leadership style) in a case study visit

■ To analyse findings from the exploration and provide feedback to the host organization in a way that adds value to whole system leadership and partnership effectiveness at the County Council

■ To identify leadership action points and priorities for participant's own leadership and organizational development.

LEADERSHIP LEARNING PORTFOLIO AND LEARNING MECHANISMS

Learning Portfolio

In order to graduate from LUK, participants are required to produce a portfolio of evidence related to how they have achieved their own learning goals and the contribution made to their LUK Learning Group peer's goals, including the Learning Group–Leadership Project Plan.

What sort of things might go into a portfolio?

1. Your Personal Leadership Development Plan.

2. Examples of real leadership activities that show you trying some new learning, making mistakes, relearning, succeeding.

3. Excerpts from a learning journal or diary that you keep. Your own thoughts, reflections, anecdotes, questions that you are seeking to answer, your own processing of leadership incidents that have puzzled or frustrated you etc.

4. Excerpts from things you have written, created, responded to; evidence of events, actions, meetings you have initiated, participated in, bits of video, transcribed recording, dialog, conversation.

5. Letters you have received, emails of colleagues' responses, comprising outcomes, intended or otherwise. Views that contradict or enrich your own.

6. Recent Leadership Diagnostics, feedback and the sense you made of it.

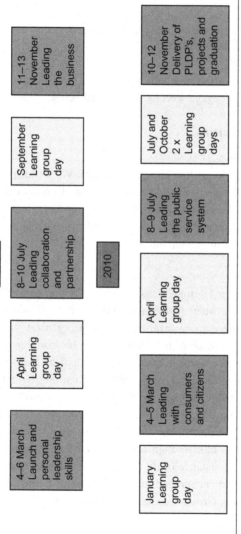

Figure 7.1 Example Learning Journey Schedule.

7. Particular insights you have had from the Learning Modules, or from your challenges faced in delivering the Learning Group–Leadership Project Plan.

8. A health check or diagnostic assessment of a team or partnership that you lead or are influential in, together with your reflections on it.

9. Learning derived from the sessions with your mentor, or from your Learning Group meetings.

10. References to significant writings on leadership that have had a demonstrable effect on how you do things.

As well as your Portfolio, which is a learning mechanism in its own right, the 12 main ways you will engage with LUK are listed below.

Learning mechanisms

1. Learning Modules
   These form the bedrock of the core program. We invite speakers who are representative of all sectors to add richness to your learning experience. We publish the content and process details of each nearer their time, preferring to remain flexible as your learning needs evolve and the external environment impacting on UK public sector leadership shifts.

2. Learning Group
   This is the major learning transfer vehicle, acting as the leadership ideas and action bridge between learning modules and application to your workplace. Peers from different organizations, parts of organizations and sectors support and challenge each other to define and act on learning goals for each person (defined in the Personal Leadership Development Plan) and for the group as a whole (using Case Study visits and the Learning Group–Leadership Project Plan to deliver the learning for the latter). Your faculty facilitator will assist you in achieving this. At each Learning Group meeting, there should also be opportunities for participants to reflect on their learning from the Learning Modules, and to talk through a critical incident or work issue on which you would like the assistance of the group. During the second year of the program, the group will be encouraged to shift their focus to the development and delivery of a Learning Group–Leadership Project Plan.

3. Personal Leadership Development Plan
   This is the mechanism through which you commit to your new purpose, goals and behavior as a leader and the challenges these hold for you. It enables you to achieve by establishing your goals, clarifying what your learning needs are from Leadership Diagnostics results (see below) and other insights and activities,

negotiating relevant support and resources and agreeing your own 'graduation' criteria with your learning group colleagues. Although we are not prescriptive about how you should write your plans, we would expect them to address, at least, the following areas:

- Where have I come from?
- Where am I now?
- Where am I going?
- How will I get there?
- Who else needs to be involved?
- How will I know when I've arrived?
- What changes will others see?

Learning goals should be SMART:

- Specific – to you and your leadership development needs within the context of LUK and detailing how you will achieve the objective;
- Measurable – in terms of the evidence you will supply to demonstrate your progress;
- Agreed – between you, your line manager (preferable) and Learning Group;
- Realistic – to stretch and challenge you but also to be attainable and
- Time-related – indicating milestones and final dates.

4. Learning Group–Leadership Project Plan
   One of your Learning Group's responsibilities will be to develop and deliver a leadership challenge project that is stretching, worthwhile and achievable in the available time. This should include a whole system perspective by crossing professional, organizational or sector boundaries. Your facilitator will help you in focusing the project aim and goals. As a group, you will be required to make a presentation about the outcomes of your project to the entire LUK cohort at the final Learning Module. An example, for guidance only, is provided below.

Background

The project should:

- Give potential for private sector and third-sector contact/insight
- Explore collaborative leadership
- Allow group members to work autonomously and bring findings together

■ Use sets of individual interviews by group members, exploring an agreed overall question and subquestions.

Those on the M.Sc. would need to write up the project for the M.Sc. and contrast the findings with what the theory says in that area. Therefore, they would also need a 'researchable question' like the example below.

Aims of the project

■ Explore collaborative leadership (public/private/third sector) and benefits, relevance, value of that.
■ Explore especially what private/third sector would regard as valuable/relevant to them (e.g. from cross-sector learning/experience).
■ Report back the findings to Leaders UK. This would give the project real relevance and a genuine 'customer'.

Overall project question

Is collaborative leadership in the public/private/third sectors comparable, and what are the pros and cons of training leaders from these sectors together?

Subquestions for interview

■ What is collaborative leadership?
■ Is it the same in private/public/third sectors in your experience?
■ What can one sector learn from another? Do you have case study examples?
■ In what circumstances does collaborative leadership work and not work?
■ What are the barriers and how do you remove them?
■ What are the characteristics of collaborative leadership (i.e. what is it?)? (We might offer a list that could then be ranked?)
■ How to you develop collaborative leadership?

Project considerations:

■ Theoretical basis for the Project Question
■ Research methodology
■ What we want to achieve by when

5. Case Study Visit

There will be at least one opportunity for your Learning Group to conduct a real-life leadership consultancy visit related to the Learning Modules. This usually involves going into an organization to act as an independent sounding board for a senior management team. Typically, part of the time is spent investigating a particular leadership issue, and a report and/or presentation is produced, which is then delivered to and discussed with the senior management. An example from previous visits, for guidance only, is provided below.

Aims of the visit are:

■ To enable participants to reflect on the content of the Leaders UK program in relation to a live example of a public service organization.

■ Through dialog with key staff in the visited organization, to enhance participants' understanding of leadership challenges within public services.

■ To improve their capacity to 'read' other organizations, summarize their learning and provide constructive feedback to other senior leaders.

■ To develop their capacity to apply this skill in their own setting.

During the program, participants have had opportunities to consider different models and theories in relation to each of the five themes, and to consider their own and their organization's practice in relation to those themes. The visits provide an opportunity to consolidate their learning from the program. A detailed briefing for an example case study visit is set out below.

Leading the Public Service System – Partnership Working
The Case Study task

We are a top performing authority but we still face significant challenges. We are constantly striving to improve the lives of children and young people particularly those in our care, the skills base, employment, business support, access to services, housing, the health and wellbeing of all our residents, the environment that we live in and support our local communities. We are also passionate about tackling deprived areas and reducing inequalities that exist across the County. The County has an agreement with Government, the Local Area Agreement, to work with partners to deliver improved outcomes for residents across all of these issues. We will succeed only through effective collaboration and partnership delivery across the County community delivery system with a wide range of partners in the public, private and Third Sectors. Under the new Comprehensive Area Assessment national performance arrangements (which replaces CPA) not only will the County Council be assessed as an organization but also the area as a whole will be assessed jointly by inspectorates to determine to what extent the area is meeting the priorities, needs and aspirations of residents. CAA will focus on outcomes and the quality of life of local residents from their perspective rather than the separate services as provided by local partners.

The Local Area Agreement and the new Comprehensive Area Assessment tie partners together in a different way and also present the County Council with a significant challenge in leading collaboration and partnership. It requires all partners to not only deliver their own corporate priorities but to reflect County wide priorities whilst doing so. This requires relationships and performance management arrangements across separate organizations (where partners are equal and autonomous) based on honesty, self awareness, constructive challenge and transparency with problems flagged and action taken to address at the appropriate level and at the earliest opportunity.

The questions to address on the Case Study visit, in the context of the Local Area Agreement and the 3 Comprehensive Area Assessment questions, are:

- Thinking about the key challenges to leading collaboration and partnership across a community delivery system, what sorts of things need to be addressed to create proactive and delivery focussed working?
- How can the key challenges be overcome?
- How do you create 'buy in' to a shared partnership vision when partners are complying with statutory requirements and national deadlines; diverse and competing priorities; difficult financial context; and different political/managerial agendas?
- How do you create honesty, self awareness and constructive challenge in partnership performance management arrangements?
- How do you encourage partners to reshape their own priorities to deliver shared objectives?
- How do you create 'collective responsibility' and a joint desire to deliver on LAA priorities amongst partners and what processes/systems could help this?
- What innovative tools and techniques could the County Council use to help deliver effective performance management across partnerships?
- Delegates should be prepared to ask supplementary questions based on their own experience of this type of leadership working. Some additional questions may be raised from reading the papers by John Seddon and Keith Grint, sent out with the Leaders UK programme.

It would be helpful if delegates were familiar with a few items that provide context for the case study. Delegates should read all the background material sent, regardless of which thematic group they will eventually be assigned to.

The Case Study Visit – aim, logistics and reporting back arrangements
Aim

To present evidence-based recommendations to a County Council senior executive team detailing what improvements could be made to the system of delivery via partnership working within and between the four themes of the case study:

■ Personalization
■ Children and Young People
■ Health and Wellbeing
■ Community Safety.

A 1 page supplementary briefing for each of the above will be provided on the morning of the visit before arriving at the County Council

Analysis and recommendations should be provided for each of the themes separately (the Council's thematic work with external partners) and then pulled together in a way which informs the executive about overall performance across the whole delivery system (including the Council's internal partnership working).

6. Leadership Learning Reflection
During the Learning Modules, time is set aside to encourage you to reflect, embed and apply your learning in the moment. Previous cohorts have found this particularly valuable, indicating that learning is often lost without quiet time because of the frantic nature of returning to work. This will be explained and practiced in the first Learning Module. A brief overview of the approach is provided below.

The Thinking-Doing Reflective Sessions
The Learning Modules are about providing you with opportunities to test and develop your own thinking. The Thinking-Doing Sessions are intended to give you the space to do that after the elements of the program where others have shared their ideas with you. The sessions will help you to:

■ Interpret and evaluate ideas
■ Compare your own ideas against others' within the group
■ Decide whether you will adjust your own thinking
■ Decide if and how what you do will change
■ Start to reveal your own existing theories on the subject

You will work in twos or threes for a proportion of the time, each taking a turn to address the following questions:

1. What is my interpretation of the ideas contained in that session?

   Identifying the ideas not evaluating them

2. What will I accept, what will I reject? Why?

   Deciding what you will accept or reject; why – what do you currently believe that means you accept or reject the ideas?

3. Will my thinking change? Why? How?

   How – specify the changes (if any)

4. Will this change what I do? How?

   How will any changes to your thinking change what you do?

7. Leadership Diagnostics (MBTI and SCHOR 360)

   MBTI Step I: The Myers–Briggs Type Indicator Instrument is a powerful and versatile indicator of personality type. It is widely used for individual, group and organizational development. You will have been issued with the questionnaire before the first learning module, where you will receive group feedback.

   SCHOR 360 is the National School of Government's instrument for enabling leaders to understand their personal impact. Its innovative format makes 360° reporting more valuable by being both robust and entirely consistent with Sir Gus O'Donnell's new framework of leadership expectations and the Professional Skills for Government (PSG) skill set.

8. E-site

   Your Leaders UK online community.

   As part of your participation on the Leaders UK program, you will be given access to the Leaders UK online community. Helping you to stay in touch and continue learning together, your Leaders UK online community provides a secure, password-protected area for you to access course materials and information, while networking with your fellow participants.

   You will find handouts, presentations and documents from the program, including joining instructions and web links and a discussion board to help you get the most from your experience at the National School of Government.

   Your Leaders UK community is accessible via our communities area (http://virtual.nationalschool.gov.uk/yourcommunities) where you will need to sign in with your communities account supplied at the start of the program.

The Virtual School

At the National School, we understand that learning must be relevant to your real-life working priorities and reflect the pressures on your time. A powerful and ever-evolving complement to more traditional learning scenarios, the Virtual School is a web-based resource allowing the busy public servant to learn quickly and conveniently at work. The result of pan-government collaboration and designed to meet Professional Skills for Government (PSG) and other standards, Virtual School content includes e-learning packages and materials, online community portals and other services.

All of our e-learning packages require you to register a personal account and sign in so you can track your progress through each package. Most of our e-learning is free to access for public servants, while some of the programs are available through a departmental subscription.

Here are some of the programs that are available to you through the Virtual School site (www.nationalschool.gov.uk/virtualschool):

- Government Select (available through subscription)
- In collaboration with GoodPractice.net – offers just-in-time desktop management resources and tools on themes chosen for their relevance to the work of those in government.
- Understanding the Civil Service (available through subscription)
- A comprehensive online induction program – the result of a cross-government consortium project led by the Ministry of Defence and the National School.
- The Organization Design and Change Framework
- Developed in partnership with DWP, this package will you to develop your organizational development capability, specifically in designing organizations and implementing changes that will achieve successful outcomes and sustainable performance. This package is freely available to Civil Servants.
- Protecting Information
- Free to access for all public servants. Developed by a cross-departmental consortium led by Cabinet Office, this course will provide you with a comprehensive guide to why information is important, the risks to its safety and what you can do to protect it.
- Finance for All
- A free, foundation-level, modular e-learning scheme developed through collaboration between the National School and HM Treasury.
- Analysis and Use of Evidence
- Provides assessment tools, free of charge, so that senior civil servants and staff working at Grade 7 (or equivalent) can test their knowledge in this PSG key skill and identify further learning.

- Successful Delivery
- Developed with the Office of Government Commerce – a free program based on PSG competencies for those requiring a broad understanding of program management.
- Managing Learning and Development
- Draws on UK and Australian public sector experience to provide learning and development professionals with a self-assessment checklist for their organizations, accompanied by recommendations for action.
- Risk and Risk Management (available through subscription)
- A subscription training program developed with PricewaterhouseCoopers
- LLP – introduces risk management, covers the key elements of a risk management framework and introduces the concepts of risk maturity and embedding risk management.
- Awareness of the Human Rights Act
- A free program covering the practical implications of the Act in a variety of contexts.
- PRIME: Leadership
- Designed specifically for government officials occupying or aspiring to senior management positions, this free program offers over 20 hours of e-learning on leadership, partnerships, strategic thinking and change and organizational learning.

9. Mentoring
    If you do not already have a coach or mentor, you are encouraged to find your own for the duration of LUK. We do have access to a pool, which is constantly changing, should you want us to assist you in finding a suitable match, although we cannot guarantee this. All proposed mentors are asked to complete the form below, having read the mentoring criteria notes first.

10. Cross-sector leadership learning experiences
    From time to time, we receive requests for LUK participants to take part in secondment opportunities. These will be circulated to the whole cohort and taken up on a strictly first-come-first-served basis.

11. Delegate Liaison Group
    There will be frequent opportunities for you to provide us with individual feedback about your LUK learning experience. You can also raise issues publicly or privately with individual faculty members at any time. In addition, Learning Groups are asked to nominate a Learning Group member to explore

more formally with the Faculty how we might improve the program. This group will meet at Learning Module events to identify program and content-related issues, and to discuss general matters arising from your participation in LUK.

12. M.Sc. (optional)

Through Leaders UK, the University of Birmingham offers participants the opportunity to register for the M.Sc. in Public Management. Further details will be provided for those students who wish to register for accreditation on completion of the Postgraduate Application Form.

Once we have processed your application form, you will be registered on the M.Sc. in Public Management program and have access to the UK Library Services, the support of a personal tutor and the services available to registered students of the University of Birmingham. Students will receive program and module handbooks and hand in dates for the completion of assessed work. Participants will need to plan time for private study and are encouraged to contact their tutors as and when they need support (by email as well as face to face). The University offers excellent services to support postgraduate students (including the library services with highly developed remote computer access).

LUK Graduation

You graduate from Leaders UK following what we might best term a critical dialog with your fellow Learning Group colleagues. You will need to demonstrate to your colleagues your leadership learning over the program as evidenced or developed in your own portfolio. This dialog takes place in the final Learning Group session. Having listened to your learning journey and engaged in a series of critical challenges to your reflections, the Learning Group itself decides whether you have engaged sufficiently in the program to graduate. Members of the Faculty do not assess your learning; rather we welcome a more collective group assessment of your personal development by those you have worked with closely in learning groups over two years.

Graduation takes place at a one-day Celebration Event when participants 'graduating' from the scheme will be presented with their certificates. Your sponsor(s) will be invited. It is an opportunity to present some of your work directly to sponsors and to reflect upon individual and collective learning over the course of the program.

Leaders UK is now approaching the intake of its 5th cohort and continues to adapt to government priorities, for example cross cutting Public Service Agreements attempting to join together separate government departments activities and outputs to deliver improved UK community outcomes.

Case 4

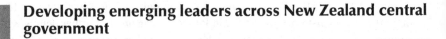

Developing emerging leaders across New Zealand central government

The Leadership Development Centre is in the business of developing public sector leadership capability.

It achieves this through a range of means, including:

■ Direct development of senior managers who are current and future leaders,

■ Indirect means, such as support for agency leadership development programs and

■ Influencing the development environment through research and promotion of leadership ideas.

Purpose and Key Roles

The case describes two original change leader development initiatives arising from two strategic New Zealand Public Service (NZPS) imperatives ('Report of the Advisory Group on the Review of the Centre', presented to the Ministers of State Services and Finance, November 2001). These are:

1. The need to prepare talented managers for more complex roles and improve the planning and development of the chief executive succession pool within the New Zealand Public Service (NZPS).

2. The message that government agencies representing the NZPS should strengthen collaborative ventures and working approaches to deliver on national goals set by the Government.

It is possible to view the focus of the first of these as building the individual capability of emerging leaders, combined with the assessment of their potential, whilst the second speaks to the goal of strengthening strategic leadership and performance capability throughout the service.

To address these imperatives, a twofold intervention was developed by the authors in conjunction with the Management Development Centre (MDC) – the forerunner of the Leadership Development Centre. The first was a Development Centre (the

Centre for Individual Management Development), designed to explore and stimulate the leadership potential of senior manager participants.

The second was a collective Leadership Program, constructed to develop the capabilities of existing leaders and reframe their thinking about their leadership role and contribution.

The overarching purpose of both programs is to contribute to NZPS strategy by developing potential leaders within a new NZPS culture that can deliver leadership at all levels, and provide cost-effective joined-up government services to the New Zealand public.

As a first step, the design group framed the strategic context for the initiatives as an attempt to shift the NZPS from 'old management culture' to 'new leadership culture', along similar lines to those described by Braich and Richardson (2001). The new capability foci and levers of this NZPS leadership and performance culture change proposition are detailed in Table 7.7 below. To support the growth of this new culture, and to make a significant contribution to the dual strategic imperatives, the CIMD was built as a 'learning centre', a new format positioned as a 'fourth generation' extension of the historical Development Centre design frameworks outlined by Griffiths & Goodge (1994) (see Table 7.8).

DESIGN FEATURES OF THE 'LEARNING CENTRE'

Examples of the additional 'fourth generation' 'learning centre' design features employed in the CIMD are represented in Table 7.9.

As is standard practice in assessment/development centres, the design was informed by a set of leader/leadership competencies. These were defined by the design team as critical for the strategic aims of the NZPS. They are summarized in the following table. The difference here is that the competencies were produced within a conceptual framework that integrated them to form an idealized and aspirational view of a NZPS chief executive role.

NZPS Leader/Leadership Competencies

The eight competencies fit naturally into three interdependent categories:
Strategy and purpose:

1. Strategic leadership
2. Leading capability building

This competency group indicates how attuned people are to the wider environment within which they operate, with a particular focus on developing strategy and human capability within and for the NZPS.

Table 7.7 CIMD & NZPS Leadership Program Value proposition – Driving the NZPS leadership culture and performance forward

From	To
Capability focus	Capability focus
■ Individual agency development strategy	■ Building whole of NZPS capability
■ Tactical and operational management development	■ Strategic change leadership learning
■ Managers of distinct functions	■ Leaders of strategic systems, processes and integrative projects
■ Partial focus on critical issues by single agencies	■ Systemic problem solving using multiple agency solutions
■ Reliance on raising organizational performance through measurement	■ Driving performance upward by sharing knowledge and best practice outcome achievement
■ Intra-agency relationships	■ Inter-agency relationships and networking
Capability levers	Capability levers
■ External course attendance by few	■ Learning organization facilitation for many
■ Passive learning or learning by osmosis	■ Active learning through the experience of leading real strategic change
■ Wait and see mechanistic succession planning	■ Active support of talented peoples' self-driven career and development management
■ Fishing for leadership capability	■ Hunting and then herding a talent pool
■ Chief executive role as the end of the learning process	■ Chief executive role – a transition point in lifelong learning, including work as coach or mentor to others
■ Ex-officios as retirees	■ Utilization as sages and mentors for other generations of NZPS leaders

Implementation and delivery:

3. Leading political/stakeholder interface and alignment
4. Leading change

Table 7.8 Characteristics of development centre design

	First generation	Second generation	Third generation
Participant involvement	Minimal – participants simply take tests	Feedback to participants at end of centre, sometimes after each exercise	Joint decision making on competencies displayed after each exercise
Exercises and tests	Off-the-shelf exercises and tests	Mainly off-the-shelf exercises and tests	Mainly real-life business problems
Development planning	Little – perhaps part of centre feedback	Some time given on the centre to planning with monitoring and support afterwards	More time given on the centre with significant monitoring and mentoring afterwards

These competencies represent the application and implementation of strategy within the political and organizational context.

Relationship and culture:

5. Intellectual leadership
6. Leading culture building
7. Building relationships, communications and reputation
8. Building personal learning and development

These elements concentrate on a more personal set of skills and behaviors.

Each competency area plays a part in reaching the potential of a strategic project or initiative. For instance, relationships determine the acceptance of strategy that in turn drives implementation. The integration of competencies appropriate to the environment and situation generates the energy, the 'X' factor that becomes the distinguishing mark of the individual chief executive and/or the leadership team.

To reinforce the new leadership cultural and performance drivers for the NZPS, the CIMD is in essence an experiential leader/leadership learning process that

Table 7.9 Some characteristics of 'fourth generation' 'learning centre' design principles employed in the CIMD

	Fourth generation 'learning centre'
Participant involvement	Open-book approach to centre material, scenarios and competencies (with one surprise for assessing some 'change leadership' competencies). Participants are encouraged to bring extra leadership and strategic topic material with them, can access more if required whilst at the centre and are asked to share it with fellow participants.
Exercises and tests	All scenarios are linked to produce a 'week in the life' of a chief executive and address a live strategic leadership issue that the business and sector is facing. Focus is on providing strategic, tactical and operational solutions generated individually and in teams. Participants own the leader psychometric results, which are not seen by observers, and build these in to their own career thinking.
Development planning	Participants are encouraged to profile themselves against the competencies before, during and after the centre using learning partners. Participants build a development solutions bank over time for ideas on exploiting strengths and building from weakness. Peer feedback is used during the centre. Participants prepare their own assessment and development report prior to feedback.
Leadership learning	Learning to learn about leadership using different media and sources: academic journals, business publications, peers, ex-chief executives is an integral part. Community of interest is established by involving current and ex-stakeholders in the centre, in this case: senior government ministers, ex-Parliamentarians of different political persuasions, current affairs journalists, current chief executives (as observers), private sector chief executives. The scenario link topic is a live strategic issue of concern to everyone and has immediate relevance for the participants with high face validity (i.e. people capability building). Corporate and operational mix of participants forces exploration of the links between strategy, tactics and operational implementation. Participants produce a working document to take back to their organization and are encouraged to live with the subject matter using centre peers in informal 'action learning' sets (Pedler, 1991).

(Continued)

Table 7.9 Continued

	Fourth generation 'learning centre'
Career options insight	Participants are encouraged to share career stories with all the contributors to the centre (over 30 people at all stages of career as a leader). This also creates an immediate career network. Corporate and operational mix of participants offers exposure to different career paths. Values and emotional intelligence are combined with a personality type measure within the context of 'Is this the role I really want'?

provides peer challenge, self-revelation and team learning in a safe environment. The design is set within the context of the future NZPS: its environment and national issues, its ethos, ethics, cooperative action and consultation. The design team set new expectations for both participants and observers by creating a cultural 'spirit' for the CIMD that mirrors this future organizational philosophy and culture. This is reflected in the following principles for the centre (which are made explicit to all participants). The culture principles (based on the value proposition in Table 7.7), as communicated to the participants and their observers, are shown in Table 7.10 below.

In essence, the overall philosophy of this 'learning centre' (which we believe illustrates a 'fourth generation' design) may be summarized as follows:

(i) The CIMD is a learning environment designed to support participants and for you each of them to support their colleagues.

(ii) The people capability theme is designed to stretch and build participants' strategic, tactical and operational thinking and action planning in different ways.

(iii) The outputs are intended to be of benefit to each and every stakeholder.

(iv) The design and construction is based on highly contextual simulations to expedite learning transfer.

(v) All the data, development techniques and coaching principles are passed to participants – this is an open-book experience.

The context within which this philosophy is implemented is one in which the intention is to share learning and experience to build you and your colleagues capability of each participant, both as individual leaders and as part of a leadership collective. In doing this, high-performance teamwork focused on stretching and relevant strategic NZPS tasks is paramount. It follows that participants will be working with each other for continuous engagement on thorny common strategic

Table 7.10 CIMD 'learning centre' culture principles

Principle	Statements
Leaders drive development	– We have built a leadership learning vehicle for you, but you have to drive it to receive the benefits – The most effective leaders seek out and convert learning stretch experiences, of which the CIMD is just one learning event – Leaders learn by asking themselves, who am I as leader, how can I add value to those I work with, from whom can I learn about myself? – Experience of the CIMD indicates that the greater the drive for learning amongst participants, the higher the quality of outputs – The CIMD has already demonstrated that it can release leadership potential, take personal responsibility for team process and own your own behavior – Put in as much reflective effort as you can, leadership and high performance teamwork is about the process of continuous learning about each other's ways of operating, as well as content outputs
Real tasks with real expectations	– Although the scenarios are built to simulate some days in the life of a Chief Executive, this is not role-playing – The observers, guest speakers and visiting Parliamentarians/Chief Executives will want to see you demonstrate high-quality thinking and outcomes from the tasks you are asked to carry out – The CIMD is learning by doing!
Leadership opportunities abound	– No one will present you with a leadership baton – Emergent leadership combined with appropriate followership can be demonstrated in the team exercises as well as the three individual scenarios – Building other peoples leadership is just as important as building your own – Focus more on creating a high-performance learning team along the lines spelled out by Katzenbach (1998) – Try some new leadership techniques, better to rehearse them here than in real life – Challenge the orthodoxy – freshness of ideas and approaches will be welcomed

(*Continued*)

Table 7.10 Continued

Principle	Statements
Your country needs you	– The people capability building theme at national level has been endorsed by the Prime Minister – The link between this and the NZPS is critical, explore it fully – No matter what the focus or size of your organization, as a potential chief executive you need to address people capability – make linkages with each other in utilizing this finite resource – Leadership around building your own capability alongside that of others you work with is self-sustaining and enhances your ability to continuously deliver to your stakeholders, clients and customers

issues. To achieve the desired outcomes, it is also essential that participants understand that competition on ideas is required, not between people. If new behaviors and mind-sets are to be acquired, it is also essential that participants are encouraged to use the 'learning centre' as a chance to experiment with different leadership tools/techniques and leader skill and style tactics. The second component of the change leadership development package is now described.

DESIGN FEATURES OF THE 'LEADERSHIP PROGRAM'

Kaore he mutunga mo nga akoranga reo me nga tikanga a te iwi Maori.

There is no end to learning (of Maori language & culture).

By the end of the formal development program, lasting approximately nine months, participants will have strived to meet the following objectives:

■ Identified and progressed their stage of development as a leader.

■ Put in place strategies to continuously improve personal and organizational effectiveness.

■ Sourced, assembled and used a range of leadership concepts, tools and techniques.

■ Lead a change leadership project, certainly for their own organization and perhaps the NZPS.

■ Actively contributed to the development of learning peers and work colleagues.

■ Enhanced their own performance and alongside this the capability of their team, organization and operating environment.

■ Learned how to continuously lead and influence the NZPS at a strategic level.

The unique principles of this leadership program:

■ Weaves together best practice leadership concepts, tools and techniques, introduced by influential speakers from around the world, within the context of NZ and the NZPS.

■ Uses real NZ and NZPS experiences and case studies, delivered by the people responsible for them.

■ Utilizes and enhances MDC leadership resources and NZPS learning networks.

■ Concentrates on putting personal leadership and leadership knowledge into action.

■ Places the onus on the participant to drive their own and others leadership development, with the support of coaching and mentoring, where sought and available.

■ Develops six critical personal effectiveness levers.

■ Tasks participants to produce demonstrable evidence of leadership behavior change alongside identifiable development of their own organization and perhaps the NZPS.

■ Results in a tangible strategic consultancy input for the sponsoring organization.

The program stages and timeline are set out in Figure 7.2 below.

The formal input consisted of five 1-day primer modules as described below:

DAY 1 – Module 1: Worldwide leadership trends and the New Zealand context

Summary: Leadership trends, NZPS purpose and context, leader development processes.

DAY 2 – Module 2: Personal leadership

Summary: Leadership and teams, leader self-knowledge, vision, values, culture and reputation building as key strategic leadership tools.

DAY 3 – Module 3: The strategic change leader

Summary: Producing personal and organizational strategies for different forms of stakeholder/customer relationships, clarifying change leadership roles/approaches.

DAY 4 – Module 4: Change leadership toolkit

Summary: Change leadership tools, techniques and best practice (personal, organizational and across the NZPS), including people capability building approaches.

DAY 5 – Module 5: Creating the future – NZPS leadership in action

Summary: NZPS leadership – future perspectives and action plans to enhance your value to stakeholders and customers.

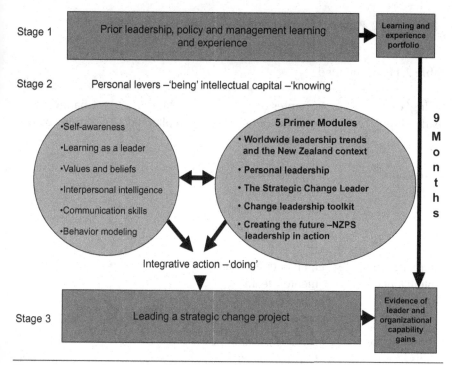

Figure 7.2 MDC – Leadership Program 'Leading in the NZPS – a Personal Journey'.

Table 7.11 Personal levers and sources of evidence

'Being' of leadership	Examples of potential data sources	Data collected	Change actions by me
Self-awareness	EI; 360° comparative results; mentor; Belbin Team Role (validated by team peers); CIMD; LP peers; partner		
Leader as learner	Learning journey milestones, achievements and plans ('knowing' gaps); action learning; completing this portfolio		

(Continued)

Table 7.11 Continued

'Being' of leadership	Examples of potential data sources	Data collected	Change actions by me
Values and beliefs	Career anchors; your own leadership philosophy; team climate and culture surveys		
Interpersonal intelligence	EI; LP peer feedback; mentor; team climate and culture surveys		
Communication skills	360° feedback; LP peer feedback; coach; team vision, focus and outcomes		
Behavior modeling	360° feedback; LP peer feedback; team climate and culture; mentor; 'doing'		

For working on personal change, participants were encouraged to address the six personal development levers described in Figure 7.3 and Table 7.11 above, which explains how to capture and measure the learning gained for 'being'.

An example of a development plan for the above is included below .

Development goals: six critical personal effectiveness levers

A. Self-awareness (I know myself – my identity matches my reputation)
I will continue to reflect on my performance, past and present, to fine-tune my understanding of myself, consciously enhance strengths and develop the rest (interpersonal skills that allow maximum development for team members including risk-managed delegation; consolidate confidence in intuitive decisions; be an enabling coordinator/leader).

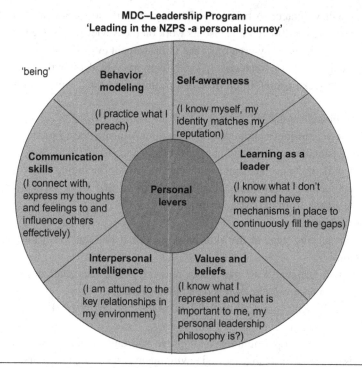

Figure 7.3 Personal development levers defined.

- I will seek specific feedback from past and present team members. I will seek specific feedback during MDC coaching sessions, and from group members.
- I will be looking for specific feedback on my reputation to check against my own view of self, looking for confirmation as well as evidence of instances where I may have acted 'against type'.
- By December 2002, I will be able to describe myself with greater accuracy, and point to specific development.

B. Learning as a Leader (I know what I don't know and have mechanisms in place to continuously fill the gaps)

Organizational issues – my own and NZPS-wide
I want to deepen my understanding of my own Ministry's formal and informal structures and processes; add to my knowledge of other agencies and sustain and extend contact networks on issues of organizational improvement.

- I will continue to learn in the key project context, and offer myself as a continuing resource to the management post-July 2002.

■ I will volunteer to be involved in my organization's Statement of Intent exercise for 2003/04 FY; also its work on the Review of the Centre.

■ I will join as many organizational improvement events as possible.

■ I will sustain my relationships with (corporate) leaders/managers.

■ I will seek material from MDC on upcoming seminars, events, resources etc.

Management/leadership

I want to contribute to the development of a Ministry 'best practice' template for divisional managers and in my own division.

■ I will trial new management/leadership ideas (including from the MDC course) with ENV team and practice those that work (seeking specific feedback from DSP3 and team).

Plugging gaps

I want to plug gaps in my skill base, including looking to my future career options.

■ I will connect with the Maori network and issues, and develop better personal knowledge of te reo and tikanga Maori.

■ I will seek opportunities to improve my Spanish (keeping posting options open).

■ I will seek opportunities to improve my understanding of trade policy issues (e.g. through trade and environment agenda, a short course).

By December 2002, I will have checked off all the above, and set new goals for learning in 2003.

C. Values and Beliefs (I know what I represent and what is important to me, my personal leadership philosophy and beliefs are...)

How will you ensure that these are made obvious to those who work for/with you?

■ Results

■ Quality

■ Hard work

■ Work/life balance

■ Respect

■ Responsibility

■ Fairness

■ Credit as soon as credit is due

■ Deal effectively (fast) with shortfalls in performance

■ Diversity – not sure what you mean by this?

The above will be touchstones for me this year, to be reviewed and adjusted when needed. I will aim to add authentic values that emerge from progress toward my development goals.

D. Interpersonal Intelligence (I am attuned to the key relationships in my environment)

I will strengthen my ability to relate well up, down, sideways, internally and externally and want to develop more 'quiet' in my approach to team members, especially those who might find me a hard taskmaster.

■ I will spend more time listening to and guiding my team, and resist reverting to the 'technical expert'. This will challenge my team to take maximum responsibility for their issues and the quality of their results, and develop their capacities for good judgment/decision making. I will be looking for feedback that says 'he/she delegates work and trusts us to deliver'.

■ I will treat seriously and spend time exploring with team members their hopes and aspirations (and not just for work) and actively guide/assist where I can. I will be looking for feedback that says 'he/she supports – with words and deeds – my progress within this Ministry and beyond'.

■ I will improve my effectiveness with Maori staff by learning how to create the best environment for their development and success. I will be looking for feedback that says 'he/she understands, respects and supports Maori staff development in this Ministry'.

This conversion of goals into what others would say (your reputation) is superb.

By December 2002, I will have checked off all the above and set new goals for learning in 2003.

E. Communication Skills (I connect with, express my thoughts and feelings to and influence others effectively)

I want to learn how to influence more subtly/indirectly so that team members have more ownership of decisions reached.

■ I will lead more than direct team members to the right approaches and decisions

Concentrate on why and what leaving your team to look after how and when?

■ I will prepare for significant meetings with team members by 'thinking in their shoes beforehand' and tuning my approach sensitively: Why not let them help you with the preparation and rotate the meeting leadership responsibility?

■ I will trial different ways of influencing Ministers, tuned to their 'learning' styles.

I will keep a checklist of my 'hit rate' to allow me to tune my approach to each individual team member/Minister.

Behavior modeling (I practice what I preach)

I will be a good match to my values and beliefs, and consciously measure these against those of my organization.

■ I will deal quickly, thoughtfully and effectively with situations where these are at risk or compromised whether by my own or others' behavior.

■ I will be looking for specific feedback on my reputation to check against my own view of self, looking for confirmation as well as any instances where I may have acted 'against type' and learn from the latter.

By December 2002, I will be able to describe myself with greater accuracy, and point to specific development.

The LDC programmes continue to be evaluated and shaped in light of shifting sector and customer demands, whilst much of the original design work continues to inform learning process alterations.

This concludes the description of some example cases reflecting a variety of applications of our core principles and practices for developing change leaders. We now turn to some important considerations for the organization in how it sets about evaluating change leadership development activity, wider considerations of who such development should be for and an overall framework for embarking on the development of change leaders.

References

Aitken, P. (2007). Walking the talk – the nature and role of leadership culture within organisation culture/s. Summer. *Journal of General Management, 32*(4).

Anderson, D. L. (2002). Dialogism and organisational change: Discourse and intertextuality in a high-tech corporation. *Ph.D thesis*. University of Colorado at Boulder.

Barrios-Choplin, B., McCarty, R., & Cryer, B. (1997). An inner quality approach to reducing stress and improving physical and emotional well-being at work. *Stress Medicine, 13*(3), 103–201.

Boje, D. M. (2001). *Narrative methods for organisational and communication research.* Thousand Oaks, CA: Sage.

Bolden, R., & Gosling, J. (July 2003). Leadership, society and the next ten years. *Report for the Windsor Leadership trust*, Centre for Leadership Studies, University of Exeter.

Boydell, T. (2005). Leadership development: current practice, future perspectives. Corporate Research Forum.

Braich, R., & Richardson, G. (2001). Emerging Leaders – a new approach to developing leadership talent February 2001. *Selection and Development Review, 17*(1).

Cammock, P. (2003). *The dance of leadership* (2nd ed.). Prentice Hall.

Clemens and Meyer (1999).

Collins, J. (2001). *Good to great*. Random House.

Drucker, P. F. (2004, June). What makes an effective executive. *Harvard Business Review, 6*, 59–63.

Fowler, J. W. (1981). *Stages of faith: The psychology of human development and the quest for meaning*. San Franciso, CA: HarperCollins.

Frey, C. (2008). Action learning intervention in a change context and commitment to organisational change. *Unpublished Henley Working Paper*, Henley Management College.

Fullan, M. (2001). *Leading in a culture of change*. San Franciso, CA: Jossey-Bass.

Gardner, W. L., & Avolio, B. J. (1998). The charismatic relationship: A dramaturgical perspective. *Academy of Management Review*, *23*, 32–58.

Goleman, D., Boyatzis, R., & McKee, A. (2001, December). Primal leadership. *Harvard Business Review, Breakthrough Leadership*, 42–51.

Grint, K. (2001). *The arts of leadership*. Oxford: Oxford University Press.

Griffiths, P., & Goodge, P. (1994). Development centres: The third generation. *Personnel Management*.

Jackson, B., & Parry, K. (2008). *A very short, fairly interesting and reasonably cheap book about studying leadership*. Sage.

Kabat-Zinn, J. (1990). *Full catastrophe living. How to cope with stress, pain and illness using mindfulness meditation*. London: Paitkus.

Kouzes, J. M., & Posner, B. Z. (Apr 1988). The leadership challenge Chicago, (2 pages). *Success*, *35*(3), 68.

Kouzes, J. M., & Posner, B. Z. (Apr 1988). The leadership challenge Chicago, (2 pages). *Success*, *35*(3), 68.

Michael, C. M. (Sep 2004). Stop wasting valuable time Boston. *Harvard Business Review*, *82*(9), 58.

Michalko, M. (2001). *Cracking creativity: The secrets of creative genius for business and beyond*. Berkeley, CA: Ten Speed Press.

McIntyre, M. G. (1999). Five ways to turn your management team into a leadership team. *The Journal for Quality and Participation*, *22*(4), 40–44.

Mumford, M. D., & Van Doorn, J. (2001). The leadership of pragmatism: Reconsidering Franklin in the age of charisma. *Leadership Quarterly*, *12*, 279–310.

Nohria, N., Joyce, W., & Roberson, B. (2003). What really works. *Harvard Business Review*, *July*, 43–52.

Parks, S. D. (2000). *Big questions, worthy dreams: Mentoring young adults in their search for meaning, purpose and faith*. San Francisco, CA: Jossey-Bass.

Parry, K. W., & Bryman, A. (2006). Leadership in organisations. In S. Clegg, C. Hardy, & W. Nord (Eds.), *Handbook of organisation studies* (2nd ed., pp. 447–468). London: Sage.

Pedler, M. (1991). *A managers guide to self-development*. Maidenhead: McGraw-Hill.

Pinker, S. (1997). *How the mind works*. New York: Norton.

Sanders, J. E., Hopkins, W. E., & Geroy, G. D. (2003). From transactional to transcendental: Toward an integrated theory of leadership. Spring. *Journal of Leadership and Organisational Studies*, *9*(4), 21–31.

Sandlin, R. T. (1992). *Rehabilitation of virtue: Foundations of moral education*. New York: Praeger.

Segal, Z. V., Williams, J. M. G., & Teasdale, J. D. (2002). *Mindfulness-based cognitive therapy for depression*. London: The Guildford Press.

Starratt, R. J. (1993). *The drama of leadership*. London: Falmer Press.

Thompson, M. C. (2000). *The congruent life: Following the inward path to fulfilling work and inspired leadership*. San Franscisco, CA: Jossey Bass.

Part 3

Organizational Considerations

Introduction

In Part 2 we focused on exploring approaches to developing change leadership capability. However, it is also important to consider the context in which the development is occurring. Part 1 set a fairly broad context for change leadership development in terms of general drivers of change and implementation challenges. Part 3 of this book examines specific organizational considerations.

Within an organization there is always a debate around the overall value of any developmental intervention. This is no different in respect of change leadership development. Chapter 8 in Part 3 focuses on issues relating to the evaluation of change leadership development interventions. In particular it explores the metrics which can be used in evaluation. Measurement is always a challenge; particularly identifying metrics which are meaningful and we explore ways in which the challenge may be met. Throughout we emphasize that the focus needs to be on assessing the impact of the change leadership development on change implementation through people. We also argue that metrics should be used throughout the development process to review progress and provide data which can be incorporated into the process in the form of a feedback loop, which we represent in our framework for change leadership development in Chapter 10.

Developing change leadership capability effectively requires considerable investment of time, effort and resources. It is important this investment is protected in terms of retaining the capability within the organization and ensuring it is deployed in areas in which optimum value can be added. Chapter 9 explores this challenge as one aspect of a broader talent-management strategy for the organization. It draws on research into talent management and lessons from organizational practice. Against the broader talent-management background the chapter examines how change leadership talent can be integrated with a talent strategy, together with considerations of the balance between line management and HR function accountabilities.

Chapter 10 in Part 3 presents an overall framework for considering change leadership development which builds on the interactive model outlined in Chapter 1. The interplay between change leaders and their context is examined through exploring a range of questions relating to leadership components and organizational context in terms of:

(i) What do we need?

(ii) How do we assess what we have (and potentially have)?

(iii) How do we use this assessment?

(iv) How do we change contextual factors to support new behaviors?

(v) How do we build leaders' capabilities to understand and respond to the dynamic between their practices and the organizational context?

Evaluating the Impact of Change Leadership Development

The quality of a leader is reflected in the standards they set for themselves.

Ray Croc (1902–1984)

Introduction

Sometimes what counts cannot be counted, and what can be counted does not count, although in the case of change leadership development it would be remiss not to try. Many companies find the market is valuing them much more, or less, than the sum of their net tangible assets. The importance of intangible assets such as brands, relationships, knowledge and communication technologies continues to grow and central to this is leadership of people. For a full account of approaches to assessing 'people value' see Print (2004).

Leadership is regarded as the key enabler in the European Foundation for Quality Management (EFQM) Business Excellence Model (EFQM, 2000) and therefore central to private, public and third-sector development initiatives. However, little attention has been paid to the impact of leadership development programs for measuring return on investment (ROI) beyond the Kirkpatrick (2006) evaluation model below. Although there is enormous annual global expenditure on leadership development, very little attention is generally paid to evaluating what 'change' actually takes place as a result. For example, all our case studies mention the aim of moving an organization's or sector's culture in a different direction, either explicitly (which is a good start) or implicitly (which is not clear enough), without determining in advance of the program what 'impact' measures will be applied to assess program developers and their participants.

In this chapter, we outline examples of change measures which can be applied at the individual, team, relational and organizational levels, so providing a menu for a more appropriate and comprehensive evaluation process which the change leaders themselves can initiate, track and review.

THE KIRKPATRICK EVALUATION MODEL

(http://www.cipd.co.uk/train/in-company/_progs/_kpevalmdl?cssversion=printable)

1. *Reaction*: how participants have reacted to the program
2. *Learning*: what participants have learnt from the program
3. *Behavior*: whether what was learnt is being applied on the job
4. *Results*: whether that application is achieving results

Level 1: Reaction

Testing the initial reactions of the participants to the program. It is important that we gain a favorable reaction in order that participants are motivated to learn. Potential ways this could be tested:

- Program evaluation sheets
- Face-to-face interviews
- General participant comments throughout the program.

Level 2: Learning

Measures the extent to which participants are learning in line with program objectives such as increase in skill or knowledge, change of attitude and/or behavior, early application of new learning. Potential ways this could be tested:

- Individual preprogram and postprogram tests for comparisons
- Observations and feedback by tutors, line managers and/or peers
- Assessment of action-based learning such as role plays and work-based projects.

Level 3: Behavior

Measures the extent to which a change in behavior has occurred, as a result of the program. Potential ways this could be tested:

- Individual preprogram and postprogram tests or surveys
- Observations and feedback from others
- Focus groups to gather quick useful information and knowledge sharing
- Face-to-face interviews.

Level 4: Results

Measures the final results that have been achieved because of the learning acquired from the program. Includes final evaluation of the program objectives. Potential indicators:

Tangible results

- Reduced costs
- Increased sales
- Increased profitability
- Reduction in employee turnover over a set period.

In-tangible results

- Positive change in management style
- Increase in engagement levels of direct reports
- Positive changes in general behavior
- Favorable feedback from peers, subordinates, customers.

A systematic review of all the literature on poor adoption of promising practices across UK organizations by The Advanced Institute of Management Research, e.g. Total Quality Management (TQM), supply-chain partnering, discovered the primary enablers of take up included commitment from top management and levels of motivation and involvement of the workforce plus, most prominently, nurturing a culture where employees were open to change and motivated to try new ways of working. Any Boardroom conversation seeking assistance with change invariably ends up focusing on leadership and employee engagement.

However, the fact that 59% of UK leaders dismiss the need for formal leadership-management training (UK Leadership Forecast 2005/2006, CIPD and DDI) means the improvement agenda may not sit highly on the list of change leaders' priorities at a time when almost a third of UK employees do not feel engaged by their employers ('What people want', Trades Union Congress – YouGov survey reported in The Independent on 1/9/2008). It is therefore rare for leaders to have a clear set of less tangible change measures which they can use to track their developmental progress when executing strategic shifts.

But on such a business journey, how might change leaders prove to themselves and skeptical onlookers that their personal and organizational change actions are bearing the desired fruit? In effect, the data sources listed below make the intangibles tangible, the implicit explicit and assist with tracking leaders' attempts to secure competitive advantage through people via change leadership development.

Impact diagnostics

The diagnostics listed below can be used as forms of evidence to assess movement in the deeper personal and organizational culture programming as change leadership unfolds, where this 'people glue' holds together the connections between organizational purpose, strategy and business plan performance. They are listed according to their suitability for use at the individual, team, relational and organizational levels. Before describing these, we begin with an overall measure of ROI on the considerable sums spent on developing change leaders:

Evidence of transfer of change intervention learning from training/development programs back to the workplace.

Most organizations invest 1%–4% of total payroll in staff training. Sometimes, the figure is even higher. Associated costs and time add to the total investment. Despite this major investment, research shows that most organizations rarely go beyond basic evaluation of training, so they do not know the actual return. When they do undertake an evaluation, organizations frequently set out to simply 'prove' what they want to know – to give credence that the current training is on the mark. They do not get an accurate picture, they get a 'positive spin' that is ultimately useless in driving successful learning transfer in the long run. Even more disturbing, evaluation that does take place often shows that a mere 10%–20% of what is learned actually results in changed on-the-job behavior. Learning transfer seldom takes place effectively and much of the investment is wasted. Figure 8.1 outlines 8 measurable factors which make up the Learning Transfer Evaluation tool.

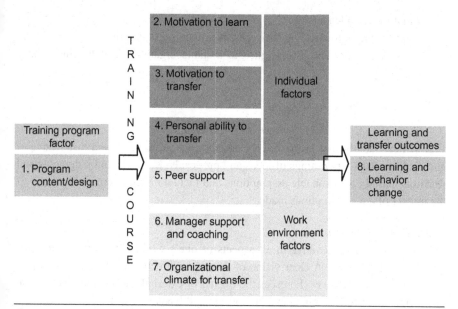

Figure 8.1   The Learning Transfer Evaluation model together with its eight evaluation factors.
Source: Concordia International Ltd.

INDIVIDUAL MEASURES

Without some way of assessing personal behavior change in becoming a more effective change leader over time, it will be difficult to justify anyone's involvement in development. For the person undergoing change development, identifying a clear start point is also necessary.

A The 'Leadership Dimensions Questionnaire' (the Emotional Dimensions – EQ were covered in Chapter 3)

Three different change leadership styles are identified within Higgs and Dulewicz's model:

(i) Engaging leadership

   A style based on a high level of empowerment and involvement appropriate in a highly transformational context. Such a style is focused on producing radical change with high levels of engagement and commitment.

(ii) Involving leadership

   A style that is based on a transitional organization that faces significant but not radical changes in its business model or 'modus operandi'.

(iii) Goal-oriented leadership
A style that is focused on delivering results within a relatively stable context. This is a leader-led style aligned to a stable organization delivering clearly understood results.

Intellectual dimensions (IQ)

A Critical Analysis and Judgment
A critical faculty that probes the facts, identifies advantages and disadvantages and discerns the shortcomings of ideas and proposals. Makes sound judgments and decisions based on reasonable assumptions and factual information, and is aware of the impact of any assumptions made.

B Vision and Imagination
Imaginative and innovative in all aspects of one's work. Establishes sound priorities for future work. A clear vision of the future direction of the organization to meet business imperatives. Foresees the impact of external and internal changes on one's vision that reflect implementation issues and business realities.

C Strategic Perspective
Sees the wider issues and broader implications. Explores a wide range of relationships, balances short- and long-term considerations. Sensitive to the impact of one's actions and decisions across the organization. Identifies opportunities and threats. Sensitive to stakeholders' needs, external developments and the implications of external factors on one's decisions and actions.

Managerial dimensions (MQ)

D Resource Management
Plans ahead, organizes all resources and coordinates them efficiently and effectively. Establishes clear objectives. Converts long-term goals into action plans. Monitors and evaluates staff's work regularly and effectively, and gives them sensitive and honest feedback.

K Engaging Communication
A lively and enthusiastic communicator, engages others and wins support. Clearly communicates instructions and vision to staff. Communications are tailored to the audience's interests and are focused. Approach inspires staff and audiences. Communication style conveys approachability and accessibility.

L Empowering
Knows one's direct report's strengths and weaknesses. Gives them autonomy, encourages them to take on personally challenging and demanding tasks.

Encourages them to solve problems, produce innovative ideas and proposals and develop their vision for their area and a broader vision for the business. Encourages a critical faculty and a broad perspective, and encourages the challenging of existing practices, assumptions and policies.

M Developing

Believes that others have potential to take on ever more-demanding tasks and roles, and encourages them to do so. Ensures direct reports have adequate support. Develops their competencies, and invests time and effort in coaching them so they can contribute effectively and develop themselves. Identifies new tasks and roles that will develop others. Believes that critical feedback and challenge are important.

P Achieving

Willing to make decisions involving significant risk to gain a business advantage. Decisions are based on core business issues and their likely impact on success. Selects and exploits activities that result in the greatest benefits to the organization and that will increase its performance. Unwavering determination to achieve objectives and implement decisions.

B 'Personal Brand Values' – Assessment of a leader's and employee's likely level of engagement given diverse values (the history and makeup of the six values was covered in Chapter 4)

The ability of a leader to release discretionary motivation during change will be dependent on their understanding of and communication–connection with people's primary drivers. A values diagnostic which captures six contemporary personal, business and societal values systems/agendas will address the current reality of work and life in the twenty-first century and can be mapped onto matching universal leadership styles as described in Figure 8.2.

By providing a measure of how important these six values systems are to leaders, the PBV tool builds a baseline and better understanding of the diversity and strength of different drivers and beliefs across a business, organization or sector. It helps leaders clarify their personal values and judge how aligned they are with the organization's and other employee's values.

Given the frequency of mergers and acquisitions and the changes these generate, the PBV can be used to assess how all the elements of the change process, e.g. key staff changes, change leaders/managers deployment, have affected the distribution of the personal values across the business, where the new organization has set out to change the ways of working.

The diagnostic can be used to produce a gap analysis between 'identity' (the values you say you hold) by self-assessment, and 'reputation' (the values you portray through your behaviour), through other's assessment. It can identify predominant

The bottom line of the diagram indicates the related 6 'Globe' leadership dimensions
Choosing your leader and the way you live your work and life

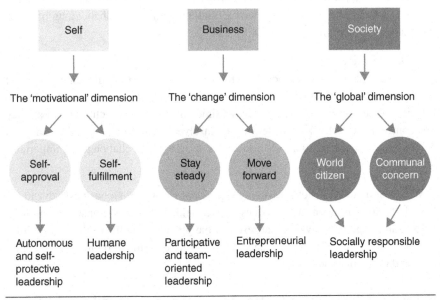

Figure 8.2 Personal Brand Values model – PBV.
Source: Copyright Concordia International Ltd.

values in particular functions or parts of a business and then be correlated with leadership/organisational performance and/or levels of employee engagement, thus providing a unique OD tool.

Likewise an organisation's espoused values (found in corporate or professional public values statements) can be compared to senior leaders and/or employee's values, giving OD and change leadership work in this area a 'reality' check. Partnership working would be another avenue to explore – with the PBV used as a dialogue facilitation device for critical relationships with key stakeholders. Finally, it can also be used for designing internal and external 'marketing' communications.

C Measure of how leaders transition to become effective change leaders ('Expert Orientation') by building long-lasting core organizational capabilities (Catherine Hayes Partnership)

This is a means of tracking the overall progress of individuals who are on fast-track and/or succession development programs, or who view a change leadership career as a longer term proposition, mainly driven by experience (Figure 8.3).

		Production orientation	Project orientation	Relationship orientation	Expert orientation
Core Purpose		Mobilizing people and other resources to deliver client needs while balancing efficiency and risk management	Nurturing ideas into action to transform the business by preparing, planning and influencing others to implement change	Connecting people to share information across boundaries and disciplines to enable both known and unknown immediate & longer term development of systems and business	Seeking and bringing cutting edge ideas and specialist knowledge and skills to the business to pre-empt new and resolve persistent problems
Core Characteristics (Being)		— Alert — Pragmatic — Proactive — Diligent — Is a role model	— Resilient, perseveres, patient — Tolerant of ambiguity — Analytic — Resourceful — Visionary/creative/innovative — Politically aware — Plans and tracks	— Open — Curious — Patient (defers gratifications) — Breadth of vision (aware of the wider organization) — Affiliative (need for contact) — Collaborative — Partners for its own sake — Sees everything as connected to everything else — Invests for the longer term	— Inquisitive — Authoritative — Autonomous — Tenacious — Restless for knowledge
Core Skills (Doing)		— Monitoring — Prioritizing — Co-ordinating — Multi-tasking Attending to detail — Contingency planning — Applying learning from the past	— Coalition building — Designing/planning/organizing/ Co-ordinating — Motivating, engaging — Establishing credibility (self/work) — Spinning many plates	— Getting people's time and attention — Handling difficult conversations — Listening, influencing, negotiating Translating (info, ideas) — Seeing patterns — Acting into the unknown — Networking	— Filtering, translating, framing, signalling — Assimilating and analysing data — Exploring, researching and probing within a particular field of expertise
Nature of Risk management		— How long will this take? — Will this reduce risk? — How much will it cost?	— How will this expose us? — What are the immediate and long term consequences of this work?	— How do we share information and maintain Risk management without diluting responsibility	— Who do we need to get to know to use our knowledge? — What makes our specialist knowledge relevant here?
Nature of Relationship		— Transactional — Requiring input to solve problems	— Temporary, requires continuous investment — Dependent on resources to get things done, without authority — Works with multiple and competing agendas	— Extensive network, multiple relationships — Focused on developing trust — Robust	— Intense — Occasional — Select — May be initiated by others
Judgement Calls		— Balancing quality, risk, cost and delivery — Where/when not to escalate issues — What is the data telling me	— Personal versus organizational needs — Whether to cut losses or perseveres — Balancing lobbying and delivering — Can people be trusted to deliver/ support	— Assessing consequences, repercussions and ripples — Weighing the political considerations — How far can I trust this information? — Can over-invest in exploring	— How to make specialist knowledge accessible and intelligible — How to support others without fostering dependence — How much expertise is necessary and sufficient?
Dilemmas		— Task versus people — Risk management versus service	— Being at the centre versus peripheral — Publicity versus reality — Innovation versus Risk management — Maintaining relationships versus impactful change	— Connected versus objective — Individual versus organisational needs — Short term versus long term	— Leading versus responding — Theory versus practice — Dependence versus independence (of clients and self)
Nature of Creativity		— Continuous improvement	— Creating new/different ways of working	— Making new/different connections with people	— New/different approaches to applying knowledge
Potential Blind Spots		— Values fire fighting over the longer term; prone to tunnel vision — Values action over reflection — Prone to either or thinking — People can become objects	— Don't know when to stop — The project becomes bigger than the solution — Prone to exaggeration and 'spin' doctoring	— Prone to get too many people on board — Can seem to take a long time to get things done — Can cloud accountability and responsibility	— Tendency to pay inadequate attention to relationships — Can exclude others through the use of jargon — Can be dismissive of non-experts — Has difficulty applying 80/20 rule
Attitude to Uncertainty		— Contain uncertainty — Set clear boundaries — Treat particular situations as distinct events	—See uncertainty until they either find a solution or someone who knows	— Acknowledge uncertainty — Contain anxiety — Work with paradoxes and allowing direction to emerge	— Solve or work around uncertainty in an attempt to move things forward

Figure 8.3 Organizational core capabilities.
Source: Copyright Catherine Haynes Partnership.

TEAM MEASURES

Leadership is rarely a sole enterprise. Indeed a critical mass of collective and distributed leadership is more likely to posses the necessary force to shift and shape organizations, as we pointed out in Chapter 5.

A 'Leadership Culture Display' (for Board, senior executive teams or management cohorts – this has also be adapted for individual assessment – examples of the behaviors were outlined in Chapter 5)

Developed by Concordia International Ltd. with underpinning research led by Aitken (2004), based on transformational, transactional and dysfunctional (for sustained business performance) collective leadership behavior. Creating a culture of excellence is all about making positive gains in people performance over time. Leadership teams must themselves champion transformative behaviors. By doing so, they will positively drive employee performance and consequently, business results. The Leadership Culture Display (see Figure 8.4) can be used to graphically illustrate the alignment of individual leader's behaviour with the rest of the leadership team – assessing whether their current focus is on future improvement, the here and now, or simply treading water.

The diagnostic:

■ Shows the type of culture the leadership team displays and the potential culture impacts on the people they lead.

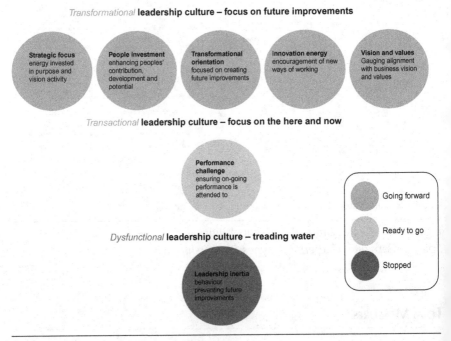

Figure 8.4   Leadership 360 model – L360.
Source: Concordia International Ltd.

■ Reveals differences in perceptions across a group of executives, and between leaders and employees about the prevailing leadership culture.

■ Raises areas of tension or conflict, for discussion and positive action.

■ Offers fresh insight into connecting the actions of each leader and their team considered as a whole – essential for a culture of sustained excellence and achievement.

■ Clarifies strategies for leadership teams to deliver their business goals.

■ Throws light onto any risks due to unfocused or inconsistent leadership.

■ Offers the knowledge to drive collective, aligned leadership at all levels of the organization.

For a change leadership team modus operandi overview, the following behavior lists can be used to assesses the transition of an executive group or management cohort from being a 'Management Group' to becoming a 'Leadership Team' (Aitken, 2004).

This is particularly useful for assessing the change leadership's fitness for current and future purpose. Invariably, a different mix of behaviors from both columns will be required for different business circumstances, e.g. in difficult trading conditions, the shorter term focus represented by the management group behaviors may be necessary (although not for too long and not to the exclusion of some appropriate leadership team behaviors).

Management group (transactional)	Leadership team (transformational)
Business units focus, drawing on 'silo' thinking, and individual accountability for line performance	Focus on stakeholder environment, across business systems and leadership/ management functioning – driven by strategy and improvement
Appears energized by competition for resources, results and sometimes favor	Energized by commitment to common purpose, goals and complementary and/ or integrated ways of working
Contributions usually based on formal organization structure, seniority and meeting process	Variety of inputs from senior management team (SMT), other leadership teams, individual initiatives and external insights
Essentially provides for the round table input of expert and/or functional reporting	Uses the diversity of know-how's, experience bases and business insights to build leadership team culture and capability

(Continued)

Process encourages relationships based mainly on contractual obligation	Process builds trust and capacity for shared learning and problem solving
Direction and motivation provided by, or sought from, single leader, e.g. the chief executive	Leadership shifts relevant to sub-teams, specialist tasks and as a possible leader learning opportunity

The above can be supplemented by the following assessments:

▪ Increases in the ratio of 'time spent leading' to 'time spent managing'.

▪ Degree of switch from individual function, to cross-functional, to global business focus.

▪ Reduction in the number of process breakdowns.

▪ Reduction in the number of change initiatives.

▪ Changes in career path and infrastructure in support of a new generation of cross-functional leaders.

▪ Equal comfort of management team members in representing functional, divisional and corporate activities and results.

▪ Sustained increases in the level and breadth of employee comittment and engagement (see Organizational Measures).

RELATIONAL MEASURES

A Trust in the change leadership relationships (Aitken and Platts)

As this is a very new but significant area in terms of relationship impact measurement, we have provided some background to its development, just as we did for the PBV and the Leadership Culture Display (LCD) in Chapters 4 and 5, respectively.

Trust is seen one of the primary contextual variables that separate successful from failed organizational interventions. Trust reduces conflict and facilitates communication and problem solving. Trust also allows for a free flow of information and learning. Low trust environments repress organizational learning by stifling communication, creativity and experimentation. Trust requires a willingness to invest our faith in others or in institutions. Trust is reciprocal and mutually reinforcing.

In other words trust underpins many common business transformation ideas, including corporate reputation building, knowledge/intellectual capital management, team transformational leadership and the networked or learning organization. On a more general note Will Hutton (The Work Foundation) calculated a daily average of 17 mentions of the word trust in the *Guardian* and *Observer* newspaper business columns throughout 2003, compared with only 6 in the previous five years. The 'fat cat' syndrome, corporate accounting malpractice, the war in Iraq and most recently the expenses claims of UK parliamentarians have all raised our interest and tested our sense of trust in leaders.

So much so that the 2003 World Economic Forum (WEF) considered 'trust and values' important enough to have as one of its five talking points alongside 'corporate challenges', 'the global economy', 'global governance' and 'security and geopolitics'. Indeed, an international poll commissioned by the WEF revealed that the most trusted organizations and institutions are those without power – NGO's and the religious bodies – whilst the least trusted are governments and companies. As for occupations, a 2002 MORI poll resulted in approval ratings of between 60% and 80% for uniformed jobs, civil servants at 40%, whilst the lowest rated were business leaders and politicians. The last decade has also seen significant falls in employee motivation, trust and loyalty.

This is alarming because as organizational performance becomes more dependent on less measurement-driven 'intangible' assets, such as leadership, shared tacit knowledge and longer term stakeholder relationships, trust becomes a 'must have' component of business life. The UK Institute of Business Ethics (IBE) sampled 350 FTSE 100 firms between 1997 and 2001 and found 'ethical' companies outperformed others on financial measures of market and economic value added. The IBE argues that this outcome occurs because the more these values are lived, 'the better and more consistent the decision making at every level, the greater the amount of trust, the more confident and motivated the employees and the less the chance of costly damage to the company's reputation'.

A virtuous cycle of trust, ethical values and reputation embraces customers, suppliers and other stakeholders. Attempts to construct corporate social responsibility and triple bottom line reporting indices may in part be a response by business to create social legitimacy for its operations. However, whether deliberate or not, the actions taken under this banner forge connections within and between internal and external business communities through establishing and renegotiating, as required, mutually beneficial and trusting relationships. Thus becoming an employer and/ or partner of choice are reinforced as key differentiators in the marketplace for employee talent, customers and preferred suppliers. Both social capital and corporate reputation are founded on trust. As a way of working, trust also encourages people to take responsibility together for remaining 'competent and ready', as business environment circumstances continually change.

If everyone wants more trust because it makes a tangible and positive difference to our work and lives, we must be clear about what we mean by trust, how much we need/already have/do not have and how we might contribute to creating a high trust environment. First what do we define as trust within business relationships, second how do we view, measure and talk about trust and third, in a work context, how can we develop and deepen trust?

What do we mean by trust within business relationships?

We are attempting to answer the question, 'To what extent do individuals feel they have an effective, enduring, trust-based working relationship with key colleagues?'

Our starting point assumes that people are predisposed to trust others, although this will vary according to early upbringing (the successful completion of the 'attachment cycle' between carer and infant) and a general trusting tendency (affirmation based on the product of past experience and the factors present in previous situations). Given these conditions, we concur with Murray et al's (2009) idea of trust being an individual's positive expectations about another individual's motives with respect to him/herself, within a situational context, entailing risk'. In this case, we are concentrating on the degree and nature of trust in critical business relationships.

Trust in me, as Mowgli in Walt Disney's *Jungle Book* and Enron stakeholders found out, is a necessary but not sufficient precondition for sound business. We need to seek out and be practiced at detecting the cues that indicate someone can be trusted in their commitment to a mutually beneficial, productive, ongoing business relationship. Leaders (and by this, we mean anyone with sufficient formal/informal power to continually influence others in adopting a particular course of action), in particular, need to trust and be trustworthy. Without this essential relationship 'firewire', the work environment becomes devoid of initiative and cynical.

But how do we know how much and what type of trust is present in a Working Trust relationship?

How to view and measure trust (using the 'Working Trust' evaluation)

For each specific critical business relationship, there has to be a reason for its existence and a desire to belong – there has to be some Tangible Needs and Personal Wants. Of course, evaluation of these needs and wants results in the first question and decision on 'Do I want to proceed?' but they also have to be reconsidered throughout the duration of the relationship, as circumstances change and the relationship itself unfolds. They remain as constant factors in two ever-present questions, 'What is the point of my involvement?' and 'How much do I want to invest in this?' Dibben et al. (2003) refer to this as 'Calculus-Based Trust', a rational determination of the relationship pros and cons, although we disagree that this only occurs during the early stages of a business relationship.

This dynamic conception of trust is also reflected in our model of Working Trust and its essential components, i.e. the type and content of the behavior cues used by parties for determining the level and nature of trust present. Whilst we agree with Bunker et al. (2004) that the development of trust might have natural stages, e.g. knowledge of the other person may come before our identification with them as trusted partners, our view is that as the lens through which the relationship is perceived becomes more sharply focused over time (because we view them more accurately, the more we get to know them), then so might be the expectations. Thus it is conceivable that we might want to revisit our 'Knowledge-Based Trust' (which allows us to predict the other parties likely behavior) once we feel more comfortable in extending this relationship to a wider range and variety of contexts. So whatever the stage of your business relationship, we believe that you can always learn how to make it more mutually satisfying and productive.

But I don't know how to talk about trust?

When you ask someone 'Do you trust me?' and the reply is 'Of course I do', you are no further forward in the relationship! Unfortunately, you are not likely to ask such a question outright or receive a useful response. It is likely your question will be more circumspect, e.g. 'You know I always do what I say I'm going to do', in which case you have not even put the topic of trust on the table. Whilst a common response might be 'Why do you ask?' a circular debate if ever there was. Discussing trust is like discussing love, you know you need to but you just cannot find the right words, or the right time or the right emotional space to find out what you really want to know.

In love you can move on with or without emotional scarring. In working relationships, the relationship pack is often already dealt, it is not easy to move on, it might also be your job to make a critical business relationship work well, and the manner of any breakdown or departure always leaves some reputation legacy. Better than to know what to look out for in a relationship built on trust (you probably think your instincts are good enough but getting this right first time, like love at first sight, is very rare – otherwise there would be little need for contract law!). Better still if you know what it is you are doing to either build or detract from such a relationship and are then able to communicate this to the other person.

What do I look for in 'Working Trust' relationships?

In our model of trust, based on an extensive literature review (available on request), organizational consulting and the development of our own business partnership, you begin by using a checklist to determine your initial Tangible Needs & Personal Wants. We then provide you with six core components of Working Trust behavior to focus your own and your parties' thoughts, actions and feelings about each critical business relationship. Our 360 degree Working Trust survey contains all the behavioral cues for establishing the current extent and nature of trust that exists in the relationship. General areas of the business relationship to consider are defined below.

■ Credibility and confidence in shared, added value delivery
   Credibility – able to make a significant contribution to joint efforts, adding real value to the relationship.

Confidence – competence can be relied upon as a product of open and constructive sharing of knowledge and experiences.

■ Responsible and dependable ongoing effective contribution
Responsible – takes personal responsibility for initiating the achievement of mutually beneficial goals.
Dependable – shows a sustained, loyal and active participation.

■ Transparency and sensitivity in progressing the business relationship
Transparency – is open, congruent and consistent in their values and behavior.
Sensitivity – is empathic and adaptive in their style of working.

Remember, at various review points along the way, you may wish to reconfirm if your initial Tangible Needs and Personal Wants are still appropriate for this relationship. Once we have assessed and reflected on the current effectiveness of our business relationship, how can we transform it?

How can we develop and deepen trust?

The good news is that by agreeing to explore how well you are doing with your colleagues, you have reinforced the sense that these relationships matter and have also demonstrated a willingness to change your behavior to jointly improve how you conduct business. In itself this builds trust. The real value, however, comes from attending to the detail of the feedback you have received. In this way, you can target your limited time and resources on those specific areas of the relationship that will secure lasting benefits. Beyond this essential communication, every situation requires a different remedy.

ORGANIZATIONAL MEASURES

A Tracking corporate reputation enhancement – Harris-Fombrun Reputation Quotient (Fombrun et al. (2000) adapted by Coombes (2007)

The least tangible asset, but possibly the most sought after in the marketplace, is the general feeling of goodwill which is generated by an enterprise. Change leaders can quickly affect reputation for good or ill and would be wise to consider the aspects of their potential reputational impact, outlined in Figure 8.5, as they embark on their own development journey.

B Changes in business culture – Concordia International Ltd – Workplace Performance Culture (WPC) Audit

The WPC survey assesses three key organizational elements that define and drive performance culture in the workforce: (1) workplace culture, (2) collaboration and

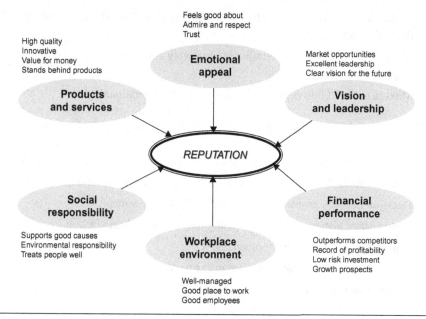

Figure 8.5 Reputation Quotient Factors (adapted by Coombes (2007)).

(3) employee engagement. Establishing an in-depth understanding of these elements, knowing their drivers and identifying strengths and opportunities for improvement are the first steps to achieving exceptional and sustained performance improvement.

The WPC survey provides:

▓ A catalyst for continual improvement in the way services are delivered.

▓ Identification of opportunities for greater efficiency and reduced operational costs.

▓ Recommendations for increased levels of engagement, commitment, productivity and employee motivation.

▓ Accurate and robust data that identifies where and why interventions are required.

▓ In-depth understanding of perceptions across a range of key organizational roles and functions, and the provision of a set of recommendations, strategies and action steps for going forward.

As a diagnostic tool, the WPC survey provides the necessary information to:

▓ Identify employee perceptions about their workplace – how they feel about working for the organization.

▓ Determine the people issues that impact on employee buy-in, productivity, performance and engagement.

▓ Improve the ability to attract and retain high performing employees.

■ Highlight issues caused by different management styles and misunderstandings that affect performance.

■ Identify where unresolved conflict is negatively affecting workplace culture and employee morale.

■ Maximize the ROI in people and reduce invisible operational costs.

The results of the WPC survey will assist the organization's leadership to improve:

■ Strategic planning and buy-in to the actions required to achieve strategic goals.

■ The identification of the cause and effect of stress, fear and bullying.

■ Decision making, problem solving and conflict management.

■ Performance management, work quality and 'customer' satisfaction.

■ Leadership and management practices.

■ Engagement, recruitment, retention and absenteeism.

■ Interpersonal skills and team functioning.

The analysis and results are grouped into three areas:

1. Workplace culture
   - Communication
   - My work
   - Our workplace
   - Conflict management
   - Participation
   - Support
   - Leadership

2. Collaboration index
   - Within teams
   - Between teams
   - Organizational

3. Employee engagement
   - Rational
   - Emotional

The WPC Audit recognizes that making positive shift in workplace culture demands more than management or leadership training alone. Positive change must be 'bottom–up' as well as 'top–down'. Moving forward demands a deep understanding of what employees think about the current culture, and what they most want for the future. The WPC speedily pinpoints strengths, opportunities for improvement, conflict points, risks and road-blocks. Both quantitative and qualitative data ensure vital information is captured.

Results are reported using clear graphical displays and comparisons. Accurate year-to-year, and cross-industry comparisons can easily be made. You will find the Audit is a powerful process in itself. Most of all, however, it will provide sure guidance for your Board/senior management to take positive action – to build shared enthusiasm, commitment and productivity across your workplace.

The WPC Audit:

■ Delivers clear facts and data on workplace perceptions, so issues can be resolved.

■ Identifies 'why' something is working or not working, so resources can be targeted at causes, not symptoms.

■ Shows differences between employee groups, allowing specific groups to be targeted.

■ Identifies gaps between what employees want and what they experience, so areas of excellence can be reinforced and gaps addressed.

■ Prioritizes actions and projects for HR and organizational development, maximizing the benefit of investment.

■ Highlights any compliance and risk management issues, allowing actions to minimize risk of claims and penalties.

■ Provides consistent benchmarking over time, comparing best practices of other organizations and ensuring your organization's initiatives maintain momentum.

A quarterly 'Dashboard' WPC snapshot can also be used to track movements related to specific change interventions instigated by change leaders.

C Measures of workplaces conducive to changing diversity, e.g. women (Concordia International Ltd – Women in the Workplace questionnaire)

Women are under-represented in many sectors facing a skills shortage; as many workplace cultures are not inclusive of women, they do not attract and retain them. Workplace culture does not affect men and women the same way; it sometimes reflects underlying attitudes or myths in the organization that make women uncomfortable, less productive and prevent them from using their potential. Some research shows that workplaces that work for women work for men and employers (study by The Conference Board of Canada and Watson Wyatt: Human Capital Index, Linking Human Capital and Shareholder Value: Summary Report (2000). The factors measure:

1. Development opportunities
2. Work–life balance/work flexibility

3. Gender-inclusive workplace
4. Participation and equal judgment
5. Harassment and bullying
6. Organizational support and trust
7. Remuneration, promotion and performance
8. Interpersonal relations and conflict management

Underpinning research includes:

■ Companies with high representation of women on their SMT have 34% higher total return to shareholders than with the lowest women's representation.
Study: The Bottom Line: Connecting Corporate Performance and Gender Diversity, Catalyst New York, 2004.

■ Women influence 80% of purchasing decisions for all products, so need to be represented in organizations – women know better that women want.
Joanne Thomas Yaccato, The 80% Minority: Reaching the Real World of Women Consumers, 2003, Toronto.

■ A women-inclusive workplace improves the ROI in people – improved retention.
Mark A. Huselid, The impact of human resource management practices on turnover, productivity and corporate financial performance, *Academy of Management Journal*.

■ Creating a culture and a workplace that attract women at the same time creates the type of workplaces that grow businesses.
   – Adaptive and participative leadership
   – 'Feminine' management qualities: more consensus and solution orientated, less combative, supportive of other staff
   Research by The International Labour Organization.

D Results demonstrating growth in 'Intellectual Capital' (IC) through change leadership actions

In line with the research on sustainable business performance by Collins, probably the most crucial task of change leaders is to leave the organization in a better position to respond to opportunities for business growth than when they found it, i.e. before they did anything different. The resource based theory of organizational strategy suggests that knowledge and skills offer dynamic capabilities for shaping the future, particularly in knowledge-intensive industries (Teece and Winter, 1984).

An example from Austrian Research Centres (ARC) breaks IC measurement down into Human, Structural & Relational Capital and Results: http://www.arcs.ac.at/downloads/ARC_Wissensbilanz_2006_englisch.pdf

Some examples from each category are provided below, whilst the full list can be found through the link above. In 2001, ARC focused on five 'knowledge goal' improvements which were: knowledge transfer, interdisciplinarity, research management, internationality and spin-offs and investments.

Human capital (from the following international Federation of Accountants categories: know-how, education, vocational qualifications, work-related knowledge, occupational assessments, psychometric assessment, work-related competencies, entrepreneurial élan, innovativeness, proactive and reactive abilities, changeability):

Human Resources
Number of researchers (headcount).
Proportion of research staff (% headcount).
Number of researchers (headcount)/number of staff (headcount).
Influx of research staff (FTE).
Number of new researchers (full-time equivalents) joining the group in the period under review.
Total research staff resignations (FTE).
Number of employees (full-time equivalents) who retired during the period under review.
Proportion of female research staff (% research staff).
Full-time equivalent women research staff/full-time equivalents of all research staff.
Women in senior positions (%).
Number of women in senior positions/total number of senior positions. Senior positions are defined as managers, authorized signatories, division heads, department heads and heads of business units.
Women on supervisory and advisory boards (%).
Number of women on supervisory and advisory boards/total number of supervisory and advisory board members.

Training
Total training days per employee.
Number of training days according to ARC training catalog excluding attendance at conferences and seminars per employee (full-time equivalent).
Expenditure for training per employee (e).

Expenditure for centrally organized seminars within the scope of the training catalog per employee (full-time equivalent) in euros.

Structural capital (from intellectual property – patents, copyrights, design rights, trade secrets, trademarks, service marks – and infrastructure assets – management philosophy, corporate culture, management processes, information systems, networking systems, financial relations):

Processes and equipment
Capital investment (% of operating revenues).
Assets acquired not including buildings and technical infrastructure (including IT infrastructure)/total operating revenues.
Hit rate for EU research programs (%).
Number of EU programs awarded/number of applications for EU programs.

Relational capital (from brands, customer loyalty, company names, backlog orders, distribution channels, business collaborations, licensing agreements, favorable contracts, franchising agreements):

Project cooperation and networking
Number of new interdepartmental contract research projects.
Number of new contract research and publicly funded research projects, or competence center projects for which cost units were established in more than one business unit.
Number of interdepartmental independent research projects.
Number of ongoing independent research projects (including projects as part of the ARC Technology Offensive) for which cost units are established in more than one business unit.
Research activities abroad.
Number of periods of at least one month spent abroad by ARC staff.
Number of international researchers.
Number of ARC researchers who are foreign nationals.
Heads of business units with teaching assignments.
Number of business unit heads who held one or more lecturing assignments at universities, technical colleges or postgraduate educational institutions in the period under review. Courses include lectures, seminars, practicals, etc. listed in the university or college catalog in an academic year, i.e. winter semester and the following summer semester.

Diffusion and networking/researcher
Presentations at scientific conferences.
Presentations given at international scientific conferences/congresses (per researcher).

Participation in committees: scientific, industrial, political.
Number of memberships in associations, etc.

Core processes
Number of competitive research projects (% of independent research projects).
Number of newly acquired contract research projects for national and international customers in the period under review, excluding small-scale projects.
Project revenues from contract research activities including small-scale projects (in euro millions).
Total revenues from contract projects for national and international customers, including small-scale projects.
Revenues/project (excluding small-scale projects, in euros)
Total revenues from contract research projects for national and international customers, excluding small-scale projects/number of projects.
Domestic customers (%).
Number of customers from Austria as a percentage of total customer projects.

Results
Commercial results
Total revenues from research contracts; nuclear financing by the Austrian Ministry of Transport, Innovation and Technology; services provided by shareholders; own work capitalized; services rendered within the ARC Group and other operating revenues.
Percentage of total costs covered by sales revenues and grants for R&D including changes in inventory.
Number of customers awarding ARC research contracts for the first time.
Proportion of new orders from industry (%).
Proportion of new projects from Austrian companies as a percentage of the total volume of new projects from industry.
Coordination of EU projects and networks.
Number of EU projects with ARC as the prime contractor and number of networks with ARC as coordinator.
Ratio of prime contractor/total EU projects (%).
Proportion of projects with ARC as prime contractor as a percentage of all ARC EU projects.
Number of customer courses and seminars.
Number of external individuals who took part in ARC courses and seminars.

Research results
Publications in peer-reviewed journals per researcher.
Articles published in journals quoted by ISI in the Science Citation Index (SCI) per researcher.
Publications in conference proceedings, trade journals and books per researcher.

Total number of conference papers published as complete articles in conference proceedings, articles in trade journals and contributions to books or published books per researcher.

Proportion of publications in future technology fields (%).

Proportion of ARC publications in scientific journals which, according to the Institute for Scientific Information (Thompson/ISI), are among the 25% of scientific fields that demonstrate the highest international growth rates in terms of publications over a period of three years.

Patents granted.

E Measures employed in the most comprehensive analysis of 'people and the bottom line' to date (Tamkin, Cowling & Hunt, 2008)

This survey of 2,905 UK organizations used the following HR measures:

Access – the effective resourcing of roles in the organization in terms of initial recruitment, ongoing job moves and succession activity:

- proportion of new appointees tested on recruitment
- proportion of new appointments having a person specification
- proportion of employees covered by a succession plan.

Ability – the skills and abilities of the workforce, the quality of the people at its disposal and the ongoing development activity of individuals to build future capacity and capability:

- proportion of workforce having a current personal development plan
- proportion of workforce having a career development plan
- proportion of workforce qualified to degree level.

Attitude – levels of engagement, motivation and morale, the meaning they find in their work, their beliefs about their workplace and their willingness to put in extra effort:

- proportion of managers that left voluntarily over the last 12 months
- proportion of workforce that receive profit-related pay
- proportion of workforce having regular appraisal
- frequency with which staff have one-to-ones with their managers.

Application – the opportunities for individuals to apply themselves, an appropriate working environment provided through information, job design, organizational structure and business strategy:

- who decides on the pace of work (ratio of managers to workers)
- who decides on task allocation (ratio of managers to workers)

These HR factor results were then correlated with measures of:

- gross profits per employee
- increase in operating profit per employee
- increase in profit margin per employee
- increase in sales growth per employee
- increase in the probability of achieving sales from new technology

The findings can be found in the reference above. Finally, and most critically, sustained performance (for measures of 'sustainability' see the Dow Jones Sustainability Indexes as a start point) is a measure of the change leader's ability to build a culture of change responsiveness into the organization's fabric so that it can respond in a timely fashion to future events. Evidence of this dynamic change readiness capability in people can be assessed using the following framework (Holt, Armenakis, Field & Harris, 2007):

Change Readiness Framework

Framework component	Statements
Self-efficacy – confident that you are capable of making the change	■ My past experiences make me confident. I will be able to perform successfully after this change is made. ■ There are some tasks that will be required when we change, I don't think I can do well. ■ I have the skills that are needed to make this change work. ■ When we implement this change, I feel I can handle it with ease. ■ When I set my mind to it, I can learn everything that will be required when this change is adopted. ■ I am intimidated by all the tasks I will have to learn because of this change. ■ When I heard about this change, I thought it suited my skills perfectly. ■ I do not anticipate any problems adjusting to the work I will have when this change is adopted. ■ After this change is implemented, I am confident I will be able to do my job.

(Continued)

Framework component	Statements
Personal valence – confident that the change will benefit the employee personally	■ When we implement this change, I can envision financial benefits coming my way. ■ This change will disrupt many of the personal relationships I have developed. ■ The prospective change will give me new career opportunities. ■ When this change is implemented, I don't believe there is anything for me to gain. ■ My future in this job will be limited because of this change. ■ In the long run, I feel it will be worthwhile for me if the organization adopts this change. ■ I am worried I will lose some of my status in the organization when this change is implemented. ■ This change makes my job easier. ■ The effort required to implement this change is rather small when compared to the benefits I will see from it.
Senior leadership support – recognition that the organization's leadership supports the change	■ Management has sent a clear signal this organization is going to change. ■ I believe management has done a great job in bringing about this change. ■ The senior leaders have served as role models for this change. ■ Our organization's top decision makers have put all their support behind this change effort. ■ This organization's most senior leader is committed to this change. ■ Every senior manager has stressed the importance of this change. ■ Our senior leaders have encouraged all of us to embrace this change. ■ The organization's senior leader has not been personally involved with the implementation of this change.

Framework component	Statements
	■ I am sure that our senior leaders will change their mind before we actually implement this change. ■ I think we are spending a lot of time on this change when the senior managers don't even want it implemented.
Organizational valence – confident that the change will lead to long-term benefits for the organization	■ I think the organization will benefit from this change. ■ Our organization is going to be more productive when we implement this change. ■ When we adopt this change, we will be better equipped to meet our customers' needs. ■ This change will improve our organization's overall efficiency. ■ Our organization will lose some valuable assets when we adopt this change. ■ This change matches the priorities of our organization.
Discrepancy – recognition of the need for change	■ There are legitimate reasons for us to make this change. ■ There are a number of rational reasons for this change to be made. ■ No one has explained why this change must be made. ■ It does not make much sense for us to initiate this change. ■ This change is clearly needed. ■ The time we are spending on this change should be spent on something else. ■ I think we are implementing this change just because we can.

This chapter offered readers some wide ranging examples, including more people-centric mechanisms, for evaluating how and what is changing through direct investment in and application of change leader's development. Given that most leadership development offerings fail to outline the type of shifts required at the outset, some of the measures above could also be used to define and then track the types of change expected of those designated as change leaders.

References

Aitken, P. (2004). The relationships between personal values, leadership behaviour and team functioning. *Doctor of Business Administration Thesis*, Henley Management College/ Brunel University.

Aitken, P., & Platts, C. (2003). Working Trust Partnership, Unpublished Research.

Bunker, B.B., Billie, T.-A., & Roy, J.-L. (Dec 2004). Ideas in currency and OD practice: Has the well gone dry? Arlington, (20 pages). *The Journal of Applied Behavioral Science, 40*(4), 403.

Coombes, P. (2007). *MBA Dissertation*, Henley Management College.

Collins, J. (2001). *Good to great*. Random House.

Dibben, M., Harris, S., & Wheeler, C. (Dec 2003). Export market development: Planning and relationship processes of entrepreneurs in different countries, Dordrecht. *Journal of International Entrepreneurship, 1*(4), 383.

Donald, L. K. (Aug 2006). Seven keys to unlock the four levels of evaluation, Hoboken, 4 pages. *Performance Improvement, 45*(7), 5.

EFQM. (2000). *Assessing for excellence: a practical guide for self-assessment*. Brussels: European Foundation for Quality Management.

Fombrun, C. J., Gardberg, N. A., & Server, J. M. (2000). The reputation quotient: a multiple stakeholder measure of corporate reputation. *Journal of Brand Management, 7*, 241–255.

Harris and Dibben (1999)

Holt, D., Armenakis, A., Field, H., & Harris, S. (June 2007). Readiness for organizational change: the systematic development of a scale. *The Journal of Applied Behavioral Science, 43*(2), 232–255.

Print, C. F. (2004). People value – there's no accounting for people. *Henley Discussion Paper Series*, HCVI HDP, No. 8, October, Henley Management College.

Sandra, L.-M., Aloni, M., John, G.-H., Jaye, L.-D., et al. (Feb 2009). Fostering partner dependence as trust insurance: The implicit contingencies of the exchange script in close relationships, Washington. *Journal of Personality and Social Psychology, 96*(2), 324.

Tamkin, P., Cowling, M., & Hunt, W. (2008). *People and the bottom line*. Institute for Employment Studies, UK.

Teece, D. J., & Winter, S. G. (May 1984). The limits of neoclassical theory in management education, Nashville, (6 pages). *The American Economic Review, 74*(2), 116.

The Conference Board of Canada and Watson Wyatt. (2000). Human capital index, Linking Human Capital and Shareholder Value: Summary Report, New York.

Chapter 9

Managing Change Leadership Talent

█ Introduction

The overall theme of this book has been concerned with developing change leaders. We have suggested throughout that this requires both concerted effort and intelligent investment of resources. Reflecting on this leads to two important questions. These are as follows:

(i) Who should we be focusing this investment on?

(ii) How do we ensure, within our organization, that we retain those leaders we have developed?

This chapter explores these two questions. Both questions arise from an underlying assumption that the capability to lead change is a discrete and identifiable capability. We do hope that, by this stage in this book, we have made a convincing case to support such an assumption. However, whilst being a distinct capability we have argued that such a capability should be a critical aspect of a broader suite of leadership capabilities. With this thought in mind we have drawn on the broader research, literature, lessons and practices which have surfaced in more general considerations around talent management. We then look at how these can be applied to the management of change leadership talent. On this basis we have organized this chapter along the following lines.

- We begin with an overall review of the challenges facing organizations in terms of talent management: What is driving the interest?; What are the major issues in talent management?; How do we define talent?

- From this background, we explore approaches and frameworks which have been shown to be helpful in the somewhat complex process of talent management.

- One important, and widely recognized, aspect of talent management is the building of a solid 'talent pipeline'. Whilst this can be considered to be a part of the broader process, we believe that it is worthy of separate consideration.

- Building from the above points we then turn to considering how the broader lessons of talent management can be integrated with the need to develop and manage change leadership talent within an organization.

- We conclude with considerations around the accountability for change leadership talent management and the range of roles and responsibilities.

The challenge of talent management

DRIVERS OF INTEREST

The term 'talent management' has been stated to be attributable to the work of a number of the partners in the consulting firm McKinsey and published in their book *The war for talent* (Michaels, Handfield-Jones & Alexrod, 2001; Williams, 2000). Indeed, in a similar vein Jack Welch (the former CEO of GE) asserted that organizations that won the war for talent would have a distinct and sustainable competitive advantage. Whilst some may see the concept, and such comments, as somewhat dramatic, there is strong evidence that organizations are taking the issue seriously. For example, in a survey conducted in the USA in 2006 by the Strategic Human Resources Society (SHRM Talent Survey, 2006) it was found that over half (53%)

of the organizations surveyed had specific talent-management policies and practices in place. Of those just over three quarters (76%) considered talent management to be a top business priority for their organizations.

This emerging focus on talent management is one aspect of a broader shift in organizational perceptions relating to the significance of people in the creation of value and the achievement of competitive advantage. As organizations increasingly adopt a resource-based view of strategy, people are more clearly seen to be significant resources and provide important capabilities that, if managed carefully, provide inimitable and non-substitutable bases for building an effective and competitive strategy.

Perhaps this shift in the significance attributed to an organization can be explained by the changing nature of the workforce. In recent years, it has become evident that the nature of workforce expectations is changing, as outlined in previous chapters. In part the shift in expectations may be seen as a consequence of changes in the psychological contract (e.g. Rousseau, 1985). Recent studies have indicated that around 70% of employees are seeking meaning and purpose in their work. This represents a manifestation of earlier views that proposed, in a work context, people to seek:

(i) psychological meaningfulness,

(ii) safety – in terms of freedom to express themselves and

(iii) the availability of the resources to enable them to perform effectively. Some would argue that the roots of such thinking can indeed be found in the earlier motivational theories.

It is perhaps the fast-changing organizational context which has created the conditions in which the basic expectations of employees are receiving greater attention from employers. This recognition is reflected in the growing literature and research into employee engagement and talent management. At a practitioner level the shift is being seen in the growth in significance which organizations place on achieving high rankings in the various 'Employer of Choice' surveys (Higgs, 2006). Interestingly, responses to the changing significance attributed to employee expectations are leading to a new way of managing and developing people at work.

THE VALUE OF HUMAN CAPITAL

Alongside the shift in the nature of the workforce we have seen a growing recognition of the financial value of people. This has been described as the human capital of the organization (Higgs, 2006). The term 'human capital' is one which has emerged from the realization that, as the knowledge economy takes hold, the value to corporations of intangible assets is growing rapidly. Research suggests that intangible assets have grown from representing 38% of a firm's total value in 1982 to representing 85% in 2000 (Conference Board, 2005). This research also provided insights into the value of human capital indicating that within the USA:

(i)   the cost of losing a 'talented person' in 2002/2003 was between $200,000 and $250,000,

(ii) the bottom line impact of a 'bad hire' was at least $300,000,

(iii) the cost of operating without a key player (technical person) at even a relatively low level (i.e. salary of $40,000) was around $500,000 per annum.

Studies such as this provide a context for considering the value of human capital and how to best manage this valuable 'people asset'.

In parallel with and closely related to, the recognition of changing employee expectations has been the development in thinking and research relating to the impact of employees, and the impact of people-management policies and practices, on the financial performance of organizations. Early work in this area was concerned with the relationship of HR/people-management practices and their impact on the bottom line which was seminally illustrated by the 'Sears case study' (Rucci, Hirn & Quinn, 1998). This study showed that within one US retail corporation a clear relationship between employee commitment, customer commitment and bottom line performance could be established. The study showed that a 5% increase in employee commitment led to a 3% increase in customer commitment and consequently to a 0.25% increase in shareholder value. This model of 'Employee Value Chain' has subsequently been adopted in a diverse range of corporations across the world. In a similar vein a range of studies within Europe, and the UK in particular, have shown a distinct link between good HR practices which are well implemented and both employee commitment and financial performance (e.g. Guest, 1997).

However, preceding these studies Allen and Meyer (1990) had clearly demonstrated a link between commitment of employees to 'go the extra mile' (affective commitment) and organizational performance. A range of more recent studies using this framework have found strong support for Allen and Meyer's original work. The more recent literature on employee engagement (a closely related concept) has built further on this work. The literature on engagement (both practitioner and academic) indicates significant financial and organizational benefits. For example:

(i)   Organizations with high levels of engagement have a more than 70% probability of achieving their goals than those with lower levels of engagement (Towers Perrin, 2005).

(ii) High engagement organizations achieve better operating margins. A 5% increase in engagement can lead to a 0.7% increase in operating margins (Towers Perrin, 2005).

(iii) Employees in high engagement organizations are twice as likely to remain with their employer than those in lower level engagement organizations (Conference Board, 2005).

(iv) Firms with higher levels of employee engagement outperform industry sector growth by 6% (Towers Perrin, 2005).

Similar patterns of benefits are encountered in the recent research into talent management. In particular organizations with good talent-management practices demonstrate more cost-effective recruitment, higher levels of motivation and retention and enhanced customer perceptions (Conference Board, 2005).

Against this background in which people are considered as a significant (and often critical) resource it has been argued that employees and, in particular, valued talent, should be managed in the same way as any other strategic resource (Ashton & Bellis, 2003).

TALENT-MANAGEMENT ISSUES

Research into how organizations are implementing talent-management policies and practices has shown that the case for talent management is widely accepted (Ashton & Bellis, 2003). There appear to be two fundamental reasons for managing talent; whether the primary focus is upon developing current and future senior leaders, or all employees. These are as follows:

(i) Respected research has demonstrated that the organization's access to superior talent is one of a few key factors in creating and sustaining a competitive advantage (Michaels et al., 2001).

(ii) The organizations that manage talent well have significantly greater access to talent than those who do not (McCall, 1998).

Thus it appears to be generally agreed that talent needs to be managed in the same manner as any other strategic resource (e.g. financial, suppliers and brand). However, in practice a number of issues and dilemmas arise in implementing this philosophy. These are as follows:

(i) The short-/long-term dilemma. Talent management requires investment of resources, time and effort with mid- to long-term outcomes. Yet organizations have to balance this with meeting short-term performance goals and shareholder expectations. A particular issue here relates to dealing with a short-term need to reduce headcount whilst maintaining, and developing a future talent pipeline.

(ii) Linked to the above dilemma is the challenge of building a 'talent culture'. This entails embedding a mind-set which recognizes the medium- to long-term process. Along with this a 'talent culture' requires leaders to accept real accountability for talent management and for top-level integration of talent management with the overall business strategy. Once again short-term challenges and, in particular difficult economic conditions, can create difficulties in sustaining a 'talent culture'

(iii) Dealing with the 'elitist' versus 'egalitarian' issue. This relates to the way in which an organization defines its talent. Whilst the majority of organizations apply talent management to senior leaders, immediate successors and 'high potentials', a few see every employee as being in the talent pool. Research by Ashton and Bellis (2003) and Higgs (2006) indicated that the arguments for a more restricted view of 'talent' were broadly outlined as follows:

- Only certain people will become leaders or produce the top performance a business may require.

- Selection will eventually have to take place given the business requirement for talent able to meet business needs.

- A dilution of focus on defined groups of talent and high potentials can put an organization's succession choices at risk.

- There is a need to focus development resource; too broad a view of talent may result in such resources being spread too thinly with consequent loss of impact.

Perhaps, to a significant extent the dilemma presents an artificial polarity. This, in part, is a consequence of terminology. An increasing number of organizations have structured effective talent-management practices focused on a relatively small group of roles and people. However, at the same time they have clear policies and practices designed to build levels of engagement and commitment amongst all employees. In broad terms this is aimed at developing and retaining employees and can thus be seen as an aspect of talent management with the label. In a number of organizations there is debate around the language and 'labels' associated with the more focused view of talent management. If an individual is not in the 'talent pool' does this mean they do not have talent. Thus, even though the case for a focused pool may be strong there is a need for care in communication.

Implementing talent management

Building from the above sections (and related research) it is evident that any talent-management strategy is likely to have a range of goals. These tend to be as follows:

(i) to ensure that the supply of talent for the business is sufficient to fund both 'leakage' (i.e. losses) and business growth,

(ii) to constantly increase the 'potency' of the talent mix to create and sustain competitive advantage,

(iii) to develop talented individuals in such a way as to enable them to realize their potential and

(iv) to deploy talent in such a way as to support the business strategy and therefore maximize value.

In implementing any talent-management process designed to realize these goals, it is essential that it is designed to align with current and future business priorities. According to the research of Ashton and Bellis (2003) this alignment can be achieved at different levels which are as follows:

(i) integrating talent propositions with key business drivers,

(ii) allowing business drivers to broadly shape the talent proposition,

(iii) aggregating a range of talent efforts to contribute to supporting the business drivers and

(iv) talent per se acting as a business driver.

None of these are inherently better than any other. However, understanding the business context and needs should underpin the frame for integration which will in turn frame the talent proposition to make a significant impact on business success it also needs to be integrated at the strategic management level (i.e. the point at which strategic execution begins to be shaped. These two points taken together indicate that there is a clear leadership dimension to any talent-management strategy. However, there is also a need for effective processes to underpin the implementation of the strategy. These two strands are explored in a little more detail below.

These two elements of talent management required for successful implementation of the strategy need to work together. However, it is clear that the success of an organization's talent-management effort is heavily influenced by the extent to which leaders carry out their role effectively. The processes need to be designed to support the leaders and to be practical, fit for purpose and not over-complex. In broad terms the areas in which line leaders have a key role to play may be summarized as being:

■ Identifying high potentials

■ Coaching high potentials

■ Participating in panels or committees established to review talent

■ Developing talent; in particular making appointments to roles designed to provide stretch and development opportunities.

Research (Ashton and Bellis, 2003; Higgs, 2006) has explored the nature of line leadership involvement which has underpinned successfully talent management. Four key areas have been identified. These are as follows:

(i) *Planning*. Ensuring that talent management is integrated with the organizations business planning process and is given equal consideration alongside other resources. This also entails ensuring that the talent strategy is clearly and visibly connected to the business drivers and that 'talent' is deployed in high value adding roles. It is in the integration process that the short-/long-term dilemmas discussed above are resolved.

(ii) *Attention.* The extent of personal attention given by senior leaders and top leadership teams to talent management and talented people is an important success factor. This attention given by the top team tends to result in high levels of attention amongst executives and HR professionals at the next level down. In organizations who are effective in talent management the issue of talent is a regular item on executive meetings agendas. The senior leaders question the HR function about talent on a regular basis and tend to talk enthusiastically about talent to direct reports and colleagues. In a sense it is this top-level leadership attention which plays an important role in building a 'talent culture'.

(iii) *Talent skill-building.* Ensuring that line managers have the skills, capabilities and confidence to operate the organization's talent-management processes. The senior leadership needs to ensure that they invest time, effort and resources to ensure that these skills are well developed throughout the line management population. An important aspect of the development is to ensure that line managers have the skills to both identify and develop talented people within their areas of accountability.

(iv) *Line accountability.* For talent management to be implemented effectively it is essential that ownership of talent needs to be embedded within the line in the organization. Including talent accountabilities in line managers' role specifications and performance contracts is an important step in embedding ownership. These accountabilities should include clear and explicit outcomes and performance measures. However, embedding ownership requires more than words in a job specification. It is important that line managers understand the importance of talent to the organization's success and that their accountability for talent is viewed as importantly as all other accountabilities.

While the above four aspects of line leadership have been identified as discrete elements of talent management it is evident that they are inter-related. In total they create a strong 'talent culture'. To be effective in talent management it is important that all four elements are in place. The leadership needs to be supported by a range of processes. Some of the key processes that are necessary to support an effective talent-management strategy are:

(i) *High potential assessment.* It is important to establish clear criteria against which people can be assessed in order to identify those with high potential for progression to leadership and other senior roles. In developing criteria it is essential to focus on those that distinguish clearly between good performance and high potential. Having identified the criteria it is important that they are communicated in a clear and understandable way to line managers. These criteria need to be clearly aligned to current and future needs of the business. Robust processes to assess people against these criteria need to be in place. It is important that these processes involve line leaders and need to be capable of being practically used for regular assessment. The assessment process should not be a one-off event. Successful organizations employ processes which enable high potentials to be assessed on a regular basis.

(ii) *Talent development*. Processes for talent development need to go beyond 'traditional' development interventions (e.g. courses and coaching). Effective processes need to focus on encouraging and facilitating talented people to be exposed to stretching and challenging experiences. In addition it is important that individuals moving into these experiences are provided with the support necessary to enable them to perform and learn successfully.

(iii) *Retention planning*. Investment in identifying and developing talent needs to be supported by processes that help to ensure the retention of the talent. Whilst reward is one factor it is widely recognized that this is less important than the organizational culture and development opportunities (Higgs, 2003). In their research into talent management, Ashton and Bellis (2003) identified the following as being the most significant retention factors:
- Challenge
- Recognition
- Opportunities for personal learning and growth
- A culture that people can identify with
- Support through coaching, mentoring and counseling
- Opportunities to take risks and freedom to an extent to make mistakes.

Against this background it is important to have processes in place to review the presence and efficacy of key retention components. In addition it is important to have processes which enable the organization to review regularly succession and retention risks. These processes should also encompass the identification of actions to monitor risks and stimulate actions to reduce the risks identified.

(iv) *Talent deployment*. An important challenge for organizations relates to ensuring that talent is deployed in a way which both develops the individual and adds value to the organization. Unless this is addressed in a structured way organizations face the dangers of line leaders 'hoarding talent'. Therefore it is important to have processes in place which focus on the planning of talent deployment. The goals of such a process should ensure that the best talent is deployed in a way that:

- they are in roles in which they can add the most value to, and have the biggest impact on, the organization; and

- they are in roles in which they can maximize their further personal development.

As with the leadership elements (see earlier) it is important to ensure that all four process areas are in place to ensure successful talent management. In considering talent processes it is important to emphasize that they should not be over-complex, rather they need to be 'fit for purpose' and to be understood to be there to support line leadership. All too often organizations create overly complex and sophisticated talent-management processes which detract from line engagement. For example one organization the authors recently worked with had a significant challenge in developing and retaining talent which was perceived as a threat to future business performance. The group HR function was tasked to address this and developed an extremely sophisticated and complex range of talent-management processes. For example talent management was conducted against a range of high leadership potential criteria covering behaviors, characteristics and values. This resulted in a list of 36 criteria. Individuals were assessed against these criteria on the basis of a 360-degree process. The assessment was carried out twice a year. After two years the suite of processes had no impact on the core talent problems.

In achieving a successful talent-management strategy it is important to focus on the leadership role and that this is supported by effective and practical processes. Processes, however sophisticated, alone will not have an impact. The logic of this is nicely illustrated by the following metaphor.

You are asked to participate in a motor race. You are provided with a formula one Ferrari and your opponent will have a Ford Focus. Who do you think will win? How would your view change if you learned that your competitor (driving the Ford Focus) is to be Lewis Hamilton or Jensen Button!!

Thus we should be clear that we need to develop leaders skilled in talent management rather than engineering 'Ferrari' quality processes.

Building a talent pipeline

In the debate outlined above there is a focus on a broad strategic approach to talent management. However, it is critical to ensure that a good pipeline of future talent is established within an organization. In order to build such a pipeline an important starting point is to embed the key criteria within the organization. This can be achieved by seeking to use the critical criteria within recruitment, selection and development processes throughout the organization. This can be illustrated by considering the example of a major international manufacturing organization. The company identified critical leadership criteria against which potential candidates for top-level leadership positions were assessed. Lower-level indicators of these criteria were employed for the assessment of potential candidates for leadership positions at the next level down. This was then repeated for a further four levels. Finally an appropriately modified set of criteria were employed as one element of the assessment process employed in graduate recruitment. In addition the organization used versions of the criteria in the design of leadership development programmes at all levels in the organization.

Further embedding took place through incorporating a 360-degree assessment against relevant versions of the criteria in the annual performance review process for all staff in any managerial or supervisory position. Development planning resulting from these annual performance reviews included development in areas relating to the core criteria. In this way the organization was able to develop a clear picture of their longer-term pipeline of potential and had processes in place to develop this talent against relatively new and junior employees.

APPLICATION IN THE CONTEXT OF CHANGE LEADERSHIP TALENT

In previous chapters we have emphasized that leading change is an increasingly important aspect of any leader's role. Indeed, in today's volatile and complex environment, it is hard to conceive a leadership role which does not require the leadership of change. Thus it is clear that the above framework could adequately provide a basis for the effective management of change leadership talent. However, in order to ensure that this happens it is important that the key talent processes are reviewed to ensure that change leadership elements of talent are properly integrated. Below we illustrate some of the key points which need to be attended to in each of the four talent processes in order to ensure that change leadership is incorporated effectively.

(i) *High potential assessment.* It is important that the assessment criteria encompass the critical change leadership capabilities which are identified as being critical for the organization.

(ii) *Talent development.* The identification of potential experiences to stretch and challenge talented people should include exposing them to experiences involving significant change. As change is frequently implemented by means of a series of projects this provides an ideal opportunity to present talented individuals with challenging assignments.

(iii) *Retention planning.* In exploring succession risks in today's environment it is important to recognize that change leadership is likely to be an essential component. In talent-management terms this means that change leadership criteria perhaps should be accorded particular priority.

(iv) *Talent deployment.* Roles within the organization in which incumbents are likely to face significant or transformational change need to be clearly identified. It is into these roles that those in the talent pool with the highest level of change leadership skills should be deployed.

In discussing talent management in general we have emphasized the importance of line management engagement and the significant positive impact of a 'talent culture'. In ensuring that change leadership talent is managed effectively it is essential to ensure that leaders understand the critical nature of this dimension of leadership talent and this becomes embedded in the 'talent culture'. This understanding requires that senior leaders appreciate that change leadership requires a range of specific skills and capabilities which are not necessarily acquired through more 'traditional' leadership development processes. All too often we find that, when working with organizations, there is a view that change is 'just another thing that leaders do'. The level of realization that there are specific capabilities required to lead change effectively is relatively low. An intervention designed to expose senior leaders to change leadership thinking and the complexities of change can be effective in bringing about a notable shift in understanding.

Who is responsible for talent management?

In their research Ashton and Bellis (2003) identified a discernible trend toward talent management becoming an important aspect of the HR function. At the same time they noted the emergence of specialist talent-management roles which tended to be located within the HR function. However, it is important to ensure that such a move does not detract from the critical nature of line engagement and the critical role of line leaders. This requires that those in the HR role do need to adopt a more enabling and facilitating role. This may be seen as a further example of HR moving into more of a 'Strategic Business Partner' relationship to the line (Ulrich, 1998). In broader terms this requires that:

(i) Participating in strategic discussions within the business and, importantly, demonstrating 'added value' to these discussions. The demonstration of 'added value' is a prerequisite for being seen as a true 'business partner'.

(ii) Developing a stronger external focus. This entails an increasing use of benchmarking against other organizations and collection and analysis of data on competitor companies. However, the external focus has to go beyond analysis of HR practices. It is essential that HR keeps in touch with business trends and issues and considers their impact on the people and talent-management practices within their organization.

(iii) Becoming more anchored in the business. This involves a move from a view that HR is representative of the employees to a view that HR is a central aspect of business and as such it contributes alongside all other functions in a way which builds commitment of employees to the business.

(iv) Anticipating changes required to people and talent-management policies and practices based on business trends, rather than responding to line management's requests for change. This does not mean ignoring the needs of line managers and their views and opinions. It does, however, mean keeping a trained eye on trends, issues and developments and considering the impact of these on business plans, strategies and performance. Such views need to be debated with line managers. HR practitioners need to be able to act as change managers through an ability to make a compelling business case for the people changes which need to take place to support the business strategy.

There also appear to be some specific capabilities required in the talent-management arena. These are as follows:

- Expert coaching, advising and counseling skills
- Skills in relationship building and relationship management
- Influencing and persuasion skills
- Resilience and persistence
- Creativity and innovation in development design
- Political awareness and acumen

In engaging with talent management, HR are frequently agents of change. It is therefore essential that they have high-level change leadership skills. By modeling these they will be better equipped to ensure that change leadership capabilities become embedded in the talent strategy.

In this chapter we have identified the growing importance for organizations of effective talent management. Whilst this is becoming more widely recognized the significance of including change leadership capabilities within talent frameworks remains relatively rare. However, given the current volatile and fast-changing environment it is critical that this changes. Overall talent-management frameworks provide a frame which can encompass the management of change leadership talent. It is critical that talent-management strategies are owned by line management and that they are actively engaged in the process. The function of HR is to support and enable the process. However, to do this effectively it is necessary that change leadership skills are developed within the function.

References

Allen, N. I., & Meyer, J. P. (1990). The measurement and antecedents of affective, continuance and normative commitment to the organization. *Journal of Occupational Psychology*, *63*(1), 1–18.

Ashton, C., & Bellis, R. (2003). *Effective talent management*. London: Careers Research Forum.

Conference Board. (2005). *"Take this Job...."*. *Executive action report*. New York: Conference Board.

Guest, D. (1997). Human resource management and performance: A review and research agenda. *The International Journal of Human Resource Management*, *8*, 263–276.

Higgs, M. J. (2003). Developments in leadership thinking. *Journal of Organizational Development and Leadership*, *24*(5), 273–284.

Higgs, M. J. (2006). Building employee engagement. *Henley Manager Update*, *18*(2), 16–23.

Michaels, E., Handfield-Jones, H., & Alexrod, B. (2001). *The war for talent*. Boston, MA: Harvard Business School Press.

McCall, M. W. (1998). *High flyers: Developing the next generation of leaders*. Boston, MA: Harvard Business School Press.

Rucci, A. J., Hirn, S. P., & Quinn, R. T. (1998). The employee – customer – profit chain at Sears. *Harvard Business Review*, *Jan–Feb*, 82–97.

Rousseau, D. M. (1985). Issues of level in organizational research: Multi-level and cross-level perspectives. *Research in Organizational Behaviour*, *7*, 1–37.

Towers Perrin. (2005). *Towers Perrin 2005 Workforce Study*. New York: Towers Perrin.

Ulrich, D. (1998). *Human resource champions: The next agenda for delivering values and results*. Cambridge: Harvard Business Press.

Williams, M. (2000). *The war for talent*. London: CIPD.

Chapter 10

A Framework for Developing 'Changing' Leadership Capability

Introduction

In exploring how thinking about leadership has been developing (see Chapter 1), we presented an overall framework that links the leader dynamically with his/her organizational context. This is shown again in Figure 10.1. The arrow pointing right represents the leadership values and culture, also embodying the leadership

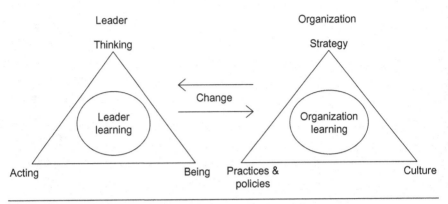

Figure 10.1   A change leadership learning framework.

capabilities, in attempts to change the organization. We covered this extensively in Chapters 4, 5 and 6 respectively. The arrow pointing left indicates the organizational impact of change attempts flowing back to the leaders in a feedback loop. We suggested ways of measuring this impact in Chapter 8. This also means that the evaluation measures themselves can be used as a menu from which to select appropriate targets for specific organizational change and change leader development exercises.

In this chapter we explore the way in which this model can provide a framework for developing change leaders. Whilst we present a range of ideas and suggestions, including our top 10 capabilities, it is important that any approach to developing change leaders is designed to ensure that the skills, behavior and practices are designed in a way that will support the organization's immediate purpose, vision and business context. In order to do this, the organization should begin by considering the current context in terms of its strategy, culture, and policies and practices. Having developed a clear understanding of this, we suggest that the key steps in building a framework for developing change leaders are as follows:

1. Based on this contextual analysis, a clear profile of what the organization will need from its change leaders and how they should be developed.

2. The profile needs to be reviewed in order to identify the range of development actions that can build these capabilities.

3. The current culture, policies and practices should be reviewed in order to establish the actions needed in these areas to support and reinforce the development of the required leader capabilities.

4. Recognizing that the business context is dynamic and volatile, the final phase is to consider how to develop leaders' capability to understand themselves and the dynamic between their behaviors and style and the changing organizational context.

These considerations provide the basis for the structure of this chapter. In essence it sets out to explore the following questions:

- What do we need?
- What do we have? – what are the gaps and how do we close these gaps, both short- to mid-term and long-term?
- What else do we need? – how do we build change leaders who are able to operate in an ever-changing context?

What do we need?

In developing leaders all too often organizations begin by either searching for best practice drawn from other organizations (or the latest high-profile publications on effective leadership) or by looking at what has been effective in the past in their own organization. When the former route is taken it frequently leads to building a framework that fails to account for the context of the organization. Equally, in the latter course, there is an assumption that what has worked in the past will also work in the future. This leads to a possibility that any framework developed on this basis will not deliver what is needed for the future. In the often-quoted definition of insanity (frequently attributed to Einstein) this amounts to:

Doing what we have always done and expecting different results.

We suggest that in order to develop a clear picture of what is needed, in terms of change leadership capability, it is important to adopt a more dynamic view.

One potential framework for achieving this is outlined below:

Where are we now?

Develop a clear picture of the current organizational context. This entails building a clear picture of the 'current reality' in terms of:

understanding our current strategic position and its implementation,

understanding the nature of our current culture,

understanding the nature and impact of our current structures, policies and practices.

From this we can assess current approaches to leadership development and the extent to which they support the achievement of current strategic goals and are anchored in existing structures, practices and culture.

Where do we need to be?

Once again this stage of the analysis begins by considering the broader organizational context and environment and identifying the extent to which in this context the strategy is (or needs to be) changing.

Against this background it is important to consider what this means in terms of the core capabilities of the business and how these can impact on the achievement of changing strategic goals. One framework for doing this is presented in Figure 10.2. This can also be used to assess the required emphasis from across the 10 change leadership capabilities we identified in Chapter 6, ensuring investment is placed to meet shifting organizational demands.

In order to conduct this analysis the organization's core capabilities are identified. These are then assessed in terms of:

1. Current performance versus the competition
2. Importance to the achievement of future strategy.

Those rated highly in terms of performance, but are in the range of medium to low in terms of importance to the achievement of competitive strategic goals, are likely to indicate capabilities in which the organization over-invests. On the other hand, those toward the higher end of importance to the achievement of competitive strategic goals, but low in terms of comparative performance, are areas in which resources need to be invested in order to build the capabilities. Those in the middle sections are broadly aligned in terms of investment of effort.

Having looked at the capabilities needed in order to achieve future strategic goals it is thus important to identify the extent to which current structures, policies and practices and the organizational culture will need to change (if at all) in order to support the development of future capabilities.

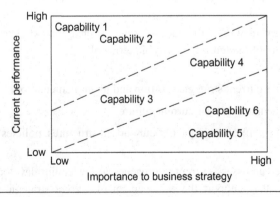

Figure 10.2 Core capability analysis.

This process can be illustrated by the following (simplified) example. This relates to a UK life assurance company. The organization was operating in an increasingly competitive market in which the speed with which new products were taken to market could have a significant impact in achieving growth in market share. A headline analysis of the core capabilities required in this market that would enable the organization to achieve a strategic change in market share through the introduction of innovative products will entail the following:

■ Speed of moving new product ideas from conception to delivery
■ Effective regulatory compliance
■ Ability to share information rapidly within the organization
■ Effective allocation of capital
■ High-quality actuarial skills
■ Optimal range of distribution channels
■ High-quality customer service.

The assessment of these (using the aforesaid model) resulted in the profile shown in Figure 10.3.

From this analysis it was evident that the company needed to build capabilities in terms of increasing the ability to get new products to market quickly and to share knowledge effectively. Both of these required effective cross-functional team working. The analysis of the culture identified the following dominant characteristics:

■ High levels of bureaucracy
■ Individualistic

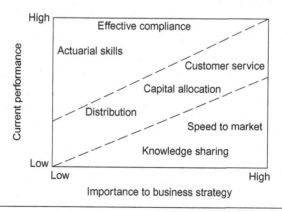

Figure 10.3   Core capability analysis – Life assurance company.

- Internally competitive
- Risk aversion
- High value on professional qualification (particularly actuarial).

In reviewing structures, policies and practices, the notable points identified were as follows:

- Large number of grades/layers
- Organization into distinct 'silos'
- Formalized communication structures
- Reward based on individual performance
- High levels of checking
- Centralized decision making.

In order to achieve the strategic goals the company needed to support the development of capabilities in the areas of speed to market and knowledge sharing by building a culture that valued team working, cross-functional working and rapid decision making. This in turn required changes to structures, systems and practices including, fluttering the structures, devolving decision making and rewarding team working as well as individual performance.

This process of analysis provides an organization with a picture of:

- What needs to change?
- Why the change is needed?
- What capabilities are required?

In addition it is important to consider the timescales of any change and the degree of the change (e.g. is it incremental or radical?).

Against this background it then becomes feasible to identify the key capabilities required of change leaders who can support the execution of the change. However, it is important this is also translated into the key leadership dimensions of Thinking, Acting and Being, in terms of:

- What are the cognitive abilities required? We know from years of research that general intelligence (IQ) is a predictor of leadership effectiveness (e.g. Higgs, 2003). However, 'Thinking' is broader than IQ alone. To what extent do we need abilities to think creatively, strategically, analytically, etc.?

■ What are the important fundamental individual personality traits, motivation or values that align with the strategic needs and cultural changes required?

■ How do we need our leaders to behave?

Below, we match Thinking, Acting and Being onto our recommended top 10 capabilities for aspiring change leaders.

	Top 10 capabilities
Thinking	Capability 2 – access broadband 'capability' from across the leadership membership Capability 4 – future sense-make combined with strategic thinking
Acting	Capability 3 – become a co-creator of a learning culture Capability 7 – develop 1:1 relational skills: coaching Capability 8 – develop 1: many dialogue skills; action learning, facilitation and process consulting Capability 10 – high-quality performance challenge culture and dialogue
Being	Capability 1 – develop mindfulness, using three capacities for leadership of change decision making Capability 5 – develop 'total' leadership Capability 6 – develop 'transcultural' competence Capability 9 – emotional intelligence

What is interesting to note is the 'Thinking' requirements, whilst still important, are outweighed by the other two. This might be worth considering when choosing the balance of activities implanted in change leadership development programmes.

What do we have?

Having developed a set of criteria for what we need in order to deliver the strategic change required by the organization, we then need to conduct a thorough assessment of how well equipped our current future leaders are to provide us with the required capabilities. This leads us into a debate that goes well beyond the scope of this book. However, two main issues can be examined briefly here. These are:

(i) How we assess individuals against our required criteria.

(ii) How we use the assessments.

ASSESSMENT

Much has been written on the subject of individual assessments, and organizational experiences of using assessment methods and techniques vary widely. Methods include testing, interviews, simulations, 360-degree questionnaires, performance reviews and assessment/development centers. Whilst there is a vast body of research and writing that contrasts differing methods and attempts to identify a 'best' model, there is no clear consensus around any one particular methodology (Herriot, 1989). Having said that, there is a degree of consensus around the view that effective assessment requires that a variety of assessment vehicles are used and individuals are assessed by a number of different raters (this is referred to as multi-source, multi-method assessment). Perhaps the most well recognized form of this is the 'classic' assessment center. Using this approach, groups of individuals undertake a variety of personality and aptitude tests, individual, paired and group tasks while being observed by a team of assessors (Thornton & Byham, 1982). The assessors rate the individuals based on the recorded and observed data against an agreed set of criteria, and an overall individual assessment of current and/or potential capability is arrived at by a process of integrating individual assessor ratings (Herriot, 1989; Thornton & Byham, 1982).

The range of potential tools and techniques for assessment is diverse. Here we cannot explore all of them or go into detail. However to indicate the range, we have indicated some typical ones under the three headings (Thinking, Being and Acting) highlighted in our framework.

■ Thinking

In relation to this aspect of the overall framework there are a range of potential dimensions including:
– general IQ
– critical reasoning ability
– decision-making ability
– creativity
– strategic perspective
– business acumen

Whilst general IQ, critical thinking and, to an extent, creativity can be assessed by means of cognitive ability tests, other dimensions require a broader range of assessment methods including simulations and business games. Furthermore, there can be elements of this dimension that are knowledge or experience based and can be assessed by means of reviews of career histories (CVs) or focused interviews.

■ Being

The 'Being' element is about who the individual is. This is a multi-faceted element that encompasses dimensions such as personality, values, beliefs, motivation, attitudes and dispositions. Assessment of this has traditionally focused on the use of well-established personality tests (e.g. SHL's OPQ; Cattells, I6PF; Costa & McCrae's 'Big 5'). However, more recently we have seen the emergence of other self-assessed values and motivation inventories and both self and other assessed emotion intelligence questionnaires.

Whilst this impact of leadership (and potential leadership) has been traditionally assessed by means of psychometrically based instruments, there has been an emerging use of psychological/in-depth interviewing to support (and in some cases) to replace such tests.

■ Acting

This dimension relates to the most observable dimensions of the leadership framework – behaviors. As such it is most amenable to assessment by direct observation or feedback from those who experience the behaviors on an on-going basis. Thus this element can be assessed by observing behaviors in simulations, performance reviews conducted by individuals' immediate managers and use of 360-degree feedback questionnaires.

In exploring the three broad areas of leadership capability within the model we have only considered assessment techniques very briefly. What is important, however, is that a range of assessments are brought to bear, building the overall profile. While there is no 'structural' way of achieving this in practice, an overall mapping of leadership requirements and assessment methods/tasks can help to establish the rigor of the process. A framework for mapping assessment is shown in Figure 10.4.

In using such a framework the criteria are reviewed and, ideally, at least two means of assessing each criterion are identified. In this way a clear multi-source assessment against each criterion is achieved.

USING THE ASSESSMENT

In making an assessment it is important to decide on how it is to be used. In a leadership context a number of organizations do focus on assessment as a tool for identifying potential leaders and employ it to make 'go/no go' decisions. In this application the assessment is used primarily to determine who (amongst the potential leadership population) goes forward into the next stage of leadership development. Further assessment processes are often completed at various stages in the

Criterion	Assessment method					
	Ability tests	Personality tests	Values/motivation questionnaire	Simulation	360° feedback	Interviews
Thinking capabilities						
				✓		
	✓				✓	✓
	✓	✓				
Being						
		✓	✓	✓	✓	
		✓			✓	✓
		✓		✓		
Acting						
			✓		✓	
				✓	✓	✓
				✓	✓	✓

Figure 10.4 Example assessment planning framework.

progression of the leadership 'potential pool' in order to focus on building a 'future senior leadership pool'.

However, increasingly organizations see the role of assessment as providing a tool to improve the ability to develop capability at all levels in the organization rather than as being primarily a promotion or retention tool. In this view assessment forms an important (if not critical) input into the overall process of building leadership capability. We would argue that in the context of developing change leaders this is a critical role of assessment.

Within the developmental context it is important that assessment is used in order to identify both individual and group development needs. To achieve this it is important to ensure that the overall development framework encompasses the following:

■ Individual feedback and associated developmental discussions

■ Formulations of individual development plans to address gaps in terms of both current roles and building future capability

■ Identification of group-wide gaps and associated development plans

■ Identification of significant gaps that cannot be covered by development and require further actions (e.g. recruitment) in order to build required future capabilities.

Development planning should be specific and not only address the 'what' has to be developed, but also the 'how'. In Chapter 7, we reviewed and outlined a range of potential development tools. In planning the 'how' of development plans, it has to be considered which of these may be appropriate to meeting individual and/or group development needs.

What else do we need to do?

Having used an understanding of the organizational context and future strategy to determine what we need in terms of leadership capabilities, it is important to re-visit this in order to identify actions needed to embed these once they have been developed. In particular, it is important to consider how well the current culture, policies and practices are likely to support the development programmes, processes and actions that are put in place. As we suggested in Chapter 5, it is difficult to change culture quickly. However, in most organizations the culture tends to be reflected in the structures, policies and practices of the organization.

Therefore, in considering what needs to be changed within the organization to embed the development of change leadership capabilities, it is useful to begin by examining the extent to which the current structures, policies and practices reinforce and reward the demonstration of these. In essence this requires that we ensure that our broader policies and practices reinforce that we are taking seriously the type of leadership behaviors that we have invested in developing. To a significant extent this will entail ensuring that the broad range of HR policies and practices (that provide a significant level in terms of underpinning the 'real' behaviors in organizations) are aligned with the leadership practices and behaviors that we are seeking to develop.

Conducting such a review entails considering an important range of questions that include:

- Are we sending signals that we are taking this development seriously?
- How do we demonstrate that we value the new capabilities?
- How do we ensure that we maintain conversations about new leadership behaviors and keep the development alive?
- Can we ensure that stories about the impact of the new capabilities spread through the organization?
- How do we ensure that we do not send conflicting messages to leaders in the organization?

Clearly in answering these questions it is important to examine a range of HR policies and practices including:

- Reward strategies and structures
- Promotions and talent-management policies

■ Performance management processes and systems

■ Recruitment and selection processes and criteria

■ Competency models and frameworks.

In addition it is essential to be able to demonstrate senior management commitment to the overall leadership capability process and to ensure their support for an active engagement with any changes in policies and practices. Although emphasizing the significance of HR policies and practices in reinforcing and embedding the new leadership capabilities, it is also important to consider broader organization and decision-making structures. As has been found in many organizations (e.g. Ashton & Bellis, 2003), unless those who have acquired such capabilities are employed in value-adding roles, the value of the development is all too often not realized. Overall we would suggest the true value from the development of new leadership capabilities becomes embedded in the organization through a combination of policies, practices and processes and (critically) senior leadership role modelling and attention as we explained in Chapter 5.

Rather than attempt to produce a checklist approach to exploring the above elements of ensuring integration of new capabilities in the organization, we will provide a few illustrations, drawn from our experience of working with organizations, that we believe illustrate the significance of attending to the organization context, to ensure that development of leadership capabilities is translated into value for the organization.

LEADERSHIP ATTENTION AND FOCUS

An international manufacturing company that had reorganised its organisational model to accommodate its core mass production business recognized a need for significant change in order to ensure full integration and the development of an effective and dominant business in their market. In order to achieve this they recognized that their leadership population would require new skills in leading their operational areas and leading the change. They went through a rigorous exercise to identify the leadership capabilities to enable this strategic direction to be implemented. In doing this they identified a set of criteria that all current and potential leaders should be assessed against. These assessments were to form the core of their overall talent-management and deployment processes. To send a message about how seriously the senior leadership team took this initiative they began the roll-out of the process with an assessment of themselves and their commitment to undertaking development based on this assessment. Furthermore they ensured that progress in terms of leadership talent development and deployment was a regular item on the agenda for top team meetings.

Having provided such a clear signal to the organization, the roll-out of the leadership development framework was successful. This success was reinforced as a result of the organization's subsequent performance, increase in shareholder value and return on assets assessed by investment analysts.

This example can be contrasted with a global pharmaceutical company that invested heavily in developing change leadership capability based on a competency framework designed to provide the basis for developing future leaders able to manage the changes necessary to compete in a volatile global market. Whilst the development process was rigorous and relevant, the CEO insisted on appointing individuals to senior leadership positions based primarily on evidence of their ability to achieve short-term performance goals. As a result the whole development effort fell into disrepute and was effectively wasted.

ALIGNING REWARDS, POLICIES AND PRACTICES

A global fast-moving consumer goods company with a strong and enduring record of profitable performance identified that its European operation was failing to perform in line with other regions. They had a strong country-based structure with high incentive rewards for country managers who achieved their goals. However, a strategic business review identified a need for a stronger team working in Europe in order to achieve a more effective Pan-European performance. Following this a new framework of leadership competencies was identified that would enable the European management team to help to build a changed and collaborative environment. A development intervention was put in place to help the European leadership team to build these new capabilities. Around three months after the development work, clear evidence of changed behaviors and improved European performance began to emerge. This lasted for a further six months. However, at the end of this period the Pan-European approach (and associated results) began to falter. In exploring the reasons for this it became apparent that one cause was that the last quarter of the individually based bonus plan had arrived. The country managers' attention reverted to their own country's performance and the Pan-European focus was lost.

Having seen this happen the organization modified the incentive structures to encompass a Pan-European component and were able to embed the new behaviors in the subsequent years.

ENSURING THAT THE LEADERSHIP CAPABILITIES ARE TAKEN SERIOUSLY

A leading UK retail organization had recognized that companies with highly committed employees tended to outperform their competitors. Building on this they developed a profile of leadership capabilities that would support the development of employee commitment and maintain this during times of significant volatility in the sector and associated change within the organization. The company had a view that leadership is widely distributed in an organization like theirs. Thus they embarked on a programme of assessing all leaders (and potential leaders) against the capability framework and putting in place development actions to address any current or future gaps identified.

In order to ensure that the investment in development achieved the desired strategic goals, they implemented a process of assessing levels of employee commitment on a quarterly basis. This metric was then used as a means of assessing the ability of leaders to deploy the capabilities that had been developed. The significance they attached to leaders' abilities to build and maintain commitment was such that it became impossible for a leader to achieve a performance bonus payment if staff commitment in his/her unit or area declined for two quarters. Similarly no leader could be considered for promotion to a higher level role if he/she had experienced employee commitment scores below the top quartile of the overall company results for more than two quarters over a two-year period.

Whilst the aforesaid examples are not exhaustive, they do reinforce the importance of embedding required leadership capabilities in the organizational policies and practices that, in turn, are manifestations of its overall culture.

Summary

In this chapter we have presented an overall framework for how we develop change leadership capabilities in our organizations. The emphasis has been on thinking about the challenges rather than offering prescriptive solutions.

The framework suggested is developed from the leadership–organization learning model first presented in Chapter 1. The emphasis throughout this book has been on the dynamic relationship between leadership values, culture, capabilities and the organizational context (in terms of strategy, culture, and policies and practices). In using this framework we have suggested that the context helps us to define the specific and generic leadership capabilities required to support current and future organizational change. We used these as a basis for assessing the extent to which we have (currently or potentially) employed these capabilities and the gap analysis informs our developmental planning.

We have suggested the framework demands change leaders and those responsible for their development return to the organizational context, in particular the strategy, culture, and policies and practices. Achieving the right balance in the spread of development activity across Thinking, Being and Acting is important and the top 10 capabilities mapped against these development domains support the view that experiential methods creating real role related personal leadership demands and organizational challenges, should be paramount. Finally, we have recommended that effective change leaders also need to understand the dynamics embedded in this framework and develop the relevant capabilities contained therein. In essence the leader's development journey continues through working with this dynamic, supported by a high level of self and organizational awareness.

References

Ashton, C., & Bellis, R. (2003). *Effective talent management*. London: Careers Research Forum.
Herriot, P. (1989). *Assessment and selection in organizations*. Chichester: John Wiley & Sons.
Higgs, M. J. (2003). Developments in leadership thinking. *Journal of Organizational Development and Leadership*, 24(5), 273–284.
Thornton, G. C., & Byham, W. C. (1982). *Assessment centers and managerial performance*. New York: Academic Press.

Chapter 11

Concluding Remarks

Introduction

Although we have used the word transformational leadership in support of change leadership development, we must be alert to 'pseudo-transformational' leadership, or leadership that appears confident even though the leader is unsure about what he/she is doing and telling followers to do, or worse, knowingly focusing followers on unattainable visions, etc. The raison d'etre of this book is to avoid the latter as this is likely to stimulate hate and conflict rather than harmony and co-operation. To create the former we need to shift our emphasis for change leadership development from self-driven needs or line manager–driven needs to one which concentrates on the relational and contextual nature of change leadership where, as Collinson (2006:187) suggests, it 'views the identities of followers and leaders as inextricably linked, mutually reinforcing, and shifting within specific contexts'. As Bolden (2004) explained, to navigate and make sense of uncertainty and complexity in internal and external organizational environments, those designated as leaders will need to become increasingly adaptable and resilient in order to win the right to lead, lead by example and share in leadership and hardship.

Leadership is not a person or a position. It is a complex moral relationship between people, based on trust, obligation, commitment, emotion and a shared vision of the good

Ciulla (2008)

Therefore it is the link between the personal, interpersonal, organizational and societal impact of change leadership development that matters most – with the developer's aim of creating learning conditions and activities which generate 'leadershipful' organizations (Vanderslice,1988) and societies.

Context is all for targeted change leadership development. In fact Hmielski & Ensley (2007) found that in dynamic industry environments, start-ups with heterogeneous top management teams (diverse backgrounds) were found to perform best when led by directive leaders whereas those with homogenous teams worked better with empowering leaders. Conversely, in more stable industry environments, heterogeneity was best matched with empowering types, whilst homogeneity responded best to directive style. Of course, role modeling and building a culture of continuous learning is the sine qua non of change leadership development as this has major implications for how change is responded to and how success and failure are treated for all to witness. To close, here are a number of business must *dos* to achieve this:

- Lead through own activity in learning (to lead and implement change)
- Model by sharing that learning
- Recognize people for the quality of reporting back to business groups on conferences, seminars, learning activities
- Support exchange of knowledge across the organization
- Be prepared to take risks with new ways of learning
- Ensure the core learning and development needs are identified in corporate and business planning
- Ensure appropriate funding and resources for learning and development based on building capacity for now and the future

■ Actively support the inclusion of learning and development issues in business decision making

■ Request learning and development data to inform business decisions, including data on level, nature and business impact of investment

■ Ensure 'reward' systems are in place for efforts by staff to encourage learning in the workplace.

Probably the most important role of a leader is to ensure a ready supply of replacement leaders. However, research on succession reveals that for every two heirs who make it to the top, one leaves early, and heirs depart notably more often than their bosses. The greater the power and influence of the chief executive (longevity, ownership of stock, combining the role of chairman), the less likely and slower the identified successor will be promoted. So, challenging this culture is vital, as well as facilitating ways to ensure leader replenishment.

Leadership development has clearly reached a critical crossroad. A number of forces – geo-politics, the carbon economy, emerging economic power bases, ideological diversity, consumer driven technology, etc. – are combining, and together they make necessary a re-think of how we raise future leaders. Through the media and their own lives, consumers and employees are becoming increasingly attuned to values-laden debates about what constitutes a 'respected' business, as well as a 'good' employer (normally based on experience of dealing with identifiable managers); particularly those arguments relating to people diversity and forces in the local and global economy and ecosystem – see Spitzeck et al. (2009). Displaying diversity and green credentials in corporate advertising may be a helpful start, but without leadership by example, the attractiveness of working for these companies is instantly damaged.

Corporate mission and values statements are worthless when not lived by the executives who proclaim them. Those executives who are the guardians of business reputation must 'collectively' share personal values representing the mission. This becomes their unique leadership 'brand'. Mealy-mouthed and inconsistently applied organizational values statements indicate a poorly crafted and non-compelling purpose, without a clear imperative to follow and focus. The catalytic nature and position of leadership culture in business (Aitken, 2007) is highlighted in Figure 11.1.

'Walking the talk' still remains the most powerful weapon in the leadership-of-change armory; it is the most personal and observable way leaders acting in concert can send out priority cues for staff, both for business outcome and culture change shifts. So, for example, if major cost reductions are required, leaders would do well to take the medicine, perhaps through salary constraint, before expecting others to do likewise – we have many recent leadership ante-heroes who have

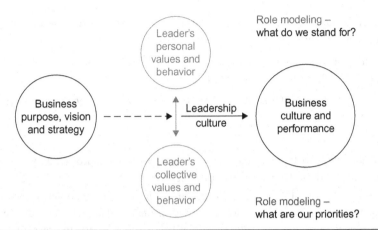

Figure 11.1 Leaders' 'walk the talk' of change.

failed spectacularly on this count. Holding up the video camera to change leaders as they go about fulfilling this everyday role may become the most profound form of change leadership development available to us.

Some questions for future research and practice concerning change leader development and change implementation through change leadership are as follows.

Research:
- Adequacy of how we currently assess the impact of leaders on business life (cross-sectional, self-report, indirect impact questionnaire measures)?
- Do we need more observational, longitudinal, qualitative and experimental studies to test the relative power of different social influence mechanisms employed in workplaces (social influence as a living, everyday process)?
- Can we learn anything about expectation/behaviour shaping from other research paradigms (family life, sports coaching, etc.)?

Practice:
- Are we training leaders with the best development methods (e.g. coaching on role modelling/communicating specific culture/s relevant to the HR/business strategy)?
- Are we selecting leaders with the most appropriate assessment methods (e.g. observing if and how they socially influence followers)?
- Are leadership teams fully aware of their own leadership culture before attempting to influence their business culture through HR strategy (can they practice what they preach)?

Forecasting twenty-first century change leadership roles

Whilst it is always dangerous to project ahead, building on the work of Dart and Stace (1999), we present some future facing change leader roles in the following table, which, when combined, would form a formidable 21st century change leadership collective.

Vision/Values/Value Leader	Blending the respective purposes of financial and societal stakeholders – generating new forms of capitalism where emotional contagion is self-regulated – rise of socioeconomic–environmental entrepreneurs, balancing making money with risk to business endurance and eco-sustainability
Techno Leader	Evolving a new generation of bio-tech, info-tech, nano-tech, clean-tech and all-tech combined companies
Capability Leader	Focused exclusively on figuring out the core capabilities required in the business, sourcing their most effective provision and deploying them smartly for the benefit of both people and the organization
Metrics Leader	Identifying the measures across the business system which can track progress in the relationships between work processes, work practices and work cultures
Manager–Leader	Ensuring business and workplace activity fits together to deliver effectively and with quality to clients and customers
Behavioral Science Leader	Behavioral economics may be the forerunner discipline of a universal approach to considering models of organization and business conduct, combining economics, psychology, sociology, politics and philosophy
Wisdom Leader	Responsible for developing the learning/ knowledge/experience/reputational 'brain' and 'heart' of the company

Looking ahead for change leadership development practitioners and researchers

Change leadership will become increasingly driven by the power of the Internet, where the 'crowdsourcing' phenomenon (Howe, 2008) is gathering pace. Business is beginning to draw down the ideas of online communities composed of like-minded enthusiasts for particular products and services that were once the sole province of employees. Crowdsourcing has its genesis in the open source movement in software, an example being the development of the Linux operating system. The social connectivity of the Internet means that work can often be organized more efficiently and effectively in the context of communities of interest rather than single corporations, based on the simple idea that the best person to do a job is the one who most wants to do that job. For example, Proctor and Gamble (P&G) had a notoriously insular corporate culture which led to stagnation in growth and reduction in market value via a poorly performing R&D function (only 15% of its new products and innovations originated outside the company).

Under a new CEO and an initiative called 'Connect and Develop' this figure ended up beyond 50%, whilst market value also since climbed dramatically. As A.G. Lafley (the CEO) explains in his book (*The game changer*): at the time P&G employed 8,500 researchers and we figured out that externally there were another 1.5 million similar researchers with pertinent areas of expertise, so why not pick their brains? To reach this community the company has either created or partnered with Internet-based engines such as YourEncore, a website where scientists can work part-time on projects posted by companies such as P&G. Recognizing that intellectual capital is increasingly found in Eastern Europe, China and India, another site called InnoCentive allows in-house P&G R&D staff to post a problem with solutions rewarded whilst P&G retains the new intellectual property created. The Apple iPhone applications production and reward system is a similar way of doing business with technology stakeholders.

Before we finish, let's remind ourselves that although no one can dispute the change leadership achievements of Richard Branson and his contemporary high profile coterie, there are legions of pioneers quietly and carefully activating change; tacitly enriching our lives for no other reason than that they believe in what they do. Here are some names worth following for the way they approach change leadership; Harriet Lamb (Executive Director of the Fairtrade Foundation), Delia Derbyshire (Composer of Electronic Music), Bill Dunster (Green Architect), Mel Young (President of the Homeless World Cup), Mohammad Yunus (Microfinance guru), Armand Hadida (fashion retailer), Neil Birnie (responsible tourism entrepreneur), Tim Smit (founder of The Eden Project), Margaret Schutte-Lihotski (inventor of the fitted kitchen) and Camila Batmanghelidjh (founder of Kids Company).

Finally, we leave you with a recent claim for the discovery of the seat of human wisdom, suggesting there may be a basis in neurobiology for wisdom's most universal traits (reported by Leake, 2009). Given it may be sometime before we introduce brain scanners into executive selection, we commend our book as a means of enhancing change leadership development wisdom in a more traditional, albeit contemporary, way.

How to find out more

Our co-authors:
Dr Paul Aitken, DBA, M. Sc., Dip. C. G., A. Dip. C., C. Psychol.
Doctor of Business Administration, M. Sc. (Applied Psychology),
Diploma in Careers Guidance,
Advanced Postgraduate Diploma in Management Consultancy,
Chartered Occupational Psychologist,
Registered Executive Coach (Henley).

PERSONAL PROFILE

Before joining the National School of Government as strategic leadership consultant and Programme Director for Leaders UK, Paul was most recently curriculum leader for Leadership and Change at Henley Business School, responsible for thought leadership and programme design/development across qualification, open executive and company programmes. He remains a Visiting Fellow at Henley. Paul is also R&D Director for Concordia International Ltd., and OD/OB consultancy assisting managers to execute strategy through culture leadership, using deep dialogue diagnostics, communication tools and impact measurement methodologies. In the UK Paul has worked as a senior human resource manager/internal consultant in local government and utilities sectors. External consulting assignments in European and New Zealand private and public sectors include senior executive team selection and development, current and future leader's talent assessment/development and culture shaping for sustainable business performance, particularly in cross-cultural and partnership working contexts. Paul combines teaching with research and writing on; how to develop change leaders, the business impact of executive's personal values, collective leadership, and leadership for sustainability. He mentors, supervises and teaches MBA, DBA, Masters and DMS programme members in his consulting/research topic interests. Paul delivers and chairs conference presentations and provides Board/executive learning facilitation, business consultancy, coaching and coaching supervision services.

As lead author Paul can be contacted at paitken@concordiaworld.com.

PROFESSOR MALCOLM HIGGS
DBA, MPhil, Chartered Psychologist, ADipC, FCIPD, FCII

Professor Malcolm Higgs is Professor of Human Resources and Organisation Behaviour at the University of Southampton School of Management.

Until 31 October 2007 Malcolm was the Director of the School of Leadership, Change and HR and Research Director of Henley Management College. He took up this position in August 2005 having for the previous four years been the College's Academic Dean. He remains a Visiting Professor at Henley Management College.

He moved to Henley from a role as Principal Partner in Towers Perrin's Human Resource Management practice. In this role he was responsible for Organisation and Management Development, Assessment, Leadership Development and Training projects for clients and for developing programmes and strategies for human resource and change management. In addition he was responsible for the firm's International leadership development practice.

Prior to joining Towers Perrin, Malcolm had eight years consulting experience with the Hay Group and Arthur Young. In 1987 he undertook a research programme into the human resource implications of the major changes in the UK financial markets and in 1988 published a book based on this research "Management Development Strategy in the Financial Sector". He has also published extensively on leadership, team development, executive assessment and change management. In addition he has published widely on the topic of Emotional Intelligence and has jointly developed a psychometric test to measure this together with a book on the topic (Making Sense of Emotional Intelligence).

Recently he has completed a major research project on change and its leadership. This has now been published in a new book (Sustaining Change: Leadership that works).

Malcolm is a member of the British Psychological Society and a Chartered Occupational Psychologist and is also is actively involved in consulting on leadership, change and assessment with a range of international companies both as an individual consultant and as the Chairman of the consulting firm Transend.

Contact Details:

Malcolm Higgs, DBA, MPhil, CPsychol, FCIPD, FCII Professor of Organisation Behaviour and HRM Southampton University School of Management Highfield, SO17 1BJ Phone 023 8059 7788 e-mail:malcolm.higgs@soton.ac.uk

References

Aitken, P. (2007). Walking the talk – the nature and role of leadership culture within organisation culture/s. *Journal of General Management, 32*(4).

Bolden, R. (2004). What is leadership? Leadership South West (University of Exeter) Research Report, South West of England Regional Development Agency, July 2004.

Ciulla, J.B. (2008). Leadership Studies and "the Fusion of Horizons". *Leadership Quarterly*, *19*, 393–395.

Collinson, D. (2006). Re-thinking followership: A post-structuralist analysis of follower identities. *Leadership Quarterly*, *17*(2), 179–189.

Dart, A., & Stace, D. (1999). Roles in the knowledge economy. *Monash Mount Aliza Business Review*, 52–57.

Hmielski, K. M., & Ensley, M. D. (2007). A contextual examination of new venture performance: Entrepreneur leadership behaviour, top management heterogeneity and environmental dynamism. *Journal of Organisational Behaviour*, *28*(7), 865–889.

Howe, J. (2008). *Crowdsourcing*. New York: Random House.

Leake, J. (2009). Found: The seat of all wisdom, *The Sunday Times*, April 5, pp. 1, 3.

Spitzeck, H., Prison, M., Amann, W., Khan, S., & von Kimakowitz, E. (2009) Humanism in Business, Cambridge university Press.

Vanderslice, V. J. (1988). Separating leadership from leaders: An assessment of the effect of leader and follower roles. *Human Relations*, *41*, 677–696.

Index

Printed in the United States
by Baker & Taylor Publisher Services